FEDERALISM AND THE CONSTITUTION OF CANADA

The Canadian system of federalism divides the power to govern between the central federal Parliament and the provincial and territorial legislative assemblies. In what can be seen as a double federation, power is also divided culturally, between English and French Canada. The divisions of power and responsibility, however, have not remained static since 1867. The federal language regime (1969), for example, reconfigured cultural federalism, generating constitutional tension as governments sought to make institutions more representative of the country's diversity.

In *Federalism and the Constitution of Canada*, award-winning author David E. Smith examines a series of royal commission and task force inquiries, a succession of federal–provincial conferences, and the competing and controversial terms of the Constitution Act of 1982 in order to evaluate both the popular and governmental understanding of federalism. In the process, Smith uncovers the reasons constitutional agreement has historically proved difficult to reach and argues that Canadian federalism 'in practice' has been more successful at accommodating foundational change than may be immediately apparent.

DAVID E. SMITH is a professor emeritus in the Department of Political Studies at the University of Saskatchewan and a policy fellow in the Johnson-Shoyama Graduate School of Public Policy at the University of Regina.

DAVID E. SMITH

# Federalism and the Constitution of Canada

UNIVERSITY OF TORONTO PRESS
Toronto Buffalo London

© University of Toronto Press Incorporated 2010
Toronto Buffalo London
www.utppublishing.com
Printed in Canada

ISBN 978-1-4426-4270-6 (cloth)
ISBN 978-1-4426-1151-1 (paper)

∞

Printed on acid-free, 100% post-consumer recycled paper
with vegetable-based inks.

**Library and Archives Canada Cataloguing in Publication**

Smith, David E., 1936–
Federalism and the constitution of Canada / David E. Smith.

Includes bibliographical references and index.
ISBN 978-1-4426-4270-6 (bound). – ISBN 978-1-4426-1151-1 (pbk.)

1. Canada – Politics and government.   2. Federal government –
Canada.   3. Constitutional history – Canada.   4. Constitutional law –
Canada.   5. Canada. Constitution Act, 1982.   I. Title.

JL65.S65 2010      320.971      C2010-906192-6

This book has been published with the help of a grant from the
Canadian Federation for the Humanities and Social Sciences, through
the Aid to Scholarly Publications Program, using funds provided by the
Social Sciences and Humanities Research Council of Canada.

University of Toronto Press acknowledges the financial assistance to its
publishing program of the Canada Council for the Arts and the Ontario
Arts Council.

 Canada Council  Conseil des Arts    ONTARIO ARTS COUNCIL
for the Arts      du Canada            CONSEIL DES ARTS DE L'ONTARIO

University of Toronto Press acknowledges the financial support of
the Government of Canada through the Canada Book Fund for its
publishing activities.

*For John C. Courtney, colleague and friend*

# Contents

# Preface

Ever since 1867, federalism and the constitution of Canada have been locked in an uneasy relationship that the passage of time has neither moderated nor clarified. One source of the problem is that unlike other Anglo-American federations to which it is often compared, Canada's is a double federation of cultures *and* territory. This book describes the first type of federation as vertical, the second as horizontal. A half-century ago that same geometric allusion was used – but not borrowed from for the purposes of this study – to describe the country's literary landscape. In a lecture he gave in 1960, Laval University sociologist Jean-Charles Falardeau said that 'if one compares the English and the French literatures in Canada, one is impressed by the fact that the former expresses itself along an axis that [is] horizontal and the latter along a vertical axis.' The first literature, he maintained, was about individuals and their milieux, the second about individuals and themselves.[1] How relevant that distinction is to the politics of Canada, particularly since 1960, is a subject for discussion in the chapters to follow. What may be said with confidence is that the two contrasting orientations to federalism present a challenge for any single constitution to accommodate.

The Constitution Act, 1867, does not speak of cultures and territory; rather it refers, on the one hand, to linguistic and denominational rights in regard to education in some but not all provinces, and, on the other hand, to jurisdiction assigned to all provinces. Even here, the allocation was not uniform. The prairie provinces, created after 1867 by acts of Parliament, were denied their natural resources for some decades, thus laying down a regional grievance that joins the present to the past, as witness the response of the governments of Alberta and Saskatchewan to the National Energy Policy in the 1980s, and that sets claim to the future in prospective intergovernmental disagreement over regulation of the environment. Nor was clarity in the relationship of centre to parts deemed necessary (or desirable): for well over a century, the constitution provided no domestic amending formula by which to discern the distribution of power necessary for agreement on union in the first place or to indicate what constituted sufficient consent for its alteration.

Similarly, there is nothing of substance in the 1867 Act to tell its reader how constitutional monarchy and parliamentary responsible government work, certainly not when joined – for the first time – to what the Preamble of the Act described as a federal union. Much depends upon the attribution given the phrase, in the Preamble, that Canada should have a 'Constitution similar in Principle to that of the United Kingdom.' In this context it is worth noting W.E. Gladstone's cautionary comment of the same period – that the British constitutional system 'had settled down ... only in the last fifty years.'[2] The conventions of the constitution as they applied to the practice of responsible government were far from settled then or for some time thereafter. More than that, how the constitution of an island realm of great antiquity that ruled an empire might be adapted to the conditions of an enormous continental state, whose origin lay in the conquest of one European people of another, remained unappreciated. Decades had to elapse before constitutional scholars acknowledged the astuteness of J.R. Mallory's epigram: 'While the seed of the plant was brought across the Atlantic ... it has grown and nourished itself in Canadian soil and become a distinctly Canadian tree.'[3]

Until the 1960s Canadian politicians were singularly taciturn when it came to elaborating their parliamentary federal form of government. Nowhere was this reticence more evident than in a document, prepared in Ottawa in 1947, to inform the Newfoundland delegation on 'the Constitution and Government of Canada and on the Canadian Federal System.'[4] Only four of its forty-three paragraphs deal with 'the division of powers' as laid down in the BNA Act; just five describe 'provincial governments': legislatures (unicameral except for Quebec), adult franchise, and the office of lieutenant governor. Parties and intergovernmental relations receive no mention. The noun federalism does not appear.

After 1960 a major change in perception of federalism occurred. The discipline of political science grew in sophistication as a result of the introduction of different approaches to its study. University departments multiplied and turned their attention toward research and public policy. Symbolic of the transformation was the work of the Royal Commission on Bilingualism and Biculturalism, appointed in 1963 to make recommendations to lessen tensions now recognized as associated with vertical federalism. As innovative as policies such as bilingualism were, and as influential as they became for the conduct of politics in Canada, equally noteworthy was a contemporaneous recognition that federalism was not the prerogative of governments alone: its web caught people as well as politicians.

For more than a century after union, federalism was detached from the constitution. Most sections of the 1867 Act dealt with the distribution of powers and the institutions associated with that distribution. It is only with the Constitution Act, 1982, that political values that inhere in individuals and minority groups appear: constitutional recognition of official languages, of minority-language educational rights, of the rights of Aboriginal peoples, of equalization, and of provincial control, exploitation, and regulation of natural resources. At the same time, the Canadian Charter of Rights and Freedoms (Part One of the 1982 Act), which guarantees pan-Canadian values, throws into question the diversity that federalism was designed to protect. Here is a further apparent contradiction between federalism and the constitution to challenge the capacity of the country's politicians.

In part because of its imprecision – a parliamentary resolution here, a prerogative act there – the constitution permits politicians to adopt an ambivalent stance when it comes to advocating or defending federalism. For that reason, it may be open to dispute whether the constitution aids or hinders the realization of federalism in Canada. Still, the promise of federalism as articulated by the Fathers of Confederation – to create one independent country out of several dependent colonies – has been realized. The evolving interpretation of federal theory to achieve that end and the role of government, commissions of inquiry, academics, and the people of Canada in that enterprise is the central theme of this study.

I have dedicated this book to John Courtney, colleague and friend for half a century. John and I met the first day of graduate school at Duke University in September 1960, where we were part of a contingent of students from the old Dominions and India and Pakistan admitted to the Commonwealth Studies Program. Few universities outside of Canada have had as strong an influence over a single academic discipline in Canada as Duke University did over political science in the 1960s and 1970s. During the years we were in Durham, our Canadian contemporaries included Ed Black, Fred Fletcher, Ken Kernaghan, Hans Lovink, and Peter Meekison. Later graduates of the Duke department who took up Canadian teaching positions included Keith Archer, Barry Cooper, Neil Nevitte, and American-born Tom Flanagan.

The primary theme of this book is the interrelationship of federalism and Canada's constitution. A secondary concern is the influence that fashions in social science analysis exert on exploring and assessing that relationship. A third topic, more implicit than explicit, is the effect that interpretation by succeeding generations of political science scholars has on public understanding of the Canadian federal system. The years at Duke, under scholars such as Taylor Cole, William Livingston, Richard Preston, Harris Proctor, and Robert Wilson, sparked my initial interest in these questions.

The Commonwealth Studies Program experienced marked change as a result of events in 1960. In February that year, Harold Macmillan, then prime minister of the United Kingdom, warned the South African Parliament of the 'wind of change' about to sweep over the continent. In October, Nigeria, the continent's most populous country, became independent, thus signalling the true beginning of the end to British colonialism in Africa. At Duke, Canada, Australia, New Zealand, and South Africa still attracted interest, but their new Commonwealth partners, along with the arrival of behaviourialism in political analysis, transformed the curriculum. Those Canadians who graduated after the mid-1960s returned to Canada not only with a very different perspective on politics from the one they had when they left but also with a different conception of what politics itself consisted.

Many people have helped me while I have been writing this book. Some were once graduate students when I was; some are former graduate students of mine who now teach in universities. Such continuity is reassuring in an era more often distinguished by rapid and dislocating change. Notwithstanding their critics, and warts, universities remain unique and beneficent institutions for learning that transcend place and time.

One unanticipated consequence of retirement, for a person who has always composed manuscripts in longhand for subsequent typing by someone else, is that if he wants a typed manuscript, he must do it himself. As a result, the customary authorial declaration of responsibility for mistakes in the pages that follow is made in this Preface with greater sense of responsibility than has heretofore been the case.

I wish to thank the Dean of the College of Arts and Sciences, University of Saskatchewan, and the Johnson-Shoyama Graduate School of Public Policy, University of Regina, for their support in the completion of this book. The Humanities Research Institute at the University of Regina has provided a subvention of funds to aid in the preparation of the index, support I gratefully acknowledge. As on former occasions, Ursula Acton has provided great assistance in preparing the manuscript for electronic submission to the press and in compiling the index to the book. Finally, I wish to thank Matthew Kudelka for his light editorial guidance.

The manuscript was completed the first week of September 2009, a period that marked the 104th anniversary of the creation of Alberta and Saskatchewan and their admission as the last of the continental provinces to the federation.

# FEDERALISM AND THE CONSTITUTION OF CANADA

# 1 Primary Matters: Federalism and the Constitution

Improbable as it may appear, the first reference in this study of Canadian federalism is to a letter from Evelyn Waugh to Osbert Sitwell. Writing at the beginning of the Second World War, Waugh invited Sitwell to join him in launching a new literary magazine: 'Its point would be the duration of the things we value – not universal suffrage or disarmament or federalism and all that but good jokes and luxurious writing.'[1] The relevance of Waugh's comment to this book lies in its timing and content. In the early 1940s, federalism as a field of study in political science was underdeveloped. This is not to say that there were no problems deserving of federal solutions: Ireland and India were obvious candidates, though Ireland, despite periodic interest in the subject, never became a federation, and though those parts of the Government of India Act, 1935, that provided for a federation on the subcontinent, failed because of objection from the princely states.[2] Organized treatment of the topic had to wait until after the war. While Waugh was no political scientist, and his opinion scarcely representative of scholars who were, still the analogy he drew between federalism and a universal good, such as disarmament, indicates the ambiguity then attached to the concept – ambiguity that had grown in the interwar period. As early as the 1920s, Harold Laski, who subscribed to a pluralist theory of the state, had pronounced 'federalism [as having] reached the limit of its creativeness.'[3]

That would change after 1946, the year K.C. Wheare's *Federal Government* was published.[4] As a result of this book, Wheare, Australian-born but Oxford-based, became the master explicator of the subject. *Federal Government* was the first and, arguably, is still the only attempt to reify a concept that remains, as the author found it six decades ago, confused and imprecise. In the first chapter, 'What Federal Government Is,' Wheare defines the 'federal principle' as 'the method of dividing powers so that the general and regional governments are each, within a sphere, co-ordinate and independent.' Few works in the vast literature on the subject over the last half-century have not begun either by adopting or disputing the Whearean principle.

Sir Kenneth Wheare died in 1979. In an appreciation of his life and work, Geoffrey Marshall, whose repute as a constitutional scholar by then rivalled that of his Oxford colleague, criticized those who labelled Wheare's federal principle as 'rigid.' Marshall thought it rigorous. Wheare, he said, preferred a 'clear and precise identification of an idea or concept.' By contrast, the dissenters treated the concept 'permissively ... less a mechanical arrangement than a state of mind.' Such imprecision, Marshall concluded, left 'no serious or clear sense for the term "federal."'[5]

The 'mechanical arrangement' – the division of powers between general and regional governments – has more substance than Waugh's undefined values. Still, the two perspectives share one characteristic in common: they are both theocentric, in the sense that the force for federalism – in Wheare's world, judicial review – is beyond and above the society contained within the boundaries the federal system establishes. In the Whearean model, the people the federation serves are remote, the link between them and government uncertain. For those who adopt Marshall's perspective, attenuation is the necessary cost of precision.

For others it is unacceptable. Almost as well-known as *Federal Government* is the book by American scholar William S. Livingston, *Federalism and Constitutional Change*, published in 1956.[6] Here the order of priorities found in Wheare is reversed: rather than law and jurisdiction being the concern, the focus of attention is on behaviour and attitudes. In Livingston's words, 'the essence of federalism lies not in the constitutional or institutional structure but in the society itself.' That premise is reflected in the title of his first chapter, 'The Character of Federalism,' and in its subject matter: the sociology of federalism, the spectrum of federal societies, and what are called diversities and instrumentalities.

The foregoing description of Wheare and Livingston might itself be described as a caricature, or at very least a stereotype, of their work. For instance, Wheare did write – but not in his famous book – about federalism as 'a device through which different nationalities could unite and ... create ... a new sense of common nationality,' and Livingston, despite his introductory discussion about 'diversities,' is elsewhere in his book quite legalistic.[7] That said, the contrast between the two approaches, as set down in the preceding paragraphs, is emblematic of the themes this book will explore.

Wheare and Livingston examine the same federations: Australia, Canada, Switzerland, and the United States. These four were the principal exemplars of federal constitutions in the 1940s; and today, in a much more populous world of federations, they are still the classical representatives of that category of governments. That status comes with age. India, newer but more densely populated than any of the classical 'four' – and parliamentary as well – has received little attention from Canadian scholars of federalism working on Royal Commissions or on their own.[8] While the literature on federalism grows yearly, the appearance of these books only a few years before the beginning of unprecedented change in Canada – specifically, the Quiet Revolution in Quebec – has conferred on them especial prominence. The contrasting importance they attribute to law on one hand and to society on the other, makes them, in the language of administrative analysis, ideal types to employ when conceptualizing federal governments, constitutions, and systems. As this book will argue, the tension that exists between a federal arrangement that emphasizes coordinate and independent spheres – one that is horizontal in its orientation and territorial in construction – and an arrangement that looks to the link between societies and governments – one that is vertical in its orientation and cultural in complexion – is central to understanding the evolution of modern Canadian politics.[9]

The inference to be drawn from Marshall's comment on federal studies that deviate from Wheare's legal principle is necessarily pejorative. Adjectival or metaphorical federalism, in such forms as open federalism, or cooperative federalism, or asymmetrical federalism, or a host of other formulations (twenty-five years ago one American political scientist compiled a list of 326 'metaphors and models of federalism'[10]) fell under his censure, and for a straightforward academic reason: they 'blunted' federalism's meaning and its 'analytic utility.' A metaphor is a descriptive term with imaginative not literal application – understanding comes through association. This is not the way of the law. It is, however, the way of politics, as witness the electoral power recently in Canada of phrases such as 'participatory democracy' and 'democratic deficit.' The contrast between law and politics in this regard deserves discussion (which it will receive later in this book) because both federalism and the constitution draw, in different and fluctuating degrees, upon each.

'The adjectival modifier "politicizes" [federalism],' says Deil Wright, an American political scientist.[11] This explains the force and originality of an article such as Alan Cairns's 'The Governments and Societies of Canadian Federalism' (1977); or the sense of a new, foundational language when Richard Simeon reinterprets the familiar and, up until then (1972), routine world of federal–provincial meetings as an exercise in 'diplomacy.'[12] At one level, it is hardly news that federalism in Canada has been politicized, if by that is meant the continuing promotion of federal and provincial interests. It was always thus, and it would be an odd federal system if this were not the case. But more is implied by the word 'politicize'; consider the range of modifiers, now so great and that convey meanings so different from that of traditional federalism. An example would be rights or Charter federalism; another would be people's federalism.

It is that transformation in understanding that explains the title of this book: *Federalism and the Constitution of Canada*, and that sets it apart from the approaches of scholars such as R. MacGregor Dawson and James Mallory (see 46–7). There are three meanings to the word *constitution*. Actually, there may be more than three, since the sense of constitution as written law (that is, the Constitution Act, 1867, and its amendments) *and* as unwritten convention (for example, except on rare occasions the Governor General only acts on advice of the prime minister) is complex, uncertain, and infinitely expandable. The Constitution Act, 1867, has 147 sections. Most deal with the structure of the federation: numbers 9 to 16 deal with the executive power; 17 to 52 with the legislative power (basically the structure and composition of the Senate and the House of Commons); and 58 to 87 and 134 to 147 with those provinces (largely Ontario and Quebec) whose provincial constitutions are found within the enactment that founds Canada. Sections 91 to 95 are the best known because they set out the divisions of powers that have been the primary source of federal–provincial legal wrangling. The remaining sections deal with taxation and revenues and the composition of the judiciary.

Nonetheless, appearances may be deceiving. How does parliamentary federalism reconcile its internal contradiction: concentrated power at the centre as a result of party discipline and the prerogatives of the prime minister; versus the distributed power that is inherent in a federal arrangement, whether it leans toward the Wheare or Livingston interpretation? Moving from the written law, what are the *conventions* of federalism in Canada? Is it in part through these unwritten understandings that the tensions implicit in parliamentary federalism are lessened? Chapter 3, 'A Constitution in Some Respects Novel,' chapter 4, 'Parliamentary Federalism,' and chapter 5, 'The Practice of Federalism' explore these questions while assessing Canada's experience with a system of parliamentary federalism. It needs to be remembered that Canada was the world's first parliamentary federation and that, largely because Australia – the monarchical, parliamentary, and federal country it most resembles – preferred American over Canadian example when the Commonwealth was created in 1901, this country remains the principal if not unique representative of its type.

Thus constitution, as in *founding*, is one meaning.

Another is constitution as in *composition*. While there is a link between the two meanings, they are not to be confused. It is important to recall, because it is essential to conceptions of modern Canada, that at this country's founding there were four provinces and that a large part of the history of Canada concerns the rounding out of the federation. Of particular note is the retention by Ottawa of the natural resources of the prairie provinces. This action, along with a protective tariff, a transcontinental railway financed through the alienation of prairie land, and freight rates that were perceived to be regionally discriminatory, created an 'empire within an empire' with, this book will argue, lasting and even irremediable effects. The imperial theme, both internally as well as in relations with Great Britain, is heard early in the history of Canada: in the Confederation Debates (the debates in the Parliament of United Canada on the 1865 Quebec Resolutions), D'Arcy McGee described the 'Imperial Government as the common arbiter of us all, in our true Federal metropolis.'[13] The contrast with Australia – a continent for a country, a country for a continent – is striking. An act of inclusion so complete was denied to Canada, at least until 1982 with the adoption of the Charter, and then the simultaneous inclusion was of individuals, not territories.

In one respect the United States is more like Canada than Australia, since it took more than a century for the frontier to move across the continent. Yet with regard to federalism and the constitution, the resemblance lies with Australia, for within a decade of the Revolution the American states had been re-created. The verbs most often used to explain this are 'reconstitute' and 'reconceive'; the favourite adverb has been 'simultaneously.' After 1787 the states owed their legitimacy to the United States Constitution. They had no prior claim to recognition based on historic, collective, or popular identity; rather, their security lay through Congress in 'the mutual recognition of the legitimacy of statehood.' More fundamental still, by accepting that recognition the American states forfeited 'the essential prerogatives of sovereign statehood.' Congress successfully claimed control of the Western lands on behalf of the nation; later those lands reappeared in the 'new status of territory' and, eventually, in a 'mechanical [and] automatic way,' as states. This process, says American historian Peter Onuf, 'debase[d] statehood.'[14]

What is the significance of the contrast between Canada, on one hand, and Australia and the United States, on the other – between sequential and simultaneous entry of states or provinces? In Canada, the entry or proposed entry of new provinces was received with unease. When in the early 1940s preliminary discussions were under way with the then British colony of Newfoundland to explore terms of union with Canada, the agent of the federal government reported that Newfoundlanders 'really [do not] appreciate or understand the workings of the Federal system of government.' More than that, said another observer, if the colony became a province, 'it would very quickly take over as its own all the old Maritime grievances.'[15] The view was that instead of creating a stronger federation, expansion might destabilize the union. How else to explain the lack of consensus, still, on how a territory becomes a province? The Constitution Act, 1982, subjected, for the first time, the admission of new provinces to the consent of seven provinces with 50 per cent of the country's population; the Meech Lake Accord would have raised the barrier to unanimous provincial approval; the Charlottetown Agreement sought to go back to the pre-1982 custom of creating new provinces by Act of Parliament following consultation with all the existing provinces.

The subject of this study, it should be emphasized, is the constitutionally established federal and ten provincial governments: 'Canada's three territories, Nunavut, the Northwest Territories, and the Yukon are in effect federal protectorates without constitutionally rooted executive authority but have been delegated much of that authority from the federal government.'[16] The decision to omit the three territories is not just a matter of convenience. As will be elaborated in chapter 4, 'Parliamentary Federalism,' the Crown is an essential element, historically and currently, in the operation of Canadian federalism. For that reason, its absence 'has both symbolic and practical consequences.' Among the latter is that 'territorial ownership of land and resources in their own Crown right' is impeded.[17] Control of land and resources is a perennial theme in the Canadian federal story.

A third meaning of constitution is *strength or vitality*. In the context of the present discussion, what is federalism's contribution to the health of Canada's constitution? The quick, because it is familiar, answer is that federalism exhausts Canadians' understanding of the constitution. More than half a century ago, Harold Innis lamented that 'multi-regional, bilingual and bireligious countries [consume] their energies in compromise.'[18] The much later complaint about 'constitutional fatigue,' after the failure of the Meech Lake and Charlottetown proposals to win approval, echoes the same sentiment. Peter Russell's *Constitutional Odyssey* is a chronicle of federalism lost, at least insofar as unanimous agreement on a constitutional form to embody it remained unobtainable.[19]

There is more to the constitution than federalism, and it is to that other dimension that Innis alludes. Few of the practices of responsible government that are usually assumed to lie at the heart of parliamentary democracy are mentioned in the Constitution Act, 1867. If not taken for granted, they are largely unknown or misunderstood by the general public and the media. It is out of this shadowland, rather than the more visible structures of Canadian federalism, that the democratic deficit of unresponsive politics appears. It is true that critics of the Senate of Canada never tire of complaining about its structure and more particularly its lack of democratic legitimacy because it is unelected. But that is part of the problem. Preoccupation with securing the unity of the federation, through mechanisms such as a distorted representation-by-population principle in the House of Commons, rigid adherence on the part of all parties in the House to party discipline, and prime ministerial domination of the legislature, has been at the cost of democratic norms, whether measured in terms of accountability, responsiveness, or representation. The controversy associated with the sponsorship program (see the Commission of Inquiry into the Sponsorship Program and Advertising Activities, 2006), which, following the near victory of separatist forces in the 1995 Quebec referendum, saw some federal officials improperly divert money to organizations in Quebec in order to promote the cause of Canadian unity, is an egregious but not unique example of the cause of federalism in conflict with the cause of the constitution.[20]

Is there a less doleful assessment to be made of federalism's effect on Canadian politics? Without a doubt. Canadian federalism – and especially the relationship between federalism and parliamentary institutions – has proven resilient and innovative. Take medicare, as one example. T.C. Douglas, the Co-operative Commonwealth Federation he led, and the government of Saskatchewan, of which he was premier after 1944, were key participants in achieving, by stages, comprehensive medical care insurance. Still, they were not alone. In the words of one who was at the centre of events, Allan Blakeney: 'Then the federal government came to the rescue.'[21] Initially, that government was Liberal, led by Louis St Laurent, but its successor, the Progressive Conservative government led by John Diefenbaker, was of the same mind. Here fiscal federalism in the form of shared-cost agreements designed by Ottawa made provincial ambition a reality. As well, it was the Diefenbaker government that appointed the Royal Commission on Health Services, headed by Mr Justice Emmett Hall of the Supreme Court of Canada. To put it bluntly, the recommendations of the Hall Commission made national what had been a provincial program. In the matter of health care, the sequence in Canada of province and then nation is not found in the United States, where such programs as Medicaid originated in Congress and have not been emulated by the states. Why are the policy hierarchies in the two North American federations different?

Another example, perhaps less universally applauded by Canadians than medicare, is the emergence of the Parti Québécois and the growth of nationalist sentiment in the province of Quebec. The journey without end in the quest for a constitutional settlement to which the government of Quebec will assent clouds judgment on the nature of the issue. True, political agreement has yet to be achieved, but in the meantime Quebec has been transformed from a province where French-speaking Quebeckers faced discrimination – for example, in the workplace because of their language – to one where the French-speaking community has taken control of the province's economy. Rather than seeing themselves as a minority in Canada, they now see themselves as a majority in Quebec. This reversal in self-perception has come at a cost, most certainly when seen through the prism of federalism: it has created a distance between French-speakers inside Quebec and French-speakers outside the province. It would be trite to say that Quebec and Canadian federalism is a large and complicated topic; but it is. Aspects of it will arise throughout the following chapters. Contrary to the jeremiad that sees the flowering of nationalist sentiment in Quebec as an index of federalism's failure in Canada, this book treats it as a mark of this country's ability to accommodate foundational change.

One of the unexamined premises held by some critics of Canadian federalism is that, among the units of a federation, equality is a necessary condition. The origin of this assumption is open to debate, but one possible source is Wheare's statement that 'the federal principle has come to mean what it does because the United States has come to be what it is.'[22] In the practice of American federalism, equality is a value much celebrated. At entry into the Union each state is guaranteed at least one member of the House of Representatives and, regardless of population, two senators. Redistricting – the decennial allocation of the 435 House seats among the fifty states – is carried out with a precision that, by Canadian standards, is unemotional, ahistorical, and illustrative of the description one American has given her fellow citizens – 'a calculating people.'[23] Historic claims do not exist. Even before Confederation, the contrast between American and British North American perspectives was noted (in Canada):

> No matter how raw and rude a territory may be when it is admitted as a State into the Union of the United States, it is at once by the popular belief invested with all the dignity of manhood and introduced into a system which … every American believes and maintains to be immortal – But how does the case stand with us? – no matter how great the advance of a British colony in wealth and civilization – no matter how absolute the powers of self Government conceded to it – it is still taught to believe that it is in a condition of pupilage from which it must pass before it can attain maturity.[24]

By contrast, in 2009 Saskatchewan had – as it has had since 1976 because of a grandfather clause in the redistribution formula – fourteen seats in the House of Commons. Since Canada has a population of around 33 million people, the House of Commons 308 seats, and Saskatchewan a population of approximately one million, the province should, by a rep-by-pop measure, have nine or at the most ten MPs. It has more members for the same reason the provinces were not treated equally at the time of their entry into Confederation. Distribution of House seats has been determined by a political calculus, not a mathematical one.[25] It was for this reason that the recent campaign for a Triple E Senate – at least the E that stood for equal number of senators per province – as opposed to the present range of twenty-four to four – was an uphill fight. Notwithstanding what people might say about wanting equality, no one wanted it achieved at the risk of losing seats in the Commons.

The constitutional adjustments that have been made over time (official bilingualism, for one) – and that are still being made, as witness the growing acceptance of the claims of Aboriginal peoples but no constitutional entrenchment of Aboriginal rights – testify to the depth as well as the breadth ('from sea to sea to sea') of Canadian federalism. They also demonstrate its elasticity in accommodating major demographic and social changes. For this reason it seems tendentious for Geoffrey Marshall to summarize Canada's experience as 'the world's most complex system of federal distribution, which remains an awe-inspiring example of what is to be avoided by any modern draftsman allocating legislative powers.'[26] Admitting, for the purposes of argument, that it is a very complex system, what – the reader of this assessment wonders – might have been 'avoided,' and with what consequences?

Perhaps the complexity lies in the different meanings of the word constitution and in how these meanings intersect with the activity associated with federalism. What happens when the constitution no longer means what its text seems to say?[27] Perhaps, too, there is a temporal dimension implicit in the remark – Canada as others once saw it and continue to see it. Here is federalism through time. But is there any communion between leaders such as Sir John A. Macdonald, Sir Wilfrid Laurier, and Pierre Trudeau on the topic of Canadian federalism? Is there a theory to weave the decades into a whole, or only a sequence of linked events?

Another possible explanation for Marshall's pessimistic judgment is related to when he uttered it – 1982. That was the year the Canadian Charter of Rights and Freedoms was adopted, as part of the much larger package of amendments found within the Constitution Act, 1982. He may have foreseen what later critics of the Charter have described as its de-federalizing influence on Canada's political culture. Rights know no jurisdiction; they transcend provincial boundaries. These arguments and the literature that expounds them are discussed in chapter 6, 'Courts and Charter: Constitution and Federalism.' Marshall could not have been familiar with either of them since they came after he passed his opinion on the condition of Canadian federalism. However, he might well have been aware of the heated debate that took place in Canada prior to adoption of the constitutional package, one aspect of which focused on the compatibility of instituting a higher law in a parliamentary federation. From his perspective at that time and from the perspective of others since then, the advent of the Charter in a system of divided jurisdictions that subscribed to the principle of parliamentary sovereignty created a conundrum that required clarification, if not solution.

Whether, and how, the Charter has affected the operation of the Canadian federation is for later consideration. What it *has* done, as discussed in chapter 7, 'The Habit of Federalism,' is reinforce the federalism of small things. The seed of that idea lies in the insight of American political scientist Daniel Elazar, who maintained that American federalism is 'an orientation [that] emphasizes each individual's place in a network of cooperative communities, where individualism is defined not through one's detachment but through partnership with others.' There is, he says, 'a federalist way' of organizing civil life.[28] Does this insight apply to Canada?

If it does, it is not because the Fathers of Confederation mapped Canadian federalism on American federalism. Indeed, there are significant differences between the two federal experiments. Nor does it mean that society on one side of the forty-ninth parallel duplicates that on the other. The degree of difference is a subject of permanent interest to Canadians.[29] In Livingston's world, constitutional federalism may recognize diversity and may promote diversity; but Elazar's perception is something different again: *within a state*, Americans organize their social clubs, their professional associations, their sports groups, and more on the federal principle. As will be shown later in this book, the same organizational sense of personal federalism prevails in the provinces of Canada, and not only for practical considerations that derive from their occupying large land areas with small concentrated populations. Federated colleges, federated Aboriginal groups, provincial athletic leagues, and provincial cooperatives are but a few examples of organizations that often ascribe to the federal idea.

On one hand, as its proponents argued it would, the Charter has nationalized values and in the process promoted an increased sense of Canadianness. It has done this through specific reference to equality between male and female persons, to the multicultural heritage of Canadians, and to minority-language educational rights. It has done it in another way – through heightened awareness of legal rights for all and of their potential for abuse. The list of individuals mistreated by the police, unlawfully confined, wrongfully imprisoned, whose names have become bywords for justice gone wrong – Neil Stonechild, David Milgaard, Donald Marshall Jr, Guy Paul Morin – makes the point.[30] The administration of justice in Canada may be a provincial matter (the practice of policing is less jurisdictionally precise, since the RCMP serves as the provincial police in eight of the ten provinces), but the publicity accompanying reports of miscarriages of justice is anything but provincial.[31] Here rights have acted as a nationalizing force that transcends the provinces.

On the other hand, and at the same time, rights and a heightened sensibility about rights work in the reverse direction, by enhancing rather than limiting the scope for activity within the provinces. The expansion of social justice networks, the growth in activity of provincial human rights commissions, the introduction in the provinces of legislation to permit class action lawsuits (which may be invoked to challenge a perceived abuse of rights or to secure recognition of a hitherto unorganized interest as a class) – these have broadened the base for federal–provincial interaction. Rights, as expressed within the boundaries of the provinces, augment federalism. Chapter 5, 'The Practice of Federalism,' will examine an argument often heard about the basic weakness of Canadian federalism – that it inadequately represents provincial concerns at the centre, with the result that federalism in Canada lies in the parts and not at the centre.[32] For the moment it may be said that as a result of the Charter and the proliferation of concern for rights, the real world of personal and social consciousness has insinuated itself into the provinces through the federalism of small things.

The effect has been to make the provinces organic to the whole. It is misleading therefore to posit federalism as institutionalized rivalry between the central and provincial governments – and leave it at that. Of course, there *is* rivalry; that is inevitable. But the persistence of seeing federalism in terms of conflict narrows the dimension of analysis in two ways: by privileging governments – usually the central and unit governments of traditional federations – over individuals, societies, and cultures as subjects of study; and, in consequence, by privileging the national over local or global perspectives. The concept of boundaries is fundamental to the approaches Wheare and Livingston adopt, just as it was to the labours of the JCPC as that body delineated the jurisdictions of the provinces and the central government, and to the Royal Commission on Dominion-Provincial Relations (Rowell-Sirois) in its search for efficiency through the elimination of legislative and bureaucratic redundancy. Yet boundaries are out of fashion today because respect for them is impractical. If, as two scholars of federalism say, it is 'impossible to sharply distinguish between federalism and intergovernmentalism,' then some adjustment in perspective is required.[33] As chapter 4, 'Parliamentary Federalism,' argues, it is no longer adequate to say that Canada is a parliamentary federation, since that designation communicates little about the operation of government at the centre or in the parts.

But the 'boundaries question' also arises when the perspective is *external*. In the postwar years the concern of scholars of federalism was inward – what went on, for example, in the Canadian (or Australian) federation, and how a country's constitution and institutions affected what went on within it. Sixty years later, in Canada in particular, the vantage is outward as well. Consider the Forum of Federations, an 'international network on federalism' launched in 1998 at the initiative of the government of Canada and, according to its mission statement, 'concerned with the contribution federalism makes and can make to the maintenance and construction of democratic societies and governments.' On its Web page, two of forum's 'three core functions' refer to 'the practice of federalism' and to 'practitioners (and future practitioners) of federalism.'[34]

The two perspectives – looking out and looking in – are not separate. Indeed, a strong motivation for the Forum of Federations initiative lay in the government's 'conviction that ... knowledge of other federations will strengthen Canadian unity.'[35] It would do this through a demonstration effect: federalism works – thus the emphasis on practice – and it does so through rich and variegated means. This catholic approach, evident in the forum's publications (as in the handbook, *Federalism: An Introduction*) and in the programs of its conferences, has rejected the hermetic and seemingly permanent categories of early federal literature.[34] For example, in the July 2008 issue of forum's magazine *Federations*, whose subtitle is 'What's New in Federalism Worldwide,' there is a 'Special Section: Decentralization and Devolution in Non-Federal Countries' as well as an article on the 'Practitioner's Page' devoted to Mexican cities.[35] By comparison, Daniel Elazar's scrupulous delineation of American federalism as neither centralized not decentralized but rather non-centralized seems laboured and overly refined.[38]

A second reason why an approach to federalism that takes rivalry as its theme is analytically deficient is that it is static. It ignores the collapse of structures of meaning that make sense of Canada's development as a federation. At one time, there was conflict of jurisdiction (the familiar division-of-powers question); at another, the internal struggles of federated political parties competing to form the national government; then there was administrative and fiscal federalism; and now societal federalism, according to which territoriality is 'represented' through myriad patterns of association (some centrally inspired, some not).

The new sense of Canadian federalism is wholly other than its antecedents. The old ideas of the federal government presiding from on high, or of the federal system being no more than a multiple of provincial unitary systems, or of the provinces and the federal government locked into an eternal quest for balance, are insufficient for understanding modern Canada. All are necessary features of that enterprise, but none alone is sufficient. It hardly needs to be said – since federalism at some level is always about doubleness – but a weakness of interpretations of the subject is that they lean toward one dimension. One explanation for this characteristic in Canada, says Richard Simeon, is 'the pull of current events,' which leads to a 'present-mindedness … in our work.'[39] Uppermost in scholars' minds, at least since the 1960s, has been Canada's survival as a nation. Variations on the theme 'must Canada fail?' and how to prevent that outcome are just that – variations on one theme, which because of its subject matter concentrates principally on the weakness of federal institutions and their capacity to change.[40] Two consequences flow from this constricted perspective: federalism as an arrangement for living that affects culture, politics, economics, and society is forsaken for attenuated mechanical descriptions – the federalism of metaphors; and discussions about federalism become a substitute for federalism, with the result that scholars loom larger than the subject itself.

After 1960 a series of proposals and a succession of conferences sought to reconcile within a single constitution cultural (that is, binational) federalism and territorial federalism. The contemporaneous tension evident between the two, relieved in part by the Constitution Act, 1982 – for example, Section 92A (provincial control over non-renewable natural resources) – but also exacerbated by Quebec's refusal to agree to its terms, along with subsequent failure to secure agreement to the 1982 Act, even in modified form, illustrates the conundrum of attempting to integrate federalism within the constitution through a deliberative process. One result has been to undermine national political parties in consequence of the formation of the Bloc Québécois and the Reform Party. Another has been to feed public frustration with government and politicians, and with the constitution and federalism itself. For those without a collective memory defined by binationalism, the more negotiators agreed on unanimity for constitutional change the more confederal – and less recognizable – the federation became. For those with a collective memory – that is, something more than the sum of individual memories – refusal by others to acknowledge the need to protect the smaller community, as through a 'historic' constitutional veto, has placed the legitimacy of the federation in doubt.

# 2 The Measure of Federalism

The power of the state is monopolized by government. In a unitary system there is one government; in a federal system there is more than one government. Modern federalism begins with the Constitution of the United States agreed to by the Founding Fathers at Philadelphia in 1787. Following American example, a federal constitution was adopted by Switzerland in 1848, by Canada in 1867, and by Australia in 1901. While some scholars trace the seed of the federal idea to the conciliar movement of medieval times or to the biblical concept of the covenant, federalism associated with a geographical division of power originated in 1787. The United States and the other three basically nineteenth-century federations remained, until the middle of the twentieth century, the singular applications of the federal idea. It was only after 1945, when the European powers, and particularly Great Britain, sought to provide their former colonies in Africa, the West Indies, and Asia with independent constitutions, that federalism ceased to be a monopoly of Western and predominantly Anglo-American countries.

As noted in chapter 1, the first attempts at examining the federal idea translated into constitutional form appeared in the decade or so after the end of the Second World War. Among the best known, but by no means unique, were the studies by K.C. Wheare and W.S. Livingston.[1] For the present discussion, what is relevant is that all of these works were comparative in their treatment of federalism. In this character-istic they were harbingers of federalist literature to follow. The com-parisons were not always international – they could be domestic: How, for instance, does one state or province of a federation fare relative to another unit of the same federation? – but there was always a compara-tive aspect to the literature, and perhaps necessarily so since federa-tions encompass more than one jurisdiction.

It is a feature of federal studies that there is always assumed to be some 'other,' to which the subject under examination should (or even must) be compared. Never, as the late Eugene Forsey once said of Canada, do 'we star[t] from the premise that Canada is not the exception to the rule but its own rule. All references to other federations or to the nature of federalism in general are beside the point.'[2] Holding this view, Forsey would never have agreed, even in the most sombre of moments such as the collapse of the Meech Lake Accord, to the following proposal: 'Faced with the realization of a potential breakup of the federation as the only alternative, a more radically asymmetrical federation [for Canada] might be accepted. The clearest example of such an arrangement is the Malaysian federation where there is a marked greater autonomy for the two Borneo [island] states.'[3]

In this respect the study of federal government is markedly different from the study of non-federal or unitary government. In fact, there is no study of unitary *systems* of government, as opposed to a particular unitary government, such as found in France. The reason why, as one Australian political scientist has observed, is that federal systems are considered to be the exception while unitary systems are treated as the norm.[4] In the Confederation Debates, John A. Macdonald's defence of his second-best alternative, a federal over a legislative union, is phrased in this way: federalism is defined by what it is not – legislative union.

This distinction between 'regular' and 'irregular' explains the attraction of federal studies. But only in part: A.V. Dicey's disparagement of federalism as 'weak,' as a system that 'limits on every side the action of government and ... splits up the strength of the state,' suggests another reason.[5] Federal systems are not just exceptional; they are treated as incomplete, handicapped, with special needs. Vinerian Professor of Law at Oxford, Dicey's opinion counted for much in academic and legal circles in the three-quarters of a century following the appearance of his *Introduction to the Study of the Law of the Constitution* (1885). The centrepiece of his great treatise was the assertion of the sovereignty of Parliament. Federalism's failing was that it undermined singular sovereignty by establishing rival jurisdictions. Marrying the two principles in one parliamentary federation, of which Canada was the first and remains a major example, could be viewed as a recipe for constitutional tension, if not turmoil.

Like Tolstoy's 'happy families,' unitary governments are all assumed to be the same, while federations, the 'unhappy families,' are considered to be different. The contrasting fate of the two governmental forms is widely attributed to the differences in structure and composition among (and, equally important, within the units of) federations. Thus the measure of federalism, both as a concept and as a practice, derives from acknowledgment, first, of difference and, second, of magnitude. The remainder of this chapter will examine the topic by answering the following questions: What is measured? Who measures? And when and where do they measure?

**What**

The capacity for difference is hinted at in the prefixes and adjectives that are commonly heard in discussions about federalism in Canada: bi-, coordinate, concurrent, divided, double, dual, inter-, intra-, quasi-, triple, two; and in such nouns as balance, compartments, jurisdictions, levels, and spheres. It is the essence of federalism that territory and power be divided. Usually, but not invariably, the powers allocated to the units of a federation are the same. Not so the geographic size of the units, which may vary enormously: Rhode Island and Texas in the United States, Tasmania and Western Australia in Australia, and Prince Edward Island (PEI) and Quebec in Canada. In Canada, the difference in geographic area has implications that extend far beyond the question of size. For reasons deriving from the country's federal parliamentary system, PEI, which today has a population one-twentieth that of Metropolitan Toronto, has contributed to the rigidification of an already rigid constitutional amending process. Because its premier sits at the federal–provincial table alongside the premier of Ontario, and because of its conventional representation in the federal cabinet, small PEI is a continuing irritant to large municipal governments, like Toronto, that under the Canadian constitution go formally unrepresented both at table and in cabinet.

The contrast between the smallest and the largest units of the respective American, Australian, and Canadian federations presents a significant challenge for economic adjustment and political accommodation. How this has been addressed in Canada is the story of fiscal federalism (particularly equalization) in the first instance, and the redistribution of House of Commons seats in the second. Both involve complex formulae that have changed over time. Equalization and redistribution are calculated on the basis of data that are collected by an agency of the federal government but that are of paramount importance to the provinces, a fact recognized early in the life of the federation. In the debate on first reading of 'An Act respecting the First Census,' Alexander Mackenzie, later to be Canada's second prime minister, cautioned that 'it was particularly important to have the personal Census taken with great accuracy as on that depended the political relations of the several Provinces under the Union Act towards each other.'[6] In an appreciation of the life and work from 1916 until 1942 of Canada's first Dominion Statistician (Robert H. Coats), the economist Nathan Keyfitz observed that 'he always saw the collection and publication of statistics as something of a judicial function to which disinterestedness was as essential as expertness.'[7]

'Towards each other' – or more precisely, how did the provinces compare to one another in relation to federal authority? That was the referent for this early comparison, as it was to be on many occasions thereafter. The most dramatic demonstration of this occurred in the same year (1870) and subsequently in 1905, when Parliament retained the natural resources of Manitoba and then Alberta and Saskatchewan (the three Canadian provinces whose constitutional root is an act of Parliament), transferring them only in 1930, while all other provinces possessed their resources from the moment of their creation. This engendered a sense of regional discrimination, grievance, and sensitivity that continues to be expressed in modern Canadian politics. Or, when the New Democratic Party (NDP) government of Saskatchewan in 2007 went to court to challenge what it claimed was discrimination in the dollar amount of equalization payment it received from Ottawa.[8] The cases for comparison were Nova Scotia and Newfoundland and Labrador, which under agreements with the federal government did not have their natural resource revenues included in their equalization calculations, while Saskatchewan did.

For Quebec, the referent is sometimes the policies and conditions of Ontario, but more usually it takes as its focus Ottawa's treatment of Quebec when compared to the rest of the country. The reason for the latter perspective – one central to understanding Canadian politics – lies in Canada's double federalism. Double federalism does not mean double government, where citizens are subject contemporaneously to the laws of two jurisdictions – for example, the provincial highway code and the Criminal Code of Canada. This is the sine qua non of a federal system. Nor does it mean dual government, where citizens are subject to the laws of one jurisdiction, which at the same time may act as an agent for another government. This was the defining feature the Articles of Confederation in the United States between 1777 and 1789.

It was this hierarchical as opposed to horizontal arrangement of power and the lack of a national voice and purpose it allowed that drove the United States into a more integrated federal constitution. Double federalism is something else again.

There are two reasons for adopting a federal constitution. One is to recognize cultural difference, defined by features such as language, religion, or ethnicity. The other is to incorporate territory. Most federations are attributable to one or other imperative. Canada is unusual in having as its origins both imperatives: one, to give Quebec jurisdiction over matters deemed essential to the preservation of its culture, which the experience of the Province of United Canada for a quarter-century before Confederation and the rise to demographic dominance of English-speaking Protestants threatened by 1867; and two, to establish the central political institutions that would make territorial expansion possible through the transfer to Canada from the Hudson's Bay Company of Rupert's Land and the North-Western Territories.[9]

Much of the complexity of *Canadian politics* and – something slightly different – of *federal politics in Canada* may be traced to double federalism. Quebec sees itself in a constitutional arrangement with Ottawa, which speaks for the rest of Canada. The other provinces see themselves individually in a bilateral relationship with Ottawa (over a range of provincially specific issues – for example, fish, lumber, and the auto industry), but they also see themselves as aligned in order to press the federal government for better terms in policy areas of mutual concern, such as health care. Nonetheless, it is important to note that the two halves of Canada's double federation are not mutually exclusive. To cite two examples, the Official Languages Act, 1969 (OLA), and the denominational educational provisions of the Constitution Act, 1867, take their meaning from the cultural dimension of the federative act of 1867. Yet they have had a direct and often disruptive impact on the life of the other, territorial federation. Denominational rights lay at the core of the original Confederation settlement, but outside of central Canada they were seen to trespass upon provincial rights. The effect of the 'schools question' that resulted was to slow down the rounding out of Confederation. The rationale offered by the Royal Commission on Bilingualism and Biculturalism for passage of the OLA (which was that English- and French-speaking Canadians were the country's two founding peoples) promoted strong opposition in western Canada to the policy as well as to the central government and Liberal party that gave it life.

The primary measure of federalism is the number of units into which a federation is divided – fifty in the United States, ten in Canada, six in Australia. The number is important, for the more there are the easier it is to form and re-form alliances among the unit governments and between the unit and central governments. However, such behaviour among the fifty states is foreign to politics in the United States, since in that country the states (and their governors) do not monopolize or even dominate the expression of state interests in national affairs. That is a key role played by members of Congress and by senators. In this vein, it would be a very different matter in Canada if twenty provincial premiers sat alongside the prime minister in federal–provincial meetings. Whether the provinces would be weaker or stronger than at present may be debated, but that their larger number would alter the behaviour of national parties (from leadership selection to election campaigning) and the practice of parliamentary government is beyond doubt. One basic example: If the number of provinces were doubled, would it be feasible for all of them to be represented in what Canadians now call a federalized cabinet?

The number of units determines the location of boundaries. Yet the subject of boundaries seldom arises in the study of Canadian politics. It comes as a surprise to learn that between 1867 and the admission of Newfoundland and Labrador to Confederation in 1949, twelve separate maps were required to depict boundary changes.[10] In 1905 the provinces of Alberta and Saskatchewan were created out of a portion of the Northwest Territories remaining after the creation of a postage-stamp sized Manitoba in 1870 and the District of Yukon in 1898. Between 1898 and 1912 vast areas taken from the Territories were added to the existing provinces of Manitoba, Ontario, and Quebec. Additions to existing provinces were made, rather than new provinces created, on the grounds of climatic conditions: the northern areas of what are now the prairie provinces were deemed by the federal government as 'absolutely unfit for agriculture,' without which there was 'little hope of "thick and permanent settlement,"' and, consequently, stable provincial government.'[11] To this practical reason were added others, such as Manitoba's claim, made 'in the spirit of confederation,' to territory equivalent in area to that held by Saskatchewan and Alberta, and Quebec's proposition that its boundaries be extended 'as compensation for any advantages that Ontario, Manitoba, and Saskatchewan would gain if they were extended to the western shore of Hudson Bay.'[12]

The following year (1913) and from a distant quarter arose another claim – whose rationale cited the extension of boundaries of Manitoba, Ontario, and Quebec – for special treatment in the allocation of seats in the House of Commons. Prince Edward Island argued that the Maritime provinces 'had as good a right to share in the public demesne of Canada as had those provinces upon which it was bestowed ... The territories added out of the public demesne will increase to a limit not now possible of calculation the representation of these provinces in the federal Parliament.'[13] To the extent this prediction proved correct it added to the problems of Canadian federalism. In 1938, when he appeared before the Royal Commission on Dominion-Provincial Relations (popularly known by the names of its chairmen, Rowell-Sirois), Mitch Hepburn, then premier of Ontario, expressed the frustration that came with seeking to reconcile the numerical claims advanced by some of the Canadian provinces:

> One could not find a more striking illustration of the impracticality of compensating provinces for the disabilities they claim (even the real ones) as a result of federal policy. The Canadian Government expended hundreds of millions ... in opening the prairies to markets; when Nova Scotia's sons (among others) went West to seize opportunity – Mr [Norman McL.]. Rogers [counsel for Nova Scotia] presented a bill for Nova Scotia's stagnation, and the Premier of Manitoba presented another one for the social services of an expanding population.[14]

Representation is intimately linked to the subject of boundaries, and for this reason political decisions may have long-term and irreversible impact. That was true when Ottawa responded to PEI's memorandum. In 1915 the Westminster Parliament – the only legislative body that at the time could alter the Constitution Act, 1867 – passed at Canada's request an amendment guaranteeing that no province should have fewer members of the House of Commons than it had Senators (S.51A). Seven decades later (1982), when Canadian politicians finally agreed on a domestic amending formula, that provision became one of four specific subjects (the others dealt with the Crown, the use of the English and French languages, and the composition of the Supreme Court of Canada) for which unanimous consent was deemed necessary for its future amendment.

Outside of the Atlantic region the Canadian provinces are large – Saskatchewan and Alberta are each almost as big as Texas. They are also vertical in their orientation, with the provincial capital and population concentrated in the South, and mineral and water resources of the Laurentian Shield in their hinterland North. (Provincial life runs, one might say, at right angles to federal or national life. Alberta and Saskatchewan each had four-lane highways between their two principal cities before they had twinned their portions of the Trans-Canada Highway.) A principal theme in the history of each province is exploitation by the south of northern resources. In this, the western provinces stand in marked contrast to the western states of the United States, for not only do the American states not control mineral resources, as the provinces do in Canada, but even where they do control resources such as water, the states are too small – except perhaps for California – to develop adequate policies to regulate or exploit them.[15]

The western provinces may be large, but they are not *too* large. Before the creation of Alberta and Saskatchewan in 1905, some territorial politicians pressed for 'one prairie province.' That proposal found little favour with the federal Liberal government, led by Sir Wilfrid Laurier, for the simple reason that such an entity would threaten the dominance of Ontario. At the time he introduced the autonomy legislation to establish the two new provinces, the prime minister told the House that 'unequal siz[e] ... is not a fatal fault ... but ... when provinces are not the result of historic tradition, when they have not come to us formed and when they have control of events, it is preferable that the provinces should be as near as possible about the same size.'[16] The territorial expansion of Ontario in 1912 created a province of over 1.0 million square kilometres; Saskatchewan and Alberta together totalled just over 1.3 million square kilometres.

In twenty-first century Canada one topic of political discussion is asymmetrical federalism – that is, disparity in the relationships that provinces have with Ottawa.[17] The cause of disparity is fuelled by a number of reasons, though one seldom mentioned now is differences in geographic size of the provinces. This element in the design of the federation distinguishes Canada from the United States, the other federation Canadians think they know. The authors of a recent book on federalism illuminate the contrast:

> In what must be deemed one of the most fortuitous and farsighted acts of the Congress, the Northwest Ordinance [1787] ... required that the United States not hold the territory it had acquired north of the Ohio River and west of the Allegheny mountain ridge as colonies, but instead provided for the admission of new states on the principle of strict equality with the

old. And rather than allow the Northwest Territory to enter as a single state ... it required democratic governance within it and set the boundaries for not less than three and not more than five new states ... In this way the United States ... avoided the kind of asymmetry that plagued the USSR and Czechoslovakia [and Canada, perhaps] two hundred years hence.[18]

The provinces of the Canadian federation – their number, size, and boundaries – remembering that two of them are actual islands, while another (British Columbia) is isolated from the rest of the country by the Rocky Mountains, and that a fourth (Quebec) is culturally distinct and was created to preserve and acknowledge that character – are less the units of measurement of federalism than the activities they contain, whether we view them demographically, in terms of ethnicity, language, or religion; or fiscally, as sources of taxation or transfers between levels of government. It is these features that deepen the otherwise flat jurisdictional or physical dimensions of federalism. And it is concern for these subjects and others, such as the quality of health care and education policy, that feeds the disposition to draw comparisons among the units of the federation and between one federation and another.

Counting leads to comparing. Taken together, those two activities account for a large part of the content of federal studies. Consider, for instance, the report (May 2008) written for the Canadian Research Policy Networks, 'The Current State of Federalism Studies in Canada (2000–2007): A Quantitative and Qualitative Review of the Scholarly Literature.'[19] The interest of the authors (Patrick Fafard, Graduate School of Public and International Affairs, and François Rocher, School of Political Studies, both of the University of Ottawa) is directed toward answering the question of who studies federalism in Canada and what aspect of the subject occupies them. Their comparisons are intra-Canada but interprovincial and interdisciplinary. The findings of the report are not relevant to the present discussion, except in the following respect: like the bulk of the literature on federalism in Canada for some decades, it is the work of social scientists.

## Who

Academics and bureaucrats – but not the general public – study federalism. Perhaps this is to be expected. One might presume that the same kinds of people study unitary systems, except (as noted earlier) no one studies that subject. As Rufus Davis has said: 'There is a treatise to be written on "the non-federal system of government."' Yet among the many respects in which a federal system is different from a non-federal one is that federalism acknowledges diversity and gives it constitutional expression. More important, that diversity is attached – not solely but nonetheless significantly – to people. Chapter 7, 'The Habit of Federalism,' will examine societal and personal federalism. Still, it gives nothing away to say that the federalism of place, as experienced by residents of Nanaimo, British Columbia, or Rimouski, Quebec, is different from the privileged perspective of the professional social scientist. For a start, the social scientist travels and meets other social scientists when conducting research. Using the metaphor of the globe, the academic, like other professionals, stands above the Arctic Circle, where the longitudes converge. Here is where accommodation happens. The average Canadian is somewhere (to continue the metaphor) between the Tropics of Cancer and Capricorn. He or she does not encounter the richness of federalism through travel but only from what is available at home. Here is another treatise to be written, this time on the relationship between mobility and perceptions of federalism. A place to start would be to ask whether academics – who travel – pay too much attention to collective rather than individual conceptions of federalism.

Canadian federalism as a subject of study has been the preoccupation of many Royal Commissions and inquiries (not just federally appointed, which is the focus of this discussion, but also as created by the provinces – for example, the Royal Commission on Constitutional Problems [Quebec], 1956, or the Royal Commission on Renewing and Strengthening Our Place in Canada [Newfoundland and Labrador], 2002). Nor should the federal exemplars be confined to the best known with the largest research agendas, such as the Royal Commission of Dominion-Provincial Relations (appointed 1937, reported 1940) or the Royal Commission on the Economic Union and Development Prospects for Canada (1982, 1985). The more focused Royal Commission on Energy (1957, 1959) recommended a National Oil Policy. That policy divided the market for oil in Canada between the consuming East and the producing West, at the Ottawa River. While the concern of that commission was the development of an industry, the implication of the policy it recommended – and which the government adopted – for Canadian federalism once world conditions changed in the 1970s can hardly be exaggerated.

The distinction between the federal and provincial provenance of

Royal Commissions is less precise than might be assumed. Consider, for instance, the archetypal inquiry on federalism, Rowell-Sirois. The genesis of that commission was the default by Alberta on debentures in 1936 (the first provincial default in Canadian history) and the possibility of further defaults there and elsewhere on the prairies, along with pressure for federal action from 'men with graduate degrees in economics and business experience occupying senior positions in the federal civil service,' particularly the newly formed Bank of Canada. The attitude such individuals held of the provinces may be gauged by the comment of J.A.C. Osborne, deputy governor of the bank, who described the provinces as incapable of 'any serious or consecutive thinking.'[20] Sectional representation of the commissioners was a paramount consideration. Initially, there were to be four commissioners, one each from Ontario, Quebec, the Maritimes and the West. The original western member was J.W. Dafoe, editor of the *Winnipeg Free Press*. At the beginning the prime minister, William Lyon Mackenzie King, had said British Columbia might be ignored on the grounds that representation according to senatorial regions was sufficient. The premier of British Columbia, Duff Pattullo, was unimpressed by this argument, while Ian Mackenzie, the province's minister in the federal cabinet, explained to King the prejudicial partisan implications of omitting British Columbia. Henry Angus, a professor of economics at the University of British Columbia, was subsequently appointed.

According to R.A. MacKay, the Maritime member of the Royal Commission and professor of political science at Dalhousie University, there was pressure from some provinces to 'federalize' the commission's staff. While denying that provincial representation on staff was a criterion, MacKay did admit, in a letter to the displeased New Brunswick premier, first, that the commission had been 'under fire to some extent in the French press on the ground of French-speaking Canadians ... being ignored,' and, second, that it was 'indeed regrettable that we are unable to find more experts in New Brunswick for the particular jobs we wanted done ... Of course it is no reflection on any province that we were unable to find in the province the experts on the particular topics we wanted investigated.'[21]

The staff MacKay was principally looking for, he said, would consist of 'economists and statisticians though there will be three or four appointments of political scientists and authorities on constitutional history and constitutional law.' If there was a problem finding such specialists in New Brunswick – according to one scholar, MacKay urged the Commission's press secretary, Wilfrid Eggleston, 'to moot it about that S.A. Saunders [a Nova Scotian economist] had been born in St. John' – there was none in Saskatchewan. George Britnell and Vernon Fowke, of the Department of Economics and Political Science at the University of Saskatchewan, and F.C. Cronkite, Dean of Law, were given an office in the legislative building in Regina and supplied with letterhead: 'The Royal Commission Brief Committee.' Here they collected data on the tariff, exchange, and monetary policy; corresponded with economists elsewhere, such as Jacob Viner at the University of Chicago; and wrote Saskatchewan's Brief to the Royal Commission. The result, said the Minister of Justice, to whom they reported, was 'more or less a Bill of Rights' for Saskatchewan.[22]

## When

If who studies federalism is important to knowledge of the topic, so too is when that study occurs. J.A. Corry's *Democratic Government and Politics*, the introductory political science text for a generation of Canadian university students, appeared in 1946.[23] One of its chapters, titled 'Federalism,' focuses on the growth of governmental activity in the twentieth century and on which level of jurisdiction in a federation should perform that activity. (It should be noted that Corry wrote two studies for the Rowell-Sirois Commission: 'Difficulties of Divided Jurisdiction' and 'Growth of Government Activities since Confederation.') Federalism is treated as an administrative convenience and federation as one stage on a continuum that runs from disunity to a unitary state, which the author describes as 'the last step in political unification.'[24]

The following year saw R. MacGregor Dawson's *The Government of Canada*. Long the premier work on Canadian politics, Dawson's book went through six editions, the last of these in 1987. Significantly for this discussion, nowhere on its contents page does the word federalism or any of its derivatives appear, though 'Confederation,' 'Dominion–Provincial,' and 'Dominion and Nation' do. In the index, there is one entry for 'Federalism, Canadian,' followed by the phrase '*see* Distribution of powers.'[25] J.R. Mallory's *The Structure of Canadian Government*, originally published in 1971, illustrates the same reticence: in the revised edition of 472 pages, four are devoted to a discussion of 'federalism and politics' and thirty-five to 'the federal distribution of legislative power,' which includes the distribution of financial resources.[26] Before and for some time after the Second World War the academic measure of federalism was pragmatic and mechanical. It dealt with who won and lost power – thus the familiar metaphor of the swinging pendulum as it arced between federal and provincial jurisdictions. All counting and no weighing, the story of Canadian federalism took the form of a sequence of linked events absent a unifying theory. Compared with what is to come after 1960, the period before is federalism minor.

Neither Dawson nor Corry was exceptional in the perspective he brought to the subject. The same could be said of another frequently cited book of the mid-1950s, *Evolving Canadian Federalism*, with contributions from leading Canadian historians, political scientists, and legal scholars.[27] It was 'ironic,' said William Livingston, who reviewed the book for the *American Political Science Review*, that 'in a volume whose central theme is the place of French Canada in the Canadian federal system, there is no contribution of any French Canadian.' (In the *Canadian Historical Review*, Eugene Forsey described the book as 'brilliantly written,' took one of its contributors, A.R.M. Lower, to task for multiple errors of fact, and said nothing of French Canada. Though received, the book was not reviewed in the *Canadian Journal of Economics and Political Science*.)[28] Here again because the emphasis is on the adjective and not the noun, the analysis is narrow and the interpretation parochial. Who can know federalism who only Canadian federalism knows? The point of this comment is not that these books are inadequate examinations of federalism today – they are – but that they are period pieces: pre-Suez and of a world defined by British-Canadian assumptions; pre-Quiet Revolution and the stretching of the constitutional imagination this entailed; pre-New West and an energy-dominated prairie economy; pre-behaviouralism as an approach to the study of politics with its heightened awareness of the political system as opposed to government. As David Malouf, the Australian author, has noted of a classic study of that country, Manning Clark's *A Short History of Australia*, originally published in 1979, works such as these 'assume an added dimension that comes from [their] place in the time when [they] were written.'[29] In that respect, they communicate a sense of the past that 'is quite as much a matter of history as what happened in it.'[30]

It would be difficult to exaggerate the role the Quiet Revolution played in contributing to what Alan Cairns has described as 'the constitutional world we have lost.'[31] As important from the perspective of the study of federalism, however, was the federal government's response: the appointment of the Royal Commission on Bilingualism and Biculturalism in 1963. Writing a decade and a half later, political scientist

Reginald Whitaker said of the commission that it 'played something of the role for political scientists that the Rowell-Sirois Commission played for political economists and historians in the 1940s.'[32] The commission gave political scientists a well-financed (certainly when compared to support for the social sciences of only a decade earlier) and highly visible forum at the very moment the discipline itself was undergoing an intellectual and demographic transformation. The behavioural approach to politics, the concept of the political system (this last the title of a prominent book published in 1953 by David Easton, Canadian-born but then University of Chicago professor of political science and later senior adviser on research to the B-and-B Commission[33]), the emphasis on the benefits to be had from adopting a comparative perspective, the introduction, elaboration, and even promotion of the idea of a civic culture – all this innovation so different from what had characterized political science a few years before but now viewed as essential tools for the study of politics in the new, independent, and predominantly federal states of Africa and Asia. In short, Canadian federalism meant one thing – division of powers – before the B-and-B Commission; it meant considerably more – language and culture – after that. One consequence of the change is that discussions of Canadian federalism before and after the Quiet Revolution and the B-and-B Commission begin with different premises and imply different expectations. The idea of a federation of cultures, in addition to whatever other assumptions interpreters might hold, was ratified by the events of the 1960s.

The early 1960s marked the beginning of the rapid growth of universities, in the number of institutions, students, and faculty. At the outset, among political scientists, the faculty were returning Canadians who had taken their graduate studies predominantly in the United States and who been trained there in behavioural and comparative methods.[34] Institutional analysis, the description that best fits Canadian political writing before 1960, was in decline if not disrepute. The B-and-B Commission, in the language of behaviouralism, offered the first opportunity to 'aggregate' – a favourite verb of the decade – the youthful, American-trained political scientists and to focus their talents and energy upon saving that aspect of Canadian federalism associated with cultural dualism but which now threatened the unity of the federation itself.

Canada may have been a double federation – of culture and of territory – from its beginning, but neither of these dimensions had been emphasized. The nineteenth century had been preoccupied with the rounding out of Confederation, the twentieth with two world wars and a devastating depression. The lens through which this almost century-long history was viewed was not that of province, or territory, or culture. Rather it was national, as in Canada's march to autonomy – fiscal, defence, and diplomatic – within the British Empire and Commonwealth. A rough measure of that development can be found in W.P.M. Kennedy's *Statutes, Treaties, and Documents of the Canadian Constitution, 1713–1929*, published in 1930.[35] Half of the thirty-one documents included in the section of the collection devoted to the period after Confederation deal with imperial relations. It should also be noted that out of a total of more than two hundred documents, only thirty-one come from the federal period. The discrepancy between the history of Canada's constitution and of its experience with federalism was cause for frustration. Kennedy commiserated with J.W. Dafoe: 'I get weary and weary of the eternal emphasis on nationhood. A nation does not go around advertising its nationhood.'[36]

The long road to Dominion autonomy, the era of the National Policy, and the years devoted to the pursuit of the war efforts focused attention on Ottawa and eclipsed interest in the provinces as sites of economic, social, and (even) political activity, except for limitedly defined events – say, the formation of protest parties. Chapter 5, 'The Practice of Federalism,' will discuss political parties and federalism, and, more particularly, third parties as vehicles for the release of pressure in a parliamentary system whose signal characteristic is discipline. It is only in the last half of the 1960s that this attitude begins to change, as signalled in the 1966 article by Edwin Black and Alan Cairns, 'A Different Perspective on Canadian Federalism.'[37] Still, interest was not consistent, as surveys of the literature on provincial politics and the program of the annual meetings of the Canadian Political Science Association reveal. Nor was federalism a principal dimension of the book-length treatments of seven provinces (but not Alberta, Quebec, or British Columbia) published in the Canadian Government Series by the University of Toronto Press between 1951 and 1975. (In Quebec there is a parallel scarcity of publications on Canadian federalism in French.[38]) A reader of these works could be excused for concluding that Canadian federalism, as seen from the provinces, was hermetic and horizontal, no more than the summation of so many unitary governments.

By contrast, and more significant for the long-term study of federalism in Canada, is the prominence Quebec assumes for academics. The coincidence of the timing of the appointment of the B-and-B Commis-

sion with the advent of a generation of social scientists less unques-
tioning of traditional institutions contributed to a heightened interest
in the potential of federalism. Stated more emphatically, rather than
being uninquisitive, social scientists actually began to voice doubts
about the adequacy of existing political institutions. If the preliminary
report of the commission was right when it said that Canada was 'passing through the greatest crisis in its history'[39]; if the voluble critics in
western Canada were right when they rejected as offensive the commission's terms of reference, which spoke of the country being composed of 'two founding peoples'; if French-speaking Quebeckers were
right that they had been treated as second-class citizens in their own
province – then the institutions of representation and federalism might
well be deemed a failure. The assumption of a homogeneous British
Canada was clearly an erroneous assumption.

For the first time the institutions created in 1867 (the House of Commons and the Senate) and the practices inherited from before Confederation (responsible government) fell under a shadow of doubts
as to their adequacy for Canada's purpose. Not immediately or all at
the same time, but the seed of the idea that institutions might require
change was planted. More than that, the view of Canada's purpose also
seemed less indisputable. After 1867, except for French-speaking Canadians living in the province of Quebec, the 'purposes of the Dominion'
(as the phrase went) were focused on the territorial expansion and integration of the northern half of North America. The policies that enabled
those purposes to be realized lie at the core of the history of Canada (for
example, the building of the Canadian Pacific Railway and the passage
of the Dominion Lands Act). All of them had one feature in common:
the realization of a transcontinental nation. That objective reinforced
another: Canada as the senior Dominion of the Empire, the largest patch
of pink on the globe. The future that Canadians early in the last century
were told belonged to them did not grant French-speaking Canada a
special, let alone an equal, voice to the rest of the country.

How different from these assumptions were the concerns of the
B-and-B Commission! Gone was the national, territorial perspective
with its long-standing assumption of a primary role for the federal
government; in its place was a new, more particular interest in identity, social integration, and accommodation, frequently in a comparative mode. The research program of the commission, the broadest of
any inquiry up to that time, supports this generalization. Paradoxically,
the site chosen to study these topics was not necessarily countries like

Canada – vast, settler societies, still (in the 1960s) significantly rural in complexion – but entities that were small, highly urban, and not always federal in constitution – Belgium and the Netherlands are examples.

It may be an exaggeration to say that the B-and-B Commission introduced into Canadian politics the concern for national unity, but it is only an exaggeration. While after 1867 relations between English- and French-speaking Canadians had been tested, usually over the manner by which provinces other than Quebec treated linguistic and denominational educational claims made by French-speaking Roman Catholics, and while Canada's participation in and support for Great Britain in the two world wars and in the Boer War had stirred anti-imperialist feeling among a portion of the Quebec population, still these tensions were not viewed as having the potential to cause national disintegration. The work of the B-and-B Commission suggested that this assumption was no longer valid. Research on countries with multi-ethnic and culturally plural populations, long ignored by Canadian social scientists, directed attention to the potential for political fragmentation where social cleavages were allowed to deepen. The unfamiliar language, concepts, and emphasis directed academic and political attention toward new concerns at the same time as the sense of a dominant British Canada was in retreat, now that the object of national autonomy and status within and outside the Commonwealth had been achieved.

A sense of a new kind of Canadian federalism with different priorities took hold in the 1960s. The centrepiece was language or, more accurately, languages – English and French – and the need to acknowledge constitutionally their pre-eminence. The policies used to reach this goal, of which passage of the Official Languages Act in 1969 was most noteworthy, lie outside this discussion, except for their influence on the climate and conduct of federalism. The reference here is not just to relations between Quebec and the rest of the country – one dimension of what this chapter earlier called Canada's double federalism – but to relations between the rest, most particularly in the West, and central Canada – that is, the other dimension of double federalism. Critics of bilingualism and biculturalism said that this innovation changed the intent of the Fathers of Confederation. This claim is indisputable. If the intent of the Fathers of Confederation had been to create a bilingual and bicultural federation, they would have acted so as to accomplish that end to some degree. Yet the provisions for language in the 1867 Act are precise and limited in their application.

Still, intent is a different matter from meaning. It could well be argued that a century after their work at Charlottetown and Quebec City, and after the creation of a transcontinental nation, the meaning of the Fathers' intent requires for its realization broader constitutional protections for language. (French in the workplace, instead of the colonization of the French language by English – in the workplace and elsewhere – is a matter the Fathers of Confederation never considered, let alone addressed.) American legal scholar Laurence Tribe, writing about the equal protection clause of the Fourteenth Amendment to the United States Constitution, makes a similar observation: 'The relevant inquiry is *not* what the original drafters and ratifiers of the Amendment imagined or even expected the concept they wrote into the Constitution would come to require, but *what concept they intended to enshrine* by the language they used, and *what that concept, rightly understood, had come to demand.*'[40]

It is important to note that the West was not party to the original understanding, however that was interpreted. And it is the West's absence from the original settlement, as reinterpreted in the 1960s, that contributes an additional strain to Canadian federalism. Province building has been one response to this strain.[41] While not confined to the West, a distinctive feature of that phenomenon in the West has been espousal of a model of Canadian federalism that sees all provinces as equal (thus rejecting claims to special status by any single province) and maturation of that view into a call for a Triple E (equal, elected, and effective) Senate.

These matters are raised in order to make the point that the response which the tensions of the 1960s and later elicited took constitutional form. Constitutional not only in the sense of the solutions sought, for instance, in restructuring institutions like the Senate or altering practices such as the amending procedure, which until 1982 looked to Westminster for authoritative action; but constitutional too in the development of a mechanism to forge agreement. While not rare before 1960, Dominion (renamed federal)–provincial conferences became a familiar feature of public life after that date, in part because for the first time they were televised. They also took place more frequently. The conferences become an integral part of the search for constitutional (some scholars called it mega-constitutional) accord.

The age of conferences began with the Confederation for Tomorrow Conference, called by the Government of Ontario in November 1967. While technically not a federal–provincial conference since Ottawa did not take part, the background papers (prepared, in the words of one participant, by 'well-known scholars'), the conference agenda, and the remarks of the provincial premiers set the tone and introduced the topics for federal–provincial conferences to come, beginning in February of the following year. Contrast, for instance, the proposition advanced by John Robarts, then premier of Ontario, that in Canada there are 'two distinct ways and philosophies of life [but] while our Constitution still contains elements which are valid for organizing Canada as a partnership of ten, we are forced to conclude that much of this other two-partner Canada remains to be invented,' with the riposte by Ernest Manning, then premier of Alberta, to the proposal that the French language and French culture be granted 'formal and constitutional status': 'You cannot … say that this particular group has a legal and constitutional right that … over five million Canadians today who are of neither Anglo-Saxon or [sic] French origin … do not possess.'[42] Not for the last time would enthusiastic promotion of dualism at the centre thwart its acceptance in the parts. The riddle this posed was also a challenge: 'How to reconcile a federalism based on provinces with one based on cultures?'

### Where

The B-and-B Commission and the Confederation for Tomorrow Conference stood apart from previous intergovernmental meetings, for where the latter had as their object to find agreement on some defined question, such as a domestic amending formula for the Constitution Act, 1867, the initiatives of the 1960s adopted as their premise institutional and constitutional failure. Initially, the flaw was presented less in purely structural terms than as a claim on rights: 'The Constitution does not provide for equality between English and French in other provinces,' said John Robarts at his conference. Short of every premier pledging to act in a complimentary manner to guarantee linguistic equality, it remained to the federal government to initiate, as it did in 1969, the Official Languages Act to ensure delivery of federal government services in both official languages across Canada. As the Canadian Charter of Rights and Freedoms a dozen years later made all residents of Canada part of a whole, so the OLA made Canada accessible to all English- and French-speaking Canadians. Both enactments transcend in their effect the internal boundaries of the federation and in this respect are analogous to the frontier in the nineteenth century in that they, too, increase the power of the federal government. Indeed, in some parts of the country the frontier, language, and the Charter may almost be perceived as stations on a continuum. The Charter as a twenty-first-century frontier is discussed in chapter 6.

Despite (or because of) the emphasis on rights, the theme of institutional failure mounted. The fact that the Senate of Canada did not offer an elected forum for the provinces, as the upper chambers in Australia and the United States did for their unit governments, was offered by critics as one example. Others pointed to the distorted partisan composition of the House of Commons owing to the single-member-district–simple-plurality-vote electoral system. Provinces and people were badly served by their representative institutions. The list might be lengthened, but the moral offered was accepted as fact. Yet the succession of constitutional conferences and reports that followed, up to the referendum on the Charlottetown Accord in 1992 – with the notable exception of the events of 1982, which saw, among other achievements, adoption of the Charter, agreement on a domestic amending formula, and reaffirmation of provincial control over non-renewable natural resources – resulted in no change. The apparent immovability of institutions and the intransigence of opponents to change, coupled with a succession of publicized but rejected constitutional schemes, deepened the sense of institutional failure.

Talk but not action marked the decades; convergence of federal theory, practice, and approval seemingly unachievable in Canada. 'Talk' needs to be understood broadly, for the word is used here to embrace both the oral and the written word. Before 1960, interpreters of federalism were few in number and concentrated mostly in law and history faculties. Their research concerns centred on struggles over the division of powers – who gained and who lost – and on the proposition, by now cliché, that federalism signified unity in diversity. What unified the federation, what diverse elements it might embrace, and whether that diversity was organic to the whole remained largely unexamined. There was no consensus in the literature on whether theory should be studied in order to understand Canadian federalism or Canadian federalism studied in order to understand federal theory.

It was against this backdrop that political scientists in Canada engaged for the first time in a sustained manner with the malleable concept of federalism. They did this in university departments, newly created institutes, and government departments and agencies, as well as in the research arms of Royal Commissions and task forces. The history of these bodies in this period has yet to be written, though there are isolated accounts of their work.[43] What a study of the era shows is an increasing appreciation of federalism not only as a horizontal arrangement of coordinate and independent governmental spheres but also one with a vertical orientation from society below to governments above. More than an appreciation of the spatial dimension of federalism is evident; there is a temporal perspective as well, one that goes beyond the familiar chronology of judicial interpretation. This approach stands out in the advisory opinions rendered by the Supreme Court of Canada on matters such as the secession of Quebec and patriation of the constitution, both of which use a language of principle unheard of in an earlier period. In the patriation reference the Court described 'the principle of federalism' as 'the dominant principle of Canadian constitutional law,' while in the secession reference the Court quoted approvingly from the submission of the Attorney General of Saskatchewan: 'The threads of a thousand acts of accommodation are the fabric of a nation.'[44] This is federalism major.

It is also a major deviation from the Whearean world of spheres. Geometry has given way to poetry, or at least to values. In the secession reference, the Court describes 'federalism [as] a legal response to the underlying political and cultural realities that existed at Confederation and continue to exist today' (Para. 43). Unusual, too, in the literature of Canadian federalism is evocation of 'the people,' whose 'elected representatives,' the Court said, 'initiated Confederation' (Para. 35). As already mentioned in this chapter, Royal Commissions have played a central role in the development of modern Canadian federalism. The scale of their research, the co-optation of scores of scholars from all parts of the country to this endeavour, the publicity associated with their reports – these and other features of commissions of inquiry made them a central mechanism in the reconceptualization of Canadian federalism.

Now they are silent. As prime ministers, Pierre Trudeau (1968–79, 1980–84) appointed forty-five Royal Commissions and Brian Mulroney (1984–93) sixteen. But in the fifteen years between 1993, when Jean Chrétien's Liberals came to office, and the re-election of Stephen Harper's Conservatives in 2008, only seven commissions were established. Part of the explanation for this change lies in criticism of the aloofness of executive federalism following the failure to reach agreement on the mega-constitutional accords of the late 1980s and early 1990s. Governments feared that commissions seemed equally remote. Consultation with the public over vital issues of policy has moved from the confines of commission hearings and commission-generated surveys to the ballot box. Referendums were at one time extremely rare in Canada. But that has not been the case over the past two decades. Referendums have been held recently on a variety of issues and in many instances have generated widespread public interest and citizen participation levels exceeding those of general elections. Their subjects have been diverse: a restructuring of the country's constitution (the Charlottetown Accord, 1992); Quebec's secession from Canada (1995); First Nations Treaty Rights in British Columbia (2002); secular and parochial schools in Newfoundland and Labrador (1995 and 1997); video lottery terminals in New Brunswick (2001); and replacement of the plurality vote with some variant of proportional representation (British Columbia, 2005 and 2009; Prince Edward Island, 2005; Ontario, 2007).

Two contrasting approaches to public consultations have also defined the shift away from Royal Commissions of the past decade and a half. On the one hand, citizens' assemblies have been convened in both British Columbia and Ontario for the purposes of studying the electoral system and recommending, if deemed appropriate, its replacement with another method of voting. (In both provinces, the assemblies recommended modifying the existing system with a form of proportional representation, and in both provinces voters rejected that proposal. How, one wonders, did citizens' assemblies become so unrepresentative of the voters?) On the other hand, concentration of power in the Prime Minister's Office (PMO) over the past two decades has dampened the enthusiasm of senior political officials for extraparliamentary consultative bodies. In their place, carefully structured focus groups and frequent government-sponsored public opinion surveys have found favour. These have replaced the open public hearings of Royal Commissions, just as outside consultants contracted by government departments and agencies for targeted research and recommendations have replaced the commissioners once called to head public inquiries.

The measure of federalism, as of politics itself, lies increasingly with the people and the courts. All generalizations are suspect, it is true. Nonetheless, there is now as much a historical aura surrounding the B-and-B and Macdonald Commissions and the Pepin-Robarts Task Force, for example, as there is around Rowell-Sirois. The articulations of the problems they were established to investigate; the methods they used to investigate those problems; and the recommendations they made in consequence of their work seem dated. Of course, through the efflux of time, they *are* 'dated'; but more than temporality is at issue.

These past commissions, each of which was central to the debate that defined modern Canadian federalism – through, for instance, the introduction of adjustment (equalization) grants, official bilingualism, and North American Free Trade – touched the constitution in all its definitions – as founding (or, in the case of bilingualism, refounding Canada), in its structure and its health.

The Canada of today and the Canada of centennial year are worlds apart. Not only the magnitude of change but its speed is remarkable to recall. In these four decades there has been a merging of federalism with the movement of time. Where once courts constrained federalism by resolving jurisdictional conflict between governments, now, by reference to the Charter and to historical citation, they augment federalism through their concern for the rights of individuals and minorities. That transformation explains in large part the disposition of political scientists to study federalism from a comparative and international perspective. While the central event of Confederation could never be ignored – nor was it – in the history of Canada, its meaning has changed. It is no longer sufficient to view Confederation as an act of unification alone. It *was* that, but for a long time the Constitution Act, 1867, was depicted as perpetuating the British political ideal within a federal framework. In the last half-century there has been a transformation in that understanding. Federalism – and not the British Parliament – made the inhabitants of British North America Canadians, just as it made the original and later colonies one country. Where once federalism was seen as a practical arrangement to facilitate Canadian unity, it is now treated as an essential attribute, however that quality might be defined, of being Canadian.

# 3 'A Constitution in Some Respects Novel'

In the first Speech from the Throne (1868) of the new Dominion Parliament, the Governor General, Viscount Monck, informed members that 'the Act of Union … imposes the duty and confers upon you the right of reducing to practice the system of Government which it has called into existence, of consolidating its institutions, harmonizing its administrative details, and of making such legislative provisions as will secure to a constitution, in some respects novel, a full, fair, and unprejudiced trial.'[1] Here was understatement, indeed; for the constitution now on trial was full of novelty, beginning with its provisions for creating the world's first parliamentary federation. In fact, almost all of the 147 sections of the 1867 Act deal with the structure of the federation. Very few deal with those practices that Canadians usually think of when they talk about government – for instance, the privileges and responsibilities of the government and of the opposition, the rules that determine who forms a government and when, the role of political parties, and the 'right' relationship between the Crown, as represented by the Governor General, and the political executive (the government).

There is one exception to that generalization, to be found in the Preamble of the Constitution Act, 1867. The first of four 'whereas' clauses reads as follows: 'Whereas the Provinces of Canada, Nova Scotia, and New Brunswick have expressed their Desire to be federally united into One Dominion under the Crown of the United Kingdom of Great Britain and Ireland, with a Constitution similar in Principle to that of the United Kingdom.' The meaning of the phrase 'Constitution similar in Principle' is open to dispute. A persuasive case may be made that it encompasses the principle of responsible government, though it must be acknowledged that in the Quebec Secession Reference (1998), the Supreme Court of Canada perceived 'an internal architecture' to the 'Constitution' comprising 'four foundational principles': constitutionalism and the rule of law, federalism, democracy, and protection of minorities.[2] The absence of responsible government in that list is surprising. While lawyers and political scientists might dispute its exact meaning, responsible government was, as James Mallory once observed, 'one of the few concepts about Canadian politics that stuck in the minds of generations of Canadian school children. It became a central part of the mythology of Canadian history, an outstanding example of the use of the past to create a sense of national identity.'[3]

A constitutional principle should not be confused with a constitutional provision, and in any case, foundational is not necessarily a synonym for exhaustive.[4] Therefore, it is reasonable to assume that the principle of responsible government still finds shelter in the Constitution Act, along with the principle of federalism. That said, the federal principle in the Canadian constitution is hardly more exact than the principle of responsible government. It is now a truism that 'the system of Government called into existence' in 1867 was not a federation like that of the United States, and for that reason was not really federal. That was the inference to be drawn from K.C. Wheare's epigrammatic comment: 'The federal principle has come to mean what it does because the United States has come to be what it is.'[5] Powers in Canada may have been divided between federal and provincial legislatures, but here, as opposed to the United States, the residual power rested at the centre. To that alignment must be added Parliament's unlimited taxing power, the Crown's enormous appointment power (for example, of lieutenant governors, senators, and senior judges) exercised on advice of the prime minister, and the power of lieutenant governors to reserve – and the federal cabinet to disallow – *any* provincial legislation, along with Parliament's capacity to declare 'Works' within a province to 'the general Advantage of Canada' and to submit the same to federal legislation.

This concentrated power led delegates to Australia's constitutional conventions of the 1890s to opine that '[Canada] is a Federation upon the centralising principle, just as the United States is a Federation on the decentralisation principle,' and to opt for the American example.[6] These adjectives echo Canadian usage in 1867: 'Our Constitution of the Dominion of Canada ... is Federal as well as Central, while that of the United Kingdom, and to which it is made "similar," as far as may be, is wholly central.'[7] As it turned out, the Australian delegates were wrong on both counts: Canadian federalism in the 1890s had begun to deviate radically from that set down by Fathers of Confederation thirty years before, while the decentralizing thrust of American federalism was already weakening. For Canada, the significance of the Australian rejection in favour of institutions and mechanisms that elevated the states and the people lay in its making the British North American federal experiment unique among major federations. It was parliamentary.

Few events in Canada's political history have received so much attention or been committed so thoroughly to memory as the transformation through judicial review of the country's original federal arrangement. The broad outline of the story is simple: the Fathers of Confederation intended to create a highly centralized federation; but the courts, particularly the Judicial Committee of the Privy Council (JCPC) in London, undid their handiwork, with the result that, say some scholars, Canada is among 'the world's most decentralized federations.'[8] The reasons for this reversal of fortune are best left for analysis in chapter 6, 'Courts and Charter: Constitution and Federalism.' In the context of the present discussion, the point to emphasize is that the 1867 Act did not create a Canadian court of appeal (one of the 'instrumentalities' that scholars, like Livingston, deem essential in the taxonomy of federations[9]), though Section 101 said that Parliament might at a later date provide for one. Parliament did this in 1875, though appeals to the JCPC continued until they were abolished in 1949.

In addition to omitting a process for domestic judicial review, the Constitution Act, 1867, said nothing about a local procedure for its amendment. The explanation usually offered is that Parliament at Westminster had enacted the 1867 statute, and it was 'natural' for any amendment to be made by the same legislative body. This is no doubt true, as far as it goes. As well, it indicates a parliamentary alignment, or cast of mind, between Canada and the United Kingdom that partly explains the failure of Canadian politicians to agree on a domestic amending formula until 1982. The Westminster model has exerted a strong hold on Canadian politics – perhaps because of the preambular statement about a 'Constitution similar in Principle to that of the United Kingdom' – one that both frustrates and complicates behaviour. As long ago as 1930, Frank Underhill expostulated that 'we in Canada are suffering from a literary theory of our constitution. It prevents us from realizing how British institutions when transplanted to America actually work.'[10]

The complicating factor is that the model proposed for emulation is not federal. Even before the entrenchment of a higher law, in the form of the Canadian Charter of Rights and Freedoms, that limits legislative autonomy, it was 'a central fallacy of Canadian constitutional law' to assume that, taken together, the Canadian Parliament and the legislatures are 'replicas of the Parliament of the United Kingdom.' The latter is 'truly a continuing functioning constitutional convention,' whereas Canada's legislatures, even within their respective jurisdictions, do not 'enjoy a supremacy of the same quality.'[11] The question that the Westminster inheritance posed – how to make parliamentary government work in a federation? – has been answered sequentially in Canada in two ways: first, through federalized national political parties, and, when these faltered after the two world wars as provinces grew more aggressive in pursuing policy and as protest parties ended the monopoly of the parties of Confederation (Liberal and Conservative), and later, through the development of extraparliamentary and extraconstitutional negotiating processes under the rubric of executive federalism.

John A. Macdonald chose his first cabinet with the federal principle, generously interpreted to embrace considerations of religion and language as well as territory, in mind and with the non-federal United Kingdom as its model: 'In the Cabinet of Great Britain there had always been representatives of England, Ireland, and Scotland. The reason was that the people of each section could not expect their interests to be sufficiently attended to unless they had representatives in Government as well as in Parliament.'[12] All subsequent prime ministers have so followed his example that a large and federalized cabinet is a convention of the constitution.[13] Political parties that were *de facto* or *de jure* federations made this practice possible, while a Senate that spoke for minority rather than provincial interests made it necessary. The further one examines Canada's constitution, the more 'novel' it becomes and the less similar to that of the United Kingdom.

The exceptionalism of Canada's federal constitution originates in the act of its creation – more specifically, in the actions of its creators. Few statements made during the debate in the Legislative Assembly of the Parliament of United Canada on the Quebec Resolutions are better known than the following by John A. Macdonald:

Now, as regards the comparative advantages of a Legislative or a Federal union ... I have again and again stated in the House that, if practicable, I thought a Legislative union would be preferable. I have always contended that if we could agree to have one government and one parliament, legislating for the whole of these peoples, it would be the best, the cheapest, the most vigorous, and the strongest system of government we could adopt.

But, he noted, opposition in Lower Canada to 'the absorption of [its legal and cultural] individuality,' and opposition in the Maritime provinces to any attempt to standardize the property law, for instance, meant that legislative union would not succeed.[14] In sum, federation was Macdonald's second choice.

If federation it must be, then the exemplar had to be the United States. Here Macdonald's comments are also memorable but at the outset also puzzling: 'The United States was in the main formed on the model of the Constitution of Great Britain, adapted to the circumstances of a new country.' Presumably, this is a reference to the balanced constitution, with its separation of powers, flowing from the Glorious Revolution of 1688.[15] That is a presumption, since he says nothing further on this matter but proceeds to assess the federation created by the Founding Fathers at Philadelphia: 'They commenced, in fact, at the wrong end. They declared by their Constitution that each state was a sovereignty in itself, and that all the powers incident to a sovereignty belonged to each state, except those powers which, by the Constitution, were conferred upon the general government and Congress. Here we have adopted a different system. We have strengthened the General Government.'[16] In this passage Macdonald is prophesizing that 'we have avoided all conflict of jurisdiction and authority,' and predicts that 'if this Constitution is carried out ... we will have ... all the advantages of a legislative union ... with ... the guarantees for local institutions and for local law.'

This is a Canadian's view of American federalism, for nowhere does Macdonald mention the primacy that the Constitution of the United States grants the people. The concept of the people as the constituent power is foreign to his sense of a constitution, nor – which is more important to this study – does he see it as having any relevance for federalism. Yet it is the people in their different localities – not the division of powers – that authorize the United States document. In No. 22 of *The Federalist*, Alexander Hamilton stated that the 'foundations of our national government [are] deeper than in the mere sanctions of delegated authority. The fabric of the American empire ought to rest on the solid basis of THE CONSENT OF THE PEOPLE.' Rephrased in comparative terms, the consequence of popular sovereignty in Canada's neighbour is this: in the English or Canadian constitution, 'the nation and the government is considered as one ...; whereas, by ours, the nation and the government are considered as distinct.'[17] Gordon Wood, the American historian, puts it this way: American governments 'were never full embodiments of the society'; rather, '*all* governments are limited agencies of the people.'[18]

The implications of this distinction are immense when comparing the constitutions of the two North American federations. The contrast is evident from the start. In the United States the events of 1787 were intended to be regenerative – to build virtue and to improve human nature: 'We, the people of the United States, in order to form a more perfect union ... do ordain.' In Canada, the intent of federation was to eradicate old problems. The United States Constitution speaks with one voice: '*In all its parts, the representative part [is] the whole of it.*'[19] In Canada, the guiding principle of Confederation was as much protection as it was representation. In fact, the two objects were combined when it came to the House of Commons (the only representative institution of government), where, until 1946, Quebec's sixty-five members of the House (divided into that province's population) determined the allocation of all other provinces' representation. Purposive federalism above the forty-ninth parallel – in the form of Section 145 (now repealed) providing for 'Construction [of the Intercolonial Railway] by the Government of Canada' (the Speech from the Throne in 1868 described it as the 'practical and physical connection' parallel to the 'legislative bond'), and Term 46 of the Terms of Union of Newfoundland with Canada (1949): 'Margarine may be manufactured or sold in the province of Newfoundland and Labrador after the date of the Union' – and representational federalism below.

Because there was no conception of the people as a constituent power in Canada, there was no conception of a limit to state power or, for that matter, of a constitution separate from the government. This is a statement of fact rather than a judgment upon the work of the Fathers of Confederation. Nor was the absence of the people from the Canadian constitution more than a matter of episodic concern – as in the farmers' revolt and the rise of the Progressive Party of the 1920s – until the advent of the Reform Party late in the twentieth century.[20] At least two reasons for this attitude may be suggested, though the first is by far the more explanatory. In his biography *Churchill*, Roy Jenkins says what has been said before but deserves repeating in this discussion. In the last half on the nineteenth century, everyone – Tories, Liberals, Labour, even Irish Nationalists, as well as many non-British observers – 'regard[ed] the House of Commons as the greatest legislative assembly in the world.'[21] Canadians shared this view; it was one reason why leaving amendments to the Constitution Act, 1867, in the hands of the Westminster Parliament proved uncontentious. On this particular point, it needs to be remembered that between 1804 and 1865 there had been no amendments to the United States Constitution. From the perspective of the Fathers of Confederation, there was good reason to see the U.S. Constitution as 'excessively rigid.'[22]

Rigidity was not a value admired by Canadians – particularly those who had tried to operate the legislature and government of United Canada – in spite of statutory and conventional requirements pressing for coalition government (sometimes with dual ministries – attorney general east and attorney general west, for example), fixed and equal representation of the two Canadas, and occasional resort to double majorities. Experience made legislative union attractive; prudence made it unrealizable. Still, in a book on Canadian federalism, Macdonald's relinquished dream of legislative union deserves more attention than it often receives.

Legislative union and unitary government are frequently discussed as if they were synonymous. They are, in the sense that both are monist in principle; but a legislative union implies the conclusion of a process of aggregation, a bringing together. The distinction is worth emphasizing, if only because Macdonald himself dwells on it. In the Confederation Debates, he says that

> the union between [England and Scotland], in matters of *legislation,* is of a federal character, because the Act of Union between the two countries provides that Scottish law cannot be altered ... No matter ... how much it may interfere with the symmetry of the general law of the United Kingdom, that law is not altered, except with the consent of the Scottish people, as expressed by their representatives in Parliament. Thus, we have, in Great Britain, to a limited extent, an example of the working and effects of a Federal Union, as we might expect to witness them in our own Confederation.[23]

Legislative union of England and Scotland occurred in 1707 (the Crowns of the two countries had united in 1603); legislative union of England and Ireland took place in 1800. Neither of these unions had received the sanction of popular opinion, and this created precedents to be cited in 1867 by those hostile to demands from British North American colonists for public consultation on Confederation. A strong voice

to this effect was Monck's, who said the demand 'betrayed a great ignorance [of] the principles of the British constitution.'[24] That opinion was
repeated, and carried the day, when, after a victory for the anti-Confed-
erates in the Nova Scotia election of 1867, Joseph Howe campaigned
unsuccessfully in Great Britain to repeal Confederation. The argument
that Nova Scotia had lost a 'noble constitution' was met with the rebut-
tal that 'this constitution had been a "gift of the Crown" revocable at
any time.'[25]

Whether public approval should have preceded the move to federation, as was the case thirty-three years later prior to the creation of the
Commonwealth of Australia, is not germane to this discussion. What *is*
of signal importance is that change of immense moment – 'by one fell
stroke [Nova Scotians were] swung out of their Constitutional orbit,
and thrown into a new system' – had occurred, and at the instigation
of politicians.[26] From being a colony of an empire, Nova Scotia had
become a colony of a colony of an empire. Howe maintained that 'we
are to have a confederacy in name, but in reality the centre of power
and influence will always be in Canada. It can be nowhere else.'[27] Howe
was invited to enter the government of John A. Macdonald in 1869.
That action, following equal treatment of the Maritime provinces with
Ontario and Quebec when it came to Senate membership, poured balm
on the province's ire. It also provided an occasion for political expression of a distinctively Canadian view of the requirements of federalism
(the speaker is George-Étienne Cartier): 'It might be thought that Nova
Scotia and New Brunswick got more than their share in the originally adopted distribution, but it must be recollected that they had been
independent provinces, and the count of heads must not always be permitted to out-weigh every other consideration.'[28]

Forty-five years later in 1915, the same reasoning – 'representation by
population … was intended to be made subservient to the right of each
colony to adequate representation in view of its surrender of a large
measure of self-government' – was advanced for an amendment to the
Constitution Act that no province should have fewer members in the
House of Commons than it had senators.[29]

Seventy-five years after that, the Supreme Court of Canada heard
on appeal a decision of the Saskatchewan Court of Appeal on electoral
redistribution. Saskatchewan's highest court spoke of 'no person's portion of sovereign power exceed[ing] that of another' and posited 'the
idea of equality [as] inherent in the right to vote.' From these egalitarian
pronouncements, and for reasons Cartier would have approved, the

Supreme Court dissented: the purpose of the right to vote in Section 3 of the Charter, it said, is not equality of voting power per se, but the right to 'effective representation.'[30]

The absence of a popular constituent power – and, more than that, the lack of concern about the absence of a popular constituent power in the constitution of Canada – whether as a legal document or an act of creation – has only become a matter of sustained debate since the failure of mega-constitutional accords, Meech Lake and Charlottetown, in the 1990s. The opinion expressed in *Canadian Monthly* as long ago as August 1872, about the weakness of the elective principle in Canada, proved rare but no less apt a century later: 'Even the reactionary founders of dynasties in Europe find it expedient, in this age, to base their power on a plebiscite ... If discontent should ever arise ... we may hear more of the omission to submit the decision of the national destiny to the direct vote of the people.'[31]

As it was, and still is, even in the age of the Charter, the constitution 'ignore[s] individual Canadians, except as they qualif[y] through membership in a ... group,' defined, for example, by church, language, or gender.[32]

Macdonald's description of Scotland's place in the United Kingdom illustrates two important features relevant to his conception of Confederation: one, legislative and federal union were located on a continuum that made no provision – because there was no need – for Livingston-like 'instrumentalities'; and two, Federal Union was about legislative and not executive power. There can be no retroactive application of Whearean or Livingstonian theories of one century to Macdonaldian practices of another. Still that is the tenor of the criticism now heard about high centralization in the 1867 Act. Where, in other words, are the coordinate and independent spheres associated today with the theory of federal government? Not all, but a significant part, of the critique focuses on the extensive powers of the central executive, as in the making of appointments.

Great powers rest in the prime minister, because in a system of responsible government, such as Canada's, the prerogative powers of the Crown are exercised by the Governor General on the advice of the prime minister. If the prerogative extended from London throughout the United Kingdom, inferentially the same held true for Canada with its 'Constitution similar in Principle.' Yet how could that be in a federation? Or, for how long could that be? Within thirty years of Confederation, as a result of JCPC opinions, the unitary Crown and its prerogatives had fractured and become territorially dispersed. The new framework for a compound monarchy took its place. These judgments, of which *Liquidators of the Maritime Bank* v. *Receiver General of New Brunswick* (1892) AC 437 is the most direct in 'federalizing' the Crown, turned as much on questions of privilege and precedence as on fields of jurisdiction. In the words of Bora Laskin, they bifurcated the Crown and established the basis of the intergovernmental rivalry that would mark Canadian federalism a hundred years later.[33]

The significance of this development for Canadian federalism lies in the familiar variations on the theme of unintended consequences accompanying judicial interpretation. Less frequently remarked is the influence this same development had for the constitution, that is, the proliferation of strong, unlimited executives. Second chambers in the provinces either never existed or, where they did, were weak. For that matter, there are no provincial constitutions, in the sense Americans use that term. Executive-centred government, the common critique heard about politics in Ottawa today, notwithstanding the revisionism of nineteenth-century courts, is also the indictment directed at provincial governments. If the representative part is the whole of American politics, then the governing part is surely the whole of Canadian politics. Here is the backdrop against which to view demands for electoral reform and Senate reform, as well as concerns about the extent of parliamentary privilege and Crown prerogative in an age that puts a premium on rights and freedoms.

But not when applied to government. Some have described the extent of executive-centredness in Canada as colonial, but with local rather than imperially appointed elites in charge.[34] Absent a traditional social hierarchy, an established church, or a second parliamentary chamber of influence like the Lords, electoral politics and its control were everything. As an aside, it is worth noting how often in the study of Canadian politics the adjective colonial arises, as here in the relationship of legislature to executive, but also as regards federal government relations with the regions and provinces, and all governments' relations with Aboriginal populations. Colonial and federal are not adjectives – or concepts – that work in harmony, as Canadian history attests.

Colonial is imperial as seen from the dependant's perspective. Canada may or may not exhibit a colonial mentality still, but there is no question that though the largest colonies of settlement before 1867 and later senior dominion of the Empire afterward, Canada took a long time maturing as a constitutionally independent entity. The Statute of Westminster, 1931, recognized the legislative independence of the five dominions (Canada, Australia, New Zealand, South Africa, and Newfoundland), but the completion of Canada's constitutional odyssey occurred fifty years later. Among other matters, the Constitution Act, 1982, provided for the Charter of Rights and Freedoms, set down a domestic amending formula, and reaffirmed provincial control of non-renewable natural resources. The chronicle of that evolution is oft-told; the consequences of its prolonged duration are less frequently remarked upon.

Premeditated or not, this strategy of distancing – both temporally and geographically – 'encourage[d] the view that constitutional interpretation [was] a matter for lawyers and judges.'[35] That assessment was made specifically about judicial review and the long hand of the JCPC, but it applies as well to the search for a made-in-Canada amending formula. While Canadian politicians (all but Quebec's) had the ultimate say in designing an amendment package, the decades-long quest that preceded agreement meant that Westminster remained the authoritative legislature. Thus the attenuating effect noted with judicial appeals was reinforced by the search for an amendment process. If in Canada there is no sense of the people as a constituent power and if at the same time there is no sense of limits in the constitution, then part of the explanation is found in the remoteness of Westminster, which for so long played a central role in the development of the Canadian constitution.

From the perspective of a book on federalism, another consequence of arrested constitutional development was the fate of the compact theory. According to this interpretation, Confederation was the agreement of 'the uniting colonies, now provinces, and ... any modification of that contract would require the consent of all the provinces.'[36] The premise that Confederation was the product of provincial agency was refuted by, among others, Norman Rogers, a refutation that quickly became orthodoxy and prevailed for some decades.[37] The nub of Rogers's view was that 'only the Imperial Parliament was behind the 1867 Act, and ... nothing in history, practice or judicial precedent had changed that.'[38] The validity of these respective positions is not the question here. Instead, it is the vanquishing of the compact theory by the so-called 'Imperial theory' that deserves attention – and for the same reasons stated in the preceding paragraphs: the heart of Canada's constitution was separated for so long from its body that an atrophy of constitutional understanding resulted.

In 1867, Westminster gave Canada 'a Constitution similar in Principle to that of the United Kingdom,' but the content of the principle was left to be inferred. The Preamble to the Act speaks of the colonies desiring to be 'federally united,' but the sections themselves provide remarkably little in the way of a recognizable federal arrangement: 'The only divided institution contemplated in law was in the legislative department.'[39] Only after 1867 was the unity of the Crown replaced by a compound monarchy that paralleled the legislative division of powers. The Act made no provision for its own amendment, nor did it establish a mechanism for judicial review. In both instances the *status quo ante* prevailed. Significantly, when in the 1880s judicial interpretation began to effect a movement away from the Act's highly centralized power, the Supreme Court of Canada, established by *statute* of the Parliament of Canada in 1875, was not caught up in the provincial rights enthusiasm. Instead, the custom developed to make appointments to the Court (by the Governor General on recommendation of the prime minister), as with the cabinet, according to the federal principle, taking into account that not every province could be represented at one time. In the Constitution Act, 1867, federalism was secured as a principle of government achieved through cabinet representation (and later through the composition of the Supreme Court of Canada); federalism was not, as it was in the Constitution of the United States, to be a check on government. This American orientation, of course, is the object of a proposal such as a Triple E Senate in Canada, and explains the practical and conceptual difficulties that arise when seeking to integrate a cardinal feature of one federal system into the operation of another, very different federal system.

The political nature of Canadian federalism is to be seen in all its manifestations, but nowhere in more striking fashion than in the composition of the Senate of Canada. For reasons to be discussed in chapter 4, 'Parliamentary Federalism,' the Senate of Canada is not an institution universally admired. The manner of its members' selection and their allocation among the provinces are reasons customarily offered for the upper chamber's poor repute. Though comparisons may be invidious, the United States Senate is usually cited to illustrate the Canadian Senate's flaws. In what might be called an illustration of aspirational federalism, critics of Canada's second chamber point to the great compromise at Philadelphia, whereby the Founding Fathers agreed that House of Representatives would be based on representation by population and the Senate on equal representation of each state. How different, and how unfederal, the composition of the Senate of Canada!

Yet the compromise on the Senate at the Quebec City Conference in 1864 was no less central to reaching agreement on federation in this country than the compromise made at Philadelphia sixty years before was to the United States. The guarantee of equal (regional but not provincial) representation with the more populous provinces of Ontario and Quebec was responsible for the entry of the Maritime provinces (Nova Scotia and New Brunswick). According to George Brown, otherwise a strong advocate of rep-by-pop: 'On no other condition could we have advanced a step.'[40] Regional equity was essential to concluding the Confederation bargain; no other issue took so long to resolve. In consequence of that agreement, it was possible for some decades after 1867 to think of the young Dominion as Christopher Dunkin, minister in charge of Canada's first census, described it in the House of Commons, that is, as 'the three kingdoms.'[41] The allusion was to the United Kingdom, which encompassed England, Scotland, and Ireland, along with the Principality of Wales, and notwithstanding whose diversity appeared to the Fathers of Confederation the paradigm of a successful nation.

But the United Kingdom, unlike Canada or the United States, was not in a position where it had to adjust its political structure to accommodate the incorporation of new territory. It is a challenge to federations to expand but at the same time not upset the terms of the original accord. The 'three kingdoms' analogy – each kingdom with its twenty-four senators – made no provision for expansion. What was to happen when the federation grew, as it was intended to grow (Section 146), since one of the purposes of Confederation was to acquire Rupert's Land and to extend westward to the Pacific Ocean? The Maritime senatorial region, with the same number of senators as Ontario and Quebec, was acceptable to the less populated Maritime provinces in 1867. And thereafter, as well, since territorial expansion was not possible and population growth unlikely. The establishment of Alberta and Saskatchewan in 1905, the addition of territory to Ontario, Quebec, and Manitoba in 1912 – rather than the formation of additional new provinces – and the creation the same year of a western senatorial region made up of the four western provinces, helped keep the Senate formula stable. The expectation was that population growth in the West would make itself felt through increased representation in the House of Commons.

In fact the representation formulae used over the years to allocate House of Commons seats among the provinces discriminated against the West. Now, in the twenty-first century, the fastest-growing provinces of the West are treated less generously than the slower-growing provinces of the region. More than that, the expectation that the Commons would be the West's chamber because its population would grow depended upon an assumption about political parties: the parties of Confederation would continue to be national parties. That assumption proved most questionable in the West. After the First World War and the rise of the Progressives on the prairies, followed by other protest parties, the West's voice was fragmented and, most often, an opposition voice.[42]

Notwithstanding the population growth in western Canada, two-thirds of Canada's population lives in Ontario and Quebec. Until the appearance of the Bloc Québécois in the early 1990s, the traditional parties dominated federal politics in the two central provinces, and they still do in Ontario. The party composition of the House has had a marginalizing effect on the expression of western interests, and explains, especially in Alberta, the popularity of slogans such as 'The West Wants In.' It also explains why in Alberta attention to Parliament shifted from the Commons to the Senate as an institution that might better express western views, if only as a limit on governmental power in a constitution that otherwise provides very little check on the executive. Since Confederation, through their organization and through the distribution of patronage, political parties have provided sustenance for the federal idea in Canada. Where they are in retreat, there is another reason to look to the Senate for protection.[43]

Through its provisions for the Senate, the Constitution Act, 1867, gave the Maritime provinces a measure of equality with the central provinces. No comparable allowance for the West was anticipated in the original scheme of Confederation. On the contrary, policies to promote the region's adhesion to the nation followed no predetermined path, a disposition at the centre which, because of its absence of forethought more than anything else, repeatedly frustrated and angered western Canadians. The contrast between treatment of the Maritime provinces and that of the West can be pressed too far, however. Joseph Howe understood from the outset the limitations of the original agreement as they affected Nova Scotia: 'In reality the centre of power and influence will always be in Canada. It can be nowhere else.'[44] The reason for this privileging is easily explained: 'The Confederation settlement set up fairly adequate safeguards for the vital interests of the Canadas and the Canadian minorities. These interests were cultural, i.e. educational, linguistic and religious. Nova Scotia being quite capable of keeping her cultural individuality, even in a centralized government, soon found that her vital interests were not cultural but economic.'[45]

Many features of the 1867 Act contributed to its distinctiveness, but none did more in this respect than the terms of the Act that made Canada a federation of cultures as well as of territory. And this in a constitution intended to be 'similar in Principle to that of the United Kingdom.' Here was the meaning of such sections of the Act as 93 (protection for denominational schools existing at the Union), 133 (provision for the use of the English and French languages in Parliament, in the legislature of Quebec, in the courts established by the 1867 Act, and in all the courts of Quebec), 22 (establishment of twenty-four senatorial divisions for Quebec), and 92(13) (property and civil rights in a province as an exclusive power of a provincial legislature). These sections, along with, for instance, the later Standing Orders of the House of Commons that require alternation in the speaker's chair of persons fluent in one or the other of the two languages, along with appointment of a deputy speaker possessing a full knowledge of the language not that of the speaker, emphasize the early and continuing prominence of language in the Canadian federation. As well, the custom emerged, once Canada took command of recommending appointments to the office of Governor General, of alternating nominees between individuals fluent in the two languages (with occasional appointments of persons coming from non-English and non-French groups of Canadians). A list of illustrations to the same effect might be made – the leadership of political parties, the position of Chief Justice of the Supreme Court of Canada – but the point is clear: the Canadian nation and, thus, Canadian federalism are about more than territory – cultural forces, too, have been at work in achieving and maintaining Canada. The Act of 1867 was not just about establishing a constitution that mirrored the United Kingdom's. It was about making a country.

Indeed, the reticence of the Act in spelling out the meaning of that phrase leaves little other choice. Yet it is imperative to note that, except for the eighteen sections of the Act setting out the legislative power of the new provinces of Ontario and Quebec, and the eight sections describing the office of lieutenant governor, the only other references to provincial government are Section 64: 'The Constitution of the Executive Authority in each of the provinces of Nova Scotia and New Brunswick shall, subject to the provisions of this Act, continue as it exists at the Union until altered under the Authority of this Act'; and Section 88, which is identical in expression except for the words 'Legislature of' in

place of 'Executive Authority in.' In the words of the consolidated Constitution Acts, 1867 to 1982: 'Similar provisions were included in each
of the instruments admitting British Columbia, Prince Edward Island
and Newfoundland.'[46] The legislatures and the executive authorities of
Manitoba, Alberta, and Saskatchewan were established by the statutes
creating those provinces.

In short, most of the provinces of Canada had a 'Constitution similar
in Principle to that of the United Kingdom' when they were still colonies, and for some decades before they entered Confederation. In other
words, the constitution preceded federation. While this is not an original observation, it is one that deserves more attention than it customarily receives.[47] It helps explain not only the strength of the provinces'
case when they came to confront the federal government in the courts
late in the nineteenth century – they considered themselves equals; but
also the confidence they exhibited in making their argument – they
were as legitimate products of English constitutional evolution as was
the government at Ottawa, actually more so, because of their longer
lineage. The relevance of these comments lies less in historical illumina-
tion – that has already been done – than in offering a new perspective
on Canadian federalism.[48]

Constitutionally, the provinces are pre- not post-federation entities.
That sequence is what explains the series of negotiations that took place
between federal and colonial (soon to be provincial) politicians. An early chapter of the history of every province recounts the terms sought
and the counter-offers made prior to the inclusion of a new province. It
was because there was no formula for admission, but instead bargaining, that the terms of entry were often contradictory: more members
of Parliament for one province, though smaller in population, than for
another province; fictitious population figures to augment the number
of MPs to be granted; special terms; extraordinary costs (the denial of
their natural resources to the prairie provinces until 1930): the list is
long, the result in the nature of what might be called conditional federalism. Arguably, with that genealogy, the conditions are never satisfac-
tory, nor are they satisfied. Back in 1868 Macdonald had said that Nova
Scotians were intent on feeling aggrieved; seventy years later a member
of the staff of the Rowell-Sirois Commission said the same thing: the
province's 'official version was that it has suffered chronic hardship
ever since Confederation.'[49]

A special instance of federalism through bargaining occurred after
the uprising at Red River and the presentation of a Bill of Rights by the

Métis leaders to the government at Ottawa. The postage-stamp province of Manitoba that resulted in 1870 looked very much like a miniature Quebec, with the same guarantees for religion, language, and law, along with institutional protections, such as a bicameral legislature. But it conformed to no blueprint past or future. In the words of David Mills, Liberal journalist and later minister in the Mackenzie government, Parliament, but more particularly the Conservatives, had in this instance failed to do what 'the theory of their system required.'[50] Mills did not expound on that theory, but taking the preceding discussion as backdrop he might have asked: 'How does this new Manitoba fit with the three kingdoms?' The answer was not immediately apparent, but neither was there one to describe the very different Manitoba that appeared late in the nineteenth century after the linguistic and denominational guarantees of the Manitoba Act, 1870, had been eviscerated.

Manitoba is the pivotal province in a discussion of Canada's double federalism. The Constitution Act, 1867, embraced two versions of federalism – cultural and territorial. After 1867, the question became whether, and if so how, the two versions were to be promulgated as the country expanded. One interpretation of Canadian federalism – when contrasting Manitoba's early history with conditions accompanying the admission of two other provinces (British Columbia in 1871 and Prince Edward Island in 1873) – is to say that provinces would enter the Union displaying the marks of cultural or territorial federalism depending upon their historical and demographical circumstances. Whether such freedom of choice was ever intended as a policy is unlikely: the rounding out of Confederation proved to be too fact specific for such an academic exercise. In any case, by the end of the century, European, British, and American immigration and settlement in the West had swamped existing demographic patterns and made such calculations moot.

The Manitoba Act, 1870, had treated confessional schools (Roman Catholic and Protestant) and the English and French languages in the same manner as they were protected in Quebec by Section 133 of the Constitution Act, 1867 – that is, equally. As far as the province was concerned, the end of this original accord began in 1890, when Manitoba's legislature statutorily withdrew the guarantees for Roman Catholics and French-speaking residents. (Events outside the province that influenced developments within included the passage in 1888 by the legislature of Quebec of the Jesuits' Estate Act, to compensate the religious order for properties confiscated after the Conquest, and the formation the following year in Ontario of the Equal Rights Association dedicated to pressing for disallowance of the Jesuits' Estate Act, and, more generally, opposed to perceived favourable treatment of French-speaking as well as Roman Catholic Canadians.[51]) It is important to note that over a period of six years, while a series of private cases challenged the constitutionality of the provincial legislation, the federal government was never a party to the litigation, nor did it seek the advice of the courts through the mechanism of a reference opinion. Whatever theory of federalism motivated the Macdonald government at Manitoba's founding as a bicultural province, had disappeared in government (and opposition) ranks in Ottawa thirty years afterward in the face of vocal provincial rights sentiment.

A coda to these events occurred ninety years later when, in *Attorney General of Manitoba* v. *Forest*, the Supreme Court of Canada found Manitoba's Official Language Act, 1890, in conflict with Section 23 of the Manitoba Act, 1870, and therefore unconstitutional.[52] As important as that restitution of rights was for French-speaking Manitobans and for those committed to official bilingualism as a public policy, more significant still for a study of Canadian federalism and the constitution was the sequence of events leading to that decision.

Crucial to this story is the executive-inspired Court Challenges Program. A history of the program describes its provenance: 'Realizing that the costs of pursuing litigation involving matters of principle and the public interest can constitute a heavy burden on individuals and groups of limited means, the federal government [in 1978] stepped forward and offered financial assistance to a number of litigants.'[53] Initially, the program was directed at clarifying the scope of language rights then protected under various provisions of Canada's constitution. Among the first litigants so supported was Forest. That decision led to a subsequent challenge, *Bilodeau* v. *Attorney General of Manitoba* (also supported by the program), on the status of Manitoba's unilingual laws. Ultimately that case was appealed to the Supreme Court of Canada, at which time the federal government joined to it the reference on the general question of the validity of the province's laws (*Re Manitoba Language Rights* [1985] 1 S.C.R. 721). In the 1980s the program was expanded to include language rights protected under new constitutional amendments (Sections 16 to 23 of the Charter) and equality rights (Section 15).[54]

Thus, by the late twentieth, as compared to the late nineteenth, century, the federal government's resolve to protect official language rights had stiffened. This was true whether the party in power was Liberal or

Progressive Conservative, at least until very recently. In the last year of its life (1992) the government of Brian Mulroney cancelled the Court Challenges Program. Restored by the Liberals under Jean Chrétien, the program lost its funding again in 2006 under Stephen Harper, only to have it partially revived by the Harper government in 2008. Certainly two decades ago, when the Manitoba language issue was being hotly debated, the federal government was a major participant. Quite unlike the 1890s, when no amount of pleading for assistance in retaining the original dual-language regime elicited federal support, in the 1980s Ottawa adopted an aggressive stance. In the words of the NDP provincial premier of the day: 'The involvement of the federal government on this issue, including its passage of two resolutions unanimously in the House of Commons, was counterproductive. It created negative rather than positive reaction throughout the province.'[55]

Omitted from this account of the Manitoba School Question is the sole instance in Canadian history of Section 93 of the Constitution Act, 1867, being activated. Subsection 4 of Section 93 says that when necessary, Parliament, following a successful appeal to the Governor General in Council, may make 'remedial laws' in the matter of denominational education to carry out the purposes of the section. In plain words, and as regards the Manitoba case, Parliament *might* pass educational measures that applied to Manitoba. Here would be another example of high centralism that, in Wheare's mind, disqualified Canada from being considered a true federation – that is, the federal government's legislating in a field of jurisdiction so transparently provincial. Except, however, when the cultural perspective of Canada's double federalism is at issue – then the central government's action may augment rather than limit the realization of the federal principle.

The preceding discussion suggests one explanation for the contrast in federal government behaviour between 1890 and 1980. The advent of bilingualism and biculturalism as organizing principles of Canadian society by 1960, and – as far as language was concerned – as official federal government policy by 1970, had reconstituted the ways that Canadians thought of themselves. The most obvious expression of this change, because it was formal and legal, was the Official Languages Act, 1969, and the ensuing agencies created to monitor its application. Of these, the best known are the Office of the Commissioner of Official Languages (an officer of Parliament) and the committees of the House of Commons and the Senate that receive the commissioner's Annual Report. Less official but equally public have been nomenclature debates over the past half-century on topics such as, How many nations comprise Canada? and Is Quebec a distinct society?[56]

For the record, it should be stated that Manitoba was the site and source of opposition to the Official Languages Act from what Senator Paul Yuzyk termed 'Canadian ethnic groups of the third element.' The leaders of these groups, he said, 'fear[ed] that they [were being] relegated to second-class citizenship.'[57]

From a societal point of view, these debates probably have more influence than formal public policy on Canadians' sense of a past, and of a future. No politician is more closely identified with these topics than Pierre Trudeau, but it is a quarter-century since he was in office and only a very small number of students read the debates of his era or are familiar with the history or operations of the language policies identified with him. Yet the enhanced legacy of language is on all sides to see – for example, on federal government buildings in every community in the country, on every piece of communication a citizen receives from the federal bureaucracy, and on Radio-Canada, which offers transcontinental radio and television networks, as opposed to local or (in some instances in the past) no French broadcasting. To this might be added changes to the school curriculum, which remains the domain of provincial departments of education: every province where English has historically predominated now, as a consequence of federal funding, offers French immersion courses.

These comments should not be interpreted as implying a wholesale transformation in Canadian attitudes toward bilingualism. No shortage of illustrations can be cited to contest that claim – most obviously the acrimonious debate that took place in Manitoba as that province's government and political parties sought to tailor their laws and practices to the Supreme Court of Canada's judgment that bilingualism in Manitoba had never been constitutionally extinguished. The comments are intended to suggest something rather less utopian: in recent decades official and unofficial learning in Canada have come to share common assumptions about the legitimacy of bilingualism. Again, it must be emphasized that these assumptions are not universally held, and in some parts of the country may be disputed or even rejected. That, too, is a legacy of official bilingualism. Nonetheless, by the 1980s, official and unofficial support for bilingualism assured a very different outcome than a century before in the contest to protect minority rights in Manitoba.

Why was there a hospitable climate then and not before? Part of the answer to that question has to do with a heightened sense of rights as an attribute of personhood, and a belief that the language one speaks is integral to definition of the self. That matter is beyond the focus of this discussion. Another that arguably goes some way to explain the change in attitudes is this: the end of Empire, Commonwealth, and Britishness itself as official categories of meaning. Of course, the Commonwealth continues, as an association of nations with British historical, cultural, and legal connections, but now there is also La Francophonie, founded in 1970 with Canada an original member and a major financial contributor. The evanescence of British Canada at the centre, though less pronounced in some provinces or regions of provinces, is an aspect of Canada's development that remains largely unexamined. The reason for mentioning it here is that bilingualism is one characteristic of modern Canada (along perhaps with the flag, the Charter, medicare, and equalization) that has come to fill the breach left by the waning of British Canada.

The relevance of this observation to the present discussion is this: the argument, advanced by those who wished to abolish both a publicly funded Roman Catholic school system and bilingualism in Manitoba, took as its first premise that Canada was an English-speaking country whose Anglo-Saxon institutions required defending. From this perspective the provision of separate schools and use of the French language were privileges that might legally be abolished *in the provinces*. Similar arguments were heard in other parts of the country on behalf of authorities who sought to limit existing practices and usages.[58] Here was one interpretation of the phrase in the 1867 Act's Preamble: 'a Constitution similar in Principle to that of the United Kingdom.' In the words of the Equal Rights Association, founded in 1889, that 'Principle' was as follows: 'Equality to all. Privileges to none.'

In an article with the practical title 'Contrasting Unitary and Federal Systems,' American political scientist Daniel Elazar defines the 'organic [unitary] model [as one where] politics takes precedence' and the 'federal model [as one where] the constitution takes precedence.'[59] As is often true in scholarly writing by non-Canadians, there are no references to Canada, even though this country possesses a constitution that borrows from both models, particularly when the subject in mind is unitary provincial government within a federal 'system,' which at the end of the nineteenth century was itself associated with a sovereign imperial authority. In the 1890s and again in the 1980s, what mixture of politics and constitution determined the outcome of those controversies? It is a striking feature of the Manitoba School Question how often events turned on legal reasoning. There was no shortage of legal reasoning nine decades later, but this time, unlike before, there was much more politics, in the form of the Court Challenges Program, references to the Supreme Court of Canada, and resolutions of Parliament to stiffen the resolve of the provincial legislature.

Half a century after the Manitoba School Question, Hugh MacLennan published his celebrated novel of English–French relations in Quebec, *Two Solitudes*.[60] But the separation MacLennan portrays between linguistic (and religious) allegiances there communicates the atmosphere that predominated in earlier debates in Manitoba. Paradoxically for Canadian unity, the distance separating cultural neighbours in Manitoba was far greater than the distance separating Anglo-Protestants in Winnipeg from the Empire's final court of appeal, the Judicial Committee of the Privy Council, at Westminster. After 1969, a linguistic line of demarcation that paid no attention to provincial boundaries appeared in Canada. Not all provinces adopted bilingualism as official public policy – in fact, only New Brunswick did; nor could the federal government force them to do so. Instead, a federal language regime was instituted, one that the Constitution Act, 1982, entrenched at the same time that it patriated (as Canadians say) the Constitution. That Act gave Canadians a domestic amending formula for the first time in the country's history and, among much else, established a law, the Charter of Rights and Freedoms, higher than Parliament, to which all legislatures and governments in Canada must conform. Here is more novelty than Viscount Monck could ever have imagined in a federal parliamentary constitution.

# 4 Parliamentary Federalism

The Parliament of Canada has three parts: Crown, Senate, and House of Commons. The history of each reflects in a distinctive manner the evolution of the federation. To take the Crown first: Macdonald's well-known desire for a highly centralized union is noted again by his most recent biographer, Richard Gwyn. In *John A.: The Man Who Made Us*, Gwyn states that the first prime minister looked upon lieutenant governors, who today are sometimes described as 'representatives of the Queen of Canada,' as 'chief executive officers' of provinces, which Macdonald viewed as 'mere municipalities.'[1] More than that, the lieutenant governors – appointed by the Governor General on advice of the prime minister – were agents of the federal government, whose principal role in the eyes of Ottawa was to keep the provinces from interfering with the interests and policies of the national government.[2] For that purpose they possessed unusual powers when it came to assenting or withholding assent to provincial legislation.

In time, due largely to judicial interpretation of Sections 91 and 92 of the Constitution Act, 1867, the Canadian federation came to resemble what K.C. Wheare would describe as a system of independent and coordinate jurisdictions. The lieutenant governors, while still federally appointed and retaining latent powers to interfere in provincial matters, exchanged their federal for an enhanced provincial identity, as evident for instance late in the twentieth century in the institution and proliferation of provincial honours.[3] Thus, from being perceived as an institution amenable to enforcing Macdonald's highly centralized federal ambitions, the Crown became a constitutional foundation for active and independently minded provinces.

Expectations for the Senate of Canada were similarly confounded but for quite different reasons. Where the Crown came to promote strong provinces, the Senate became in the eyes of a legion of critics a bastion of central dominance. Like lieutenant governors, senators were appointed by the Governor General on advice of the prime minister; unlike them, senators were appointed for life (since 1965, until age seventy-five). In a democratic age, critics of the Senate scorn its appointive selection and the partisan patronage this has encouraged every prime minister to wield. Still, the signal characteristics of the Senate lie not in its manner of selection but rather in its fixed upper limit on members and in their equal distribution among senatorial 'divisions' rather than among the individual provinces. Exceptions to that general statement are, first, that Section 26 of the Constitution Act, 1867, provides for the appointment of four or eight additional senators 'representing equally the Four divisions of Canada' – a provision invoked only once, in 1990 at the time of the passage of the Goods and Services Tax legislation; and, second, that the senators for Newfoundland and Labrador (six) and the three northern territories (one each) are members of no 'division.'

The upper limit means that the Senate can never be swamped or, more practically, threatened to be swamped, as the House of Lords has been threatened at rare moments of political passion, such as during the introduction of the Parliament Act, 1911, which reduced the Lords' power by limiting it to a suspensive veto. Fixed numbers divided equally among regions so disparate in population as Ontario, Quebec, and the Maritime provinces in 1867 was an essential condition for agreement on union. The object of Confederation for many Upper Canadians was to break out of the straightjacket of United Canada with its own fixed and equal representation of the two Canadas in a single assembly. A federal parliament with the lower chamber based on representation by population was the answer, but only realizable if the vulnerable parts of the new federation received added protection. That was the purpose of the Senate – and it still is. This is the reason why reform of the Senate has proven a conundrum: its structure is the consequence of a bargain, made by the Fathers of Confederation, the terms of which included both chambers of Parliament. Reforms that do not contemplate the same breadth of change will not succeed.

There is another way of expressing the point, though it takes as its logic the proposition that Canada is a double federation of cultures and territory. Yes, there is jurisdictional federalism to protect the provinces; yes, there is jurisdictional federalism with special provisions of language, religion, and law to protect the unique culture of Quebec; yes, there are other constitutional arrangements to acknowledge the French presence in Canada – but in Parliament, the institutional duty to protect sectional interests rests disproportionately with the Senate. This is one reason why in 2000 the Senate proved so obdurate about the Clarity Bill; that bill made the House of Commons the sole arbiter of whether the question and results of a secession referendum in a province were clear.

Again, when in 2006 the government of Stephen Harper introduced Bill S-4, 'An Act to Amend the Constitution Act, 1867 (Senate Tenure),' to set terms for senators rather than having them retire at age seventy-five, opposition from east of the Ottawa River was especially strong. In the words of the New Brunswick presentation, over the signature of the province's premier, term limits would 'dilute the independence [of senators]' and 'would lead to a further marginalization of small Provinces at the federal level.'[4] 'Small Provinces' comprise one category of the federation's units; Quebec (by itself) another. Both look to the Senate, as currently constructed, for protection; both see little attraction in proposals, such as Triple E, that among other results would give every province an equal number of senators.

An earlier chapter posited a contradiction between responsible and federal government. The first is centripetal in its effect, gathering power to the centre. The second is centrifugal, dispersing power to the parts. How does parliamentary federalism reconcile these conflicting tendencies? Or is the question quite that simple? The centrifugal character of federalism may require further examination. Is power dispersed differently in a cultural as opposed to a territorial federation? What happens in a country such as Canada, where both types of federal principles are at work? Do the different institutions of parliamentary federalism privilege one principle over another – the Crown and territorial federalism, the Senate and cultural federalism? Is it the role of the House of Commons, or other bodies, such as those of executive federalism, to moderate these disparate tendencies?

Whatever the answer to that question today – which, in light of the complex redistribution formulae with grandfather clauses and irreducible minimums that apply following every decennial census, is probably yes – that was not the object articulated at the Charlottetown and Quebec conferences. The House of Commons was to be the popular, democratic organ of Parliament. Through it would be realized the principle of representation by population, long sought but hitherto unachievable in the institutional balance statutorily mandated in the Act of Union, 1840. More than that, until rep-by-pop obtained, responsible government was at best an approximation to what happened in the United Kingdom. Coalition governments, double-headed ministries, and the occasional double majority saw to that. An elected lower house based on the principle of representation by population would provide the atmosphere essential to the prospering of responsible government; in short, it would give that essential principle of the nineteenth-century British constitution a chance to flourish for the first time in central Canada.

Yet even in 1867 the House of Commons was no instrument of pure rep-by-pop – if only because the government sat in that chamber and from the first the composition of cabinet acknowledged the different parts of the federation in a manner dismissive of population. But there were other reasons why the House deviated from the principle championed by advocates like George Brown. The Fathers of Confederation had agreed that the ratio of Quebec's population per member would determine the number of members each province would have in the new lower chamber – the effect being an unintended melding of the cultural and territorial approaches to federalism. A consequence of this practice was a chamber with no fixed ceiling on its numbers (until a new redistribution formula, introduced in 1946, did just that, only to be abandoned three decades later for a series of agreements that saw some provinces increase their number of seats but no province lose) and, more fundamental still, an attitude toward representation that might be described as malleable.

The contrast between the inelastic Senate and the infinitely expandable Commons is striking when compared to the relationship between the two chambers of the Australian Parliament, where a nexus provision in the Commonwealth of Australia Constitution Act, 1900 (Section 24), requires the number of seats in the House of Representatives to be 'as nearly as practicable twice the number of the senators'; or in the United States, where, except for the entry of Hawaii and Alaska into the Union, both chambers of Congress seem to be almost fixed in number. In 2008 the House of Representatives is the same size as it was in 1941. (In that year the House of Commons had 245 members; today its membership is 308.) More than just striking, the contrast, first, in composition between the upper and lower chambers of Canada's Parliament, and, second, in magnitude of bicameral difference between the Canadian Parliament and the legislatures of the federations with which Canada has most in common, reveals political and constitutional differences between Canada and the other countries.

In Australia the nexus provision means that, short of the hurdle of a constitutional amendment, growth in the size of the lower (rep-by-pop) chamber necessitates growth in upper chamber, with implications for the electoral fortunes of the (same) two parties that dominate the chambers. In the United States, the static House numbers, along with a disregard for any rationale but population when it comes to determining state representation in Congress, leads to dramatic changes in the allocation of seats among the states: New York, the state with the largest contingent of congressmen in 1941, now trails California by twenty-four seats and Texas by three. In Canada, under the current redistribution formula, Quebec is guaranteed seventy-five seats in perpetuity and six other provinces are assured, by one or another guarantee, that they will not lose seats in any subsequent redistribution. The only way by which provinces that are growing in population – that is, Ontario, Alberta, and British Columbia – may receive additional seats is by adding to the size of the House of Commons.

Like the Crown, the House of Commons has not worked out quite as anticipated, and for somewhat analogous reasons. If the Crown, as opined by the courts, emboldened the provinces in their conflicts with the federal government, the Commons with its popular base ought to have exerted a countervailing influence. But it did not: instead, protection of provincial representation in the Commons became more important than realizing the principle of rep-by-pop. That happened because the sudden expansion in population at the end on the nineteenth century came outside the original 'three kingdoms.' 'Rep-by-pop' as the slogan of growth was heard most distinctly from the West – and not infrequently thwarted: the census of 1911 gave the prairies sixteen additional seats, but these did not take effect until 1917; eleven more seats after 1921 only appeared at the 1925 election. Federalism for westerners has always been at some point about redistribution.

Protection from 'rep-by-pop' was the mantra of small provinces, whose measure of federalism lay in their contemplated relative decline in population compared to the rest of the country. History, it is said, repeats itself: in 1850, in a debate in the Legislative Assembly of the Parliament of United Canada on the baleful effects of fixed, equal representation of the two parts of the colony, Henry Boulton posed what appears to be an evergreen question in Canadian politics: 'Was this curse to be perpetuated, like the balance of power between Free and Slave States – intelligence sacrificed to dead votes?'[5]

The Canadian constitution is a world of illusion and allusion. It establishes a monarchy that in practice is a parliamentary democracy. It claims to be a constitution like that of the United Kingdom, but it does not specify what that means – an intriguing omission since Canada is a federation and the United Kingdom is not. It creates a highly centralized federal government, but in practice the Canadian federation is said to be one of the world's most decentralized. The Canadian constitution is a study in contrasts, and parliamentary federalism extends the range of that study: Does the Crown strengthen or weaken Canadian federalism? Does Canadian federalism undermine the Canadian constitution, or is it the reverse? Is the near paralysis on Senate reform a tribute to or a travesty of the work of the Fathers of Confederation? Need electoral democratic norms always be viewed as inimical to parliamentary and federal government? Do the institutions of parliamentary federalism serve what this book describes as vertical (cultural) federalism better than they do horizontal (territorial) federalism?

The parts of Parliament are not of a piece in their influence on federalism. This is not true of the United States and Australian constitutions, whose legislative parts seem to reinforce or refine a common norm, be it consultation or representation. In Canada the Crown, Senate, and Commons exert influences that are at cross-purposes to the health of the federation. It is this intraparliamentary discordance that explains Canada's long quest for agreement on myriad constitutional matters. A discussion of parliamentary federalism as if it were analogous to congressional federalism, with its unifying core principle (representation), would be futile. Different principles and behaviour animate each of the three parts of Parliament. This, and the fact that different perspectives on federalism are associated with each of the three parts, explains at least some of the reasons for the failure to carry through reforms to the institutions and procedures of Parliament and federalism.

This overview is intended to provide context for the discussion of the Crown, Senate, and Commons that follows. In examining any one of the three, it is possible to lose sight of how each complements or contradicts the activities of the others. Proposals for constitutional reform tend to be narrow in their focus: term limits here, codified prerogative there. Also, because the majority of Canadians are more democratic than parliamentary in their interests, they treat the Crown and the Senate as of diminished significance when compared to the Commons. This presumption is less than accurate when the matter at hand is constitutional negotiations.

## The Crown

The subject of this part of the chapter on parliamentary federalism is more accurately designated the Crown-in-Parliament. While long understood as part of the whole, the constitutional monarchy that emerged after the Glorious Revolution (1688) was now accepted to be subject to the will of its parliamentary partners. The independence of the sovereign, as witnessed during the time of the Tudors and Stuarts, was at an end. It is important to underline the telescoping of parts represented in this powerful image of a three-in-one parliament. For that mixture of constitutional elements should caution against making assumptions about what is executive or what is legislative power. As opposed to a system like that of the United States, which is based on the principle of separation of offices, in a constitutional monarchy with a Westminster-style parliament, the government of the day is no mere executive. The achievement of responsible government did not empower the legislature so much as transfer the Crown's control of the executive to a small group of persons who commanded the support of the legislature.

As evidence of the difficulty that follows from an absence of caution, see the report of the *Task Force on Canadian Unity: A Future Together, Observations and Recommendations* (1979). Co-chaired by Jean-Luc Pepin and John Robarts, and appointed shortly after the victory of the Parti Québécois in 1976, the Task Force adopted for its analytical perspective the challenges of Canadian dualism and regionalism. The validity of this approach is not a subject for present discussion, except to note a specific recommendation (no. 30) of the Task Force, which calls for 'the present distribution of legislative and executive powers [to] be clarified and adjusted to contemporary needs and realities.' The assumption that these powers may be readily categorized is just that, an assumption.

In a monarchy, where there is a 'real' executive and a 'formal' executive, where the real executive is made up of members of the legislature, where that real executive exercises prerogative power inherent in the formal executive, where the formal executive in a province (the lieutenant governor) is constitutionally empowered (Section 90) to reserve provincial legislation for the 'Signification of Pleasure,' that is, approval, by the federal real executive (cabinet), where the same body (the federal cabinet) may direct Parliament to make remedial laws in the matter of denominational education in a province, then the ready distinction presumed to exist between legislative and executive powers, in the Canadian constitution at least, is not immediately apparent. Arguably, this imprecision is a source of great power – usually to the executive. The unconvinced might reply that, the prerogative aside, these are archaic, moribund powers, relics of the quasi-federal system the Fathers created. In addition to the obvious retort that there have been a number of opportunities to remove these provisions, yet they remain in the Constitution – in the case of Section 90, entrenched after 1982 by a unanimity amendment provision – there is Eugene Forsey's oft-repeated pronouncement that provisions in respect of lieutenant governors give to the central government power to preserve, in each province, the system of responsible cabinet government.[6] Forsey repeated this view in 1979 following the appearance of a Canadian Bar Association recommendation that the lieutenant governor should be renamed 'the Chief Executive Officer of the province [and] should not be subject to federal control.' That recommendation he termed 'objectionable,' because it would 'remove one of the few safeguards against a province playing ducks and drakes with the Constitution.'[7] Excerpts of the CBA recommendations (*Towards a New Canada*, 1978) are reprinted, one presumes approvingly, in the *Coming to Terms* volume of the report of the Task Force on Canadian Unity.

Unlike the B-and-B Commission of the 1960s or the Royal Commission on the Economic Union and Development Prospects for Canada of the 1970s, the Task Force on Canadian Unity did not publish any of its research reports, of which a number examine the reform of central government institutions. It is commonly said that the emphasis the Task Force gave to dualism in the Canadian federation did not find favour with the Trudeau government and its more expansive depiction of Canada as a nation with two official languages and cultural diversity.[8] Research studies completed for the Task Force, now housed in Library and Archives Canada, indicate the nature of the difference. In a paper titled 'Politics and the Constitution' written by Robert Décary, within a chapter titled 'Attribution of Power,' and after a Cartesian-like enumeration of elements of ever-decreasing amplitude (from 'Principles of Federalism' to 'Total Sovereignty' to 'Appointment of Lieutenant-Governors and Judges'), are found the following two statements: 'The right to appoint lieutenant-governors and judges is another remnant of the supremacy of the Federal Government which should disappear if constituent states are to be considered as equals, in their own sphere'; and 'Section 58 of the British North America Act (appointment of lieuten-ant-governors) and 96 (appointment of judges) are totally incompatible with the concept of provincial sovereignty.'[9] (The volume of the Task Force report titled *A Future Together* transposes this language, describing Section 96 as 'a questionable remnant of federal centralization.'[10])

Of these statements, two comments are required. First, appointment of lieutenant governors and judges is not a 'remnant' of a once-dominant federal power but an integral element of a British-styled monarchical form of government. To date, proposals for alternative mechanisms to broaden consultation in the appointment process –for instance, by incorporating Parliament into judicial nominations – have proved difficult to implement. Second, whether or not Sections 58 and 96 are 'totally incompatible with the concept of provincial sovereignty' is, as Macdonald would in other contexts say, *à propos de rien*, since provincial sovereignty is not a foundational concept in the Canadian constitution.

The inference otherwise in the Task Force study is presumably to the JCPC opinion *Maritime Bank* v. *the Receiver General of New Brunswick (1892)*. The following passage, composed by Lord Watson, from this much-cited opinion in the literature of Canadian federalism deserves extensive quotation:

> The object of the [Constitution] Act [1867] was neither to weld the prov-inces into one, not to subordinate provincial governments to a central authority, but to create a federal government in which they should all be represented, entrusted with the exclusive administration of affairs in which they had a common interest, each province retaining its independence and autonomy. That object was accomplished by distributing, between the Dominion and the provinces all powers executive and legislative, and all public property and revenues which had previously belonged to the provinces, so that the Dominion government should be vested with such of these powers, property and revenues as were necessary for the due per-formance of its constitutional functions, and that the remainder should be retained by the provinces for the purposes of the provincial government.[11]

Here was judicial heralding of the Whearean federal analysis that was to appear half a century later. For that reason it should not be presumed that provincial sovereignty is a necessary condition for fed-eralism. Wheare makes no such claim, nor, for that matter, did Lord Watson. Saywell observes that '[Watson] neither explicitly nor implicitly questioned the statutory provisions for Dominion control of provincial legislation.'[12]

The challenge in the claim to provincial sovereignty is the same challenge that would arise if a claim were made to federal sovereignty. Sovereignty in a constitutional monarchy rests in the Crown-in-Parliament (or, legislature), except when the subject is the reserve powers (dissolution of Parliament, for instance) that remain as a matter of prerogative in the hands of the Crown's representative. Interference with the prerogative is impermissible, the JCPC determined in 1919. At issue was a Manitoba statute (Initiative and Referendum Act) that required the lieutenant governor to submit proposed laws to voters instead of to the legislature. (The years following the First World War were a time of enthusiasm for direct democratic mechanisms.) In the words of Lord Haldane, because the lieutenant governor represents the Sovereign in the province it 'renders natural the exclusion of his office from the power conferred on the Provincial Legislature to amend the constitution of the Province. The analogy of the British Constitution is that on which the entire scheme is founded, and that analogy points to the impropriety of construing section 92 as permitting the abrogation of any power which the Crown possesses through a person who directly represents it.'[13] Section 92(1) of the Constitution Act, 1867, said specifically (but Section 41(a) of the Constitution Act, 1982, has the same effect) that the legislature of a province may not unilaterally amend the office of lieutenant governor. In short, under the Canadian constitution the executive is not a creature of legislation but independent of it. The implications of that status or placement are central in an era, such as the early twenty-first century, concerned with enforcing executive accountability.

In the decades after the Second World War the Crown became increasingly Canadianized, as evident in multiple ways, including the appointment after 1952 of native-born Canadians to the office of Governor General.[14] The symbolic significance of this practice is clear: it placed Canadianizing the Crown in the same category of initiatives as ending appeals to the JCPC; seeking, but not totally achieving until 1982, a domestic amendment formula; adopting a Canadian flag; bringing Newfoundland and Labrador into the federation; and building public works of transcontinental importance, such as the Trans-Canada Highway and the St Lawrence Seaway. This is the familiar, and to a large extent official, depiction of the Crown as an instrument of national cohesion buttressed at the same time by the solidity of its English constitutional lineage. From the perspective of Canadian politics and federalism there is another, less frequently acknowledged, dimension to this development. The Crown's Canadianization has separated the person of the monarch from the concept of the Crown. That division helps explain both the lassitude of Canadians to the attractions of republicanism and their apparent indifference to the existing constitutional arrangement.

A dramatic exception to that generalization, and one with potential repercussions for the federation, occurred late in 2008. The general election in October 2008 produced a Parliament in which the governing Conservatives retained the largest number of seats (143) but not a majority. The three opposition parties (Liberal, NDP, and Bloc Québécois) commanded the remaining 165 seats. Less than two months after the election and only two weeks into the new Parliament, the leaders of the opposition parties announced (for reasons unrelated to this study) a plan to topple the government and replace it with a Liberal-NDP coalition supported by the Bloc. They sent a letter to the Governor General indicating that were the government defeated in the House, they stood ready to form a new government. For its realization, the plan depended upon the Governor General's refusing a request from the current prime minister for dissolution of Parliament (a prerogative power that indubitably rests with the Crown) and turning to the putative coalition.

The literature on the power of dissolution is extensive, and opinions on the Crown's discretion in granting or refusing a request varied. What was striking, unexpected, and unprecedented, however, was the interposition of federalism, or of federal sensitivities, into the controversy surrounding the choices facing the Governor General. The four western provinces send ninety-two members to the House of Commons. In October 2008 the Conservatives captured seventy-one of these seats. Fourteen of the remaining twenty-one seats, divided between Liberals and NDP, were located in British Columbia. To these statistics was added the fact that the Conservative vote had increased in the October election in seven of the ten provinces and in all three of the territories. (The Liberal vote had declined in eight provinces and three territories.) A view widely expressed was that if the Governor General were to refuse a request for dissolution from the sitting prime minister and invite the coalition parties to form a government, western Canada would be disenfranchised by the exercise of the prerogative. As it happened, the prime minister sought and received from the Governor General Parliament's prorogation. When Parliament next met, a new leader of the Liberal Party (Michael Ignatieff) decided to support the

Conservative government, thus ending for the time being talk of a coalition. The reason he gave for this change of strategy was as follows: 'I felt it would divide the country. I want to be someone who unites the country and that includes the West.'[15]

Until 2008, the exercise of the Crown's prerogative had not been perceived to have an effect on federalism. Instead the literature on the prerogative of dissolution is preoccupied with the effect of its exercise on relations between the political and the formal executives. What a succession of minority governments, culminating in the controversy of 2008, has demonstrated is that fragmented and regionally based political parties may, through the quite constitutional negotiations of their parliamentary leaders, expose the Governor General, in a manner hitherto unseen, to the vicissitudes of Canadian federalism. Noting that the coalition could be 'kept in power only with the support of the Bloc, whose raison d'être is the dismemberment of Canada,' Thomas Flanagan argued that 'gross violations of democratic principles would be involved in handing government over to the coalition without getting the approval from the voter.'[16]

Canadian governors general have been indefatigable travellers at home and, more recently, abroad. Through these journeys, often to less populated parts of the country, through the award of honours, such as the Order of Canada, and through patronage of the arts, the sciences, and sport, the work of the Governor General touches all Canadians. Though the travel itineraries and honours allocations use the provinces as their categories for reporting, the activities of the Governor General are more intentionally national than federal in character. With one exception: Quebec. There is a special relationship between the Crown and Quebec, evident in, among other factors, the interest that British governors general (who were inevitably bilingual) took in the historic fabric of Quebec City; symbolized in the Governor General's summer home at the Quebec Citadel; reflected in the custom of alternating in the office persons who are English- and French-speaking; and replicated, to an extent not true of other provinces, in the provenance of Rideau Hall staff. A study written for the Task Force on Canadian Unity spoke of alternation as 'a symbol of Canadian duality' and recommended that it continue 'as an inviolable custom of the Canadian constitution.'[17]

At Confederation, the Crown in the provinces was expected to strengthen the centre. This was the rationale behind the manner of the lieutenant governors' selection, as well as behind their power to reserve provincial legislation for federal government approval or rejection (because of the political costs associated with taking a decision, Ottawa often did nothing, since after one year a provincial bill caught in this limbo lapsed). By contrast, the Crown at the centre of Empire was not expected to exercise similar power over the federal government – that had been the whole object in achieving responsible government. While London still had power in some constitutional fields, such as foreign affairs, it was understood that it was only a matter of time before these too would be transferred to Canada (and other Dominions). It is significant that when that day eventually came, in the form of the Statute of Westminster, 1931, the complete autonomy that came with Dominion status did not affect the Canadian federal system. The Statute of Westminster 'expressly repudiated' any suggestion that it might.[18] Section 52(2) of the Constitution Act, 1982, itemizes the contents of the Constitution of Canada, one part of which is 'the Acts and orders referred to in the schedule [to the Constitution Act, 1982].' The Statute of Westminster is one of those 'Acts.'

Provincial ownership of natural resources (delayed in the case of the three prairie provinces until 1930), jurisdictional responsibility for social legislation, as well as in other fields such as education and transportation, but most of all judicial interpretation of Sections 91 and 92 in such a manner (that is, via the Crown) as to make the executive power of a province coterminous with its legislative power, strengthened the autonomy of the parts to a degree unimagined by the Fathers of Confederation. Canadian federalism is about jurisdiction rather than representation. The Crown has made a large contribution to that feature of Canadian politics, just as it has, in the opposite direction, restrained expression of the popular will. Like the English, the Canadian constitutional formula links the public to the executive power through Parliament. As Enoch Powell, master parliamentarian, once explained, parliamentary government on the Westminster model is not about representation so much as it is 'a means of arriving at valid sustainable decisions' whose validity rests upon their public acceptance.[19]

## The Senate

The Crown underwrites the autonomy of the provinces and helps make the federative principle in Canada one of jurisdiction (in the parts) rather than representation (at the centre). As a result, it weakens the argument of those who would introduce, more directly than at present, the federal principle into the organization of Parliament's second chamber.

While it is true that talk of reform of the Senate can be found in the nineteenth century, it is only in the last forty years that reform of the upper house has been linked in a sustained way to the subject of federalism. The B-and-B Commission said nothing about institutional reform, nor did it perceive the problem of Canadian federalism to be inadequate representation of provincial interests at the centre. In the 1970s, however, proposals were made to use the Senate to transform the federation and Parliament: the Task Force on Canadian Unity (1979) recommended that 'the Senate should be abolished and replaced by a new second chamber to be called the Council of the Federation.' The Council would be composed of 'delegations representing the provincial governments' (Recommendations 47 and 48). Thus the council would not be a legislative body, as found in Westminster-modelled parliaments, nor would it be a popular body, a chamber of the people (albeit an unrepresentative one), as the Senate of Canada is currently.

In essence, the council was patterned after the German Bundesrat, a model elaborated upon in a number of unpublished studies written for the Task Force.[20] Significant, in light of later proposals to reform the Senate, was a document titled 'Some Notes on the Alternatives for a Revised Second Chamber,' compiled by R.L. Watts, a member of the Task Force and the Canadian academic who has written most about comparative federalism. Summarizing 'apparent consensus from previous discussions,' he noted the following: 'rejection of an all centrally appointed Senate; rejection of an elected Senate as inappropriate where the cabinet is responsible to the House of Commons; and preference for a majority of regional (provincial) members but also some centrally appointed members.' He concluded that 'the central institutions need to be revitalized to express better the distinctive provincial interests which have come to the forefront and reached even critical proportions in the last decade.'[21]

That comment reflects a central feature of the Senate reform debate of the last four decades – its present mindedness. The phrase 'distinctive provincial interests' may be ambiguous: Are the interests those of one or more than one province? Still, the Task Force, appointed a year after the Parti Québécois came to power, is in no doubt: its deliberations, research studies, and report and recommendations communicate a sense of urgency to respond to that particular event. The report may speak of 'regionalism' and 'duality' as cleavages in Canadian society, but for its authors in the late 1970s, vertical or dual federalism is in the ascendant. Less than a decade later and in the context of another

inquiry, the Royal Commission on the Economic Union and Development Prospects for Canada, a study of *Intrastate Federalism in Canada* by
Donald Smiley and Ronald Watts adopted an opposite view: as far as
Parliament's second chamber was concerned, 'the proposal for replac-
ing the existing Senate with a body of provincial delegates has some
serious disadvantages, [while] a persuasive case can be made for a
popularly elected Senate, especially one with strong powers to influence and even obstruct governments backed by House of Commons
majorities.'[22] A document released by the Government of Canada (1991)
in the course of discussions leading to the Charlottetown Accord reiter-
ated that reconsidered view even more strongly: 'It is important to bear
in mind that constitutions do not operate in a vacuum. The basic law
of a federation reflects the customs, values, traditions and history of its
people ... The principle on which the constitution of Germany is built
is ... quite different from Canada's.'[23]

What had happened in those few years to explain the reversal of
opinion on Senate reform? First, the Parti Québécois had failed, in the
face of strong federal Liberal opposition, to carry the 1980 provincial
referendum on Quebec sovereignty, while the province's Liberals had
subsequently displaced the Parti Québécois government. The sense of
urgency had abated. Second, a wave of reform sentiment directed at
achieving a Triple E Senate (elected, equal, and effective) had become
identified with the new Reform Party then emerging in Alberta. No
longer was the priority to respond to the pressure exerted by cultural federalism; rather, it was to accommodate the conflicting interests
associated with territorial federalism. Within another two decades the
momentum behind Triple E had flagged as well. Nonetheless, in that
interval intense debate surrounding the Meech Lake and Charlottetown
accords had spawned an atmosphere receptive to provincial claims for
equality of legislative status in the upper chamber and for a basis of
electoral legitimacy analogous to that seen in Australia and the United
States. Triple E became the most widely discussed proposed reform to
the Senate in Canada's history.

In contrast to a Bundesrat-like upper house made up of provincial
governmental delegations – the institutional apotheosis of intergovernmental relations – Triple E would create a popularly elected legislative
second chamber. Proponents of Triple E wanted the Senate to check
the Commons, where the government sits. Federalism and the constitution would come together in the upper chamber, only now federalism
would be a check on – rather than a principle of – government achieved

through cabinet representation in the lower chamber. The implications of such a transformation for the conduct of responsible government and for parliamentary federalism were vast and seldom explored by advocates of the reform.

By the first decade of the twenty-first century, though no one was promoting Triple E, one of the Es – election – was still finding favour. As prime minister, Paul Martin introduced the concept of the democratic deficit as a problem in need of a solution. An appointed Senate was not only 'indefensible,' said another Liberal, Tom Kent, but an imperative for change.[24] It fell to the succeeding, Conservative government, led by Stephen Harper, to introduce but fail (as of 2009) to carry through Parliament legislation (Bill S-4, An Act to Amend the Constitution Act, 1867, that is, the Senate Tenure Bill, tabled May 2006; and Bill C-20 [39th Parliament], Senate Appointment Consultations Act, tabled December 2006) to institute both terms for senators and consultative elections in the provinces, the winners of which the prime minister would propose to the Governor General for appointment to the Senate. Like the marriage of statutorily fixed election dates to the Crown's continuing prerogative to dissolve Parliament, even in the absence of a vote of want of confidence, consultative elections subject to regulation by a variety of provincial statutes to select nominees for appointment to one chamber of Canada's Parliament lack theoretical coherence and are subject to legal challenge.[25]

The Senate is constantly criticized but rarely subjected to close scrutiny.[26] Its recent history is distinguished by a sequence of new though not original proposals for reform, none of which has come to fruition. Federalism inclines its students to comparative analysis, a disposition of singular importance when the subject being discussed is the upper chamber of the legislature. In federations that body is the federal house, a presumption the Senate of the United States in the eighteenth century and comparable legislative bodies elsewhere two hundred years later appear to support. This same reasoning has led critics of the Senate of Canada to say that it is a failed federal chamber and to promote an alternative composition analogous to that found in the United States, or Australia, or Germany, the traditional 'others' of Canadian federal analysis.

The flaw in analysis is that Canada is not a federation like these others. It is a double federation – of culture and territory, and, most important in the 1860s, of limited territory. It seems almost an oxymoron to speak in the same breath of Canada and limited size: the country is so

huge and so much of its post-Confederation history focused on pulling
the parts together through one or another transcontinental enterprise.
But in the mid-1860s that activity was in the future. Of course, the original four-province federation was large compared to the countries of
Europe. Still, it was only a fraction of what was to come. More than
that, the two Maritime provinces, along with Prince Edward Island and
Newfoundland and Labrador, which were confidently expected to join
at some later date, could not expand territorially, since they did not lie
adjacent to the vast 'Rupert's Land and the North-western Territory,'
which Section 146 of the Constitution Act, 1867, anticipated would enter
the union; nor could they expect an increase in population through in-
migration, since that population would necessarily be agrarian in economic pursuit and require access to land. Thus did the moving frontier
in time change the terms of the original union.

Combine that Maritime future of constrained expectations with the
protection and institutional autonomy secured to Quebec by the 1867
Act; then place both of these perspectives alongside that of Ontario,
which anticipated economic and demographic expansion as a result of
Canada's acquisition of the North-west. This range of disparate futures
combined with equally disparate populations (in 1861, fewer than
600,000 people in Nova Scotia and New Brunswick, and over one million each in Ontario and Quebec) help explain the composition of the
Senate. Ontario and the provinces of settlement to the west had less
reason to look to the upper chamber of Parliament as a bulwark. This is
an oversimplification, of course, since the success of political parties at
capturing Quebec's share of Commons seats has always been a major
calculation in national elections. Nonetheless, the initial construction
of the Senate, which continues to the present, was determined by the
competing claims of those parts of Canada that expected to grow or
languish.

It was these 'parts,' or sections or regions, that became the senatorial 'divisions' described in Section 22 of the Constitution Act, 1867.
Initially three (Ontario, Quebec, and the Maritime provinces), a fourth
division, comprised of the four western provinces, was added in 1915,
after a parliamentary debate over the course of some months during
which maintenance of the divisional structure was never in question.
Along with the manner of appointment and the fixed upper limit on
senatorial numbers, the divisional structure is a distinctive feature of
the Canadian Senate. It was the disparity in population between divisions (in the 2006 census, less than two million in the Maritime, more

than nine-and-a-half million in the western) and within (British Columbia 4.1 million, Saskatchewan approximately 1 million) that animated
proponents of Triple E.[27] It was the latter imbalance that led two senators, Jack Austin and Lowell Murray, in 2007 to propose making British Columbia a separate division with 12 members of the upper house,
while its six senators would be divided among the remaining three
western provinces: four to Alberta, one each to the other provinces.[28]

What is notable about the divisional structure is how readily Senate reformers dismiss its significance. Like the federal government's
appointment of lieutenant governors, it too is treated as an inconse-
quential remnant based on antiquated assumptions. Dunkin's three-
kingdom metaphor of 1869 (or four-kingdom after the uncontentious
constitutional amendment of 1915) is deemed no longer to apply.
Instead, the strains of territorial federalism require provincial governments to act as advocates in conflicts with the federal government. The
strains became manifest only in the period after the Second World War,
largely because the issues concerned natural resources, and these were
transferred to the prairie provinces only in 1930 on the eve of a decade of depression and drought that was followed by another decade
of war and postwar adjustment. The revolts of the organized farmers
in the 1920s were of a different order: their objective was to force government to help farmers as they struggled with banks, railways, and
grain companies. After the collapse of the provincial wheat pools in
the early 1930s, the federal government assumed a monopoly position with regard to the marketing of grains that it still retains to some
degree. Using political economy literature as markers of the transition,
Seymour Martin Lipset's *Agrarian Socialism* and the ten-volume Social
Credit series, published by the University of Toronto Press, signify
the past and *Prairie Capitalism: Power and Influence in the New West* the
present.[29]

The divisional basis of the Senate is less esoteric and antique than
criticism of that arrangement implies. The Victoria Charter, 1971, negotiated but not passed by the federal and provincial governments, devised
a domestic amending formula using a modified divisional structure.
Proposed amendments would have required the support of each of
the federal government and Ontario and Quebec, at least two of the
western provinces containing half or more of the region's population,
and two provinces in Atlantic Canada. *An Act Respecting Constitutional
Amendments* (SC 1996, c. 1), the so-called 'regional veto act,' though
an ordinary statute, prohibits the government from proposing certain

amendments to the constitution unless the amendment has first been consented to by Ontario, Quebec, British Columbia, and at least two Atlantic and at least two Prairie provinces comprising in each instance at least 50 per cent of the region's population. The point of noting these examples of a divisional calculus is to recall an important documented feature of Canada – its regionalism.[30] In the case of Ontario and Quebec, region and province may be coterminous concepts. That is not true to the west or east of the populous St Lawrence heartland. Here was the conundrum the Fathers of Confederation faced when designing an upper chamber for the new federal Parliament; here too the challenge that Canadian politicians encountered for fifty-five years while trying to devise a domestic amending formula, finally agreed to in 1982 but only in the absence of acknowledging Quebec's claim to a historic veto; and here as well is the enigma that reformers of the Senate of Canada themselves acknowledge – by virtue of the changes they propose – but have never resolved.

In this context it is worth noting the contrast in practice between Canada and United States. In 1787 the Congress of the Confederation of the United States passed the Northwest Ordinance, which prohibited slavery north and west of the Ohio River but also set the terms for admission of new states from the region. The defining criterion for entry was a population of 60,000; with admission came two senators and at least one Congressman, and together those numbers determined the state's vote in the electoral college to select the president and vice-president. The simplicity of these terms was further emphasized by the precedent the ordinance set: expansion would occur through the admission of new states and not the expansion of existing states. The contrast with Canada on both counts is striking and suggests that caution be exercised when contemplating models of reform drawn from the United States. The words of one MP of more than a century ago remain apt: 'The smaller provinces have representation in the Senate, so that to radically change the constitution of that House would disarrange our whole system.'[31] He would have been more accurate had he added the adjective 'disproportionate' to modify the noun 'representation.'

Arraignment of the Senate has concentrated on the chamber's failings as a federal rather than a parliamentary body. Critics are so numerous that to quote one is invidious. Still, Ronald Watts communicates well the general sentiment in his *Comparing Federal Systems in the 1990s*: 'Where senators are appointed by the federal government, as in Canada, they have the least credibility as spokesmen for regional interests, even when they are residents of the regions they represent.' He concludes that 'of all the federal second chambers, the Canadian Senate has the least public legitimacy.'[32] The comparative lack of interest in the Senate as a legislative body – its primary function is as a deliberative and investigative body that complements the House of Commons – deserves notice. Canada is unusual among federal systems in that bicameralism at the centre is not duplicated in the parts. Five provinces once had upper chambers, but only one of these (Quebec) lasted past 1928, and it was abolished in 1969. The absence of provincial upper chambers, in company with a federal government monopoly on appointment of senators, cannot fail to influence the attitude that provincial politicians adopt toward the Senate and toward proposals for its reform. Whether this institutional asymmetry makes the provinces more or less amenable to proposed reform of the Senate is not among the purposes of this book to decide.

Arguments for election build on two themes: the democratic ethos of the times and the practice of others. The case advanced by Triple E proponents and, more recently, by the supporters of the *Senate Appointment Consultations Act* adopts territorial rather than cultural federalism for its perspective. There is reason to doubt the efficacy of that premise, which may explain why Triple E has never garnered universal provincial support. The story of Confederation is one of special deals for the provinces, though few provincial politicians have been as candid in this regard as Richard McBride, premier of British Columbia from 1903 to 1915, whose opinion was cited by a later premier (Duff Pattullo) before the Rowell-Sirois Commission: 'The Terms of Union, in each instance, represented a separate and distinct treaty with Canada.' For this reason, provinces should deal with Canada alone. To force British Columbia to accept terms as agreed to by other provinces would 'coerce [her] and seriously invade provincial rights.' In short, equality was not enough.[33]

The prospect of election presents a special challenge to vertical federalism, one that even the minimalist proposal of consultative elections lays bare. In a study commissioned by the Office of the Commissioner of Official Languages (2007), political scientist Louis Massicotte concluded that 'official language minorities have little to gain but much to lose if the selection process for senators is amended.'[34] He noted that 'official language minority communities are proportionately *better represented* [emphasis in original] in the Senate than in the House of Commons.' Two reasons explain the contrast between the chambers. First, senators are appointed on the recommendation of prime ministers, who, whether Liberal or Conservative, have treated the appointment of French-speaking senators (and not only from Quebec) as important – consider the French in the West and the Acadians in the Maritime provinces. Second, MPs are elected, and in the absence of a territorial concentration of French-speaking voters – as occurs in New Brunswick and parts of Manitoba and Ontario – it is unlikely that French-speaking candidates will be elected.

The same result would occur with an elected Senate, perhaps in an even more pronounced fashion since the senatorial districts would be larger than those for the House. It is possible that district boundaries might be drawn in a manner to facilitate the election of French-speaking candidates, though that would be difficult in a province where the French-speaking population is small and dispersed. More than that, the rationale for doing this would seem to vitiate introducing the elective principle in the first place. To those who would suggest adopting a list system of proportional representation as a solution to the quandry, that would place the onus back where it began – with the nominating procedures of the political parties – and the result would resemble the dual or multimember provincial constituencies that at one time prevailed on Prince Edward Island and in New Brunswick. Their rationale lay in linguistic and religious divisions that demanded acknowledgment by Liberals and Conservatives when they nominated candidates.

One consequence of an elected Senate, says Massicotte, would be that 'the French fact in Canada will depend on the senators in Quebec.'[35] The implication of that outcome for the policy of bilingualism – of which, according to the Annual Report (2007–8) of the Commissioner of Official Languages, the Senate increasingly sees itself as 'protector' – scarcely requires elaboration.[36]

In 1980 the Supreme Court of Canada was asked by the federal government to give its opinion on the authority of Parliament to amend the constitution unilaterally as regards the Senate.[37] At issue was the Trudeau government's constitutional reform package of 1978 (Bill C-60, the 'Constitutional Amendment Bill'), which among other matters provided for a House of the Provinces, in place of the Senate, with members indirectly elected by provincial legislative assemblies and the House of Commons. The details of that proposed reform of thirty years ago are immaterial, except for the long reach of the Court's opinion in two respects. First, it said that 'it is clear that the intention [of the Fathers of Confederation] was to make the Senate a thoroughly independent body which could canvass dispassionately the measures of the House of Commons.' Further, it stated that 'the Senate has a vital role as an institution forming part of the federal system ... Thus, the body which has been created as a means of protecting sectional and provincial interests was made a participant of the legislative process.'

'Thoroughly independent,' and 'an institution forming part of the federal system [as well as] a participant in the legislative process.' These phrases have come to severely test proposals for Senate reform. Unlike the general procedure for amending the constitution, as set down in Section 42 (that is, support from seven provinces with 50 per cent of the population), which applies to the powers of the Senate and to the method of selecting senators, threats to independence are less easy to calculate, though not to imagine. At the same time, the Court's 1980 advisory opinion made clear that the Senate was already a part of the federal system and an actor in the legislative process. Schemes to alter the upper chamber in a manner that could be said to weaken these judicially ascribed characteristics face informed opposition from their outset. For instance, would Triple E with its emphasis on representation undermine the dispassionate contemplative role envisioned for the Senate by the Supreme Court? Or again, are senatorial terms compatible with 'thorough independence'?

Of course, it might be argued that 'the standards established by the Supreme Court prior to the constitutionalization of a formal amending procedure in 1982 have [no] bearing on how the terms of that new procedure are to be interpreted.' That suggests an important question for which at the present time there is no authoritative answer. Nor is the matter limited in its applicability to the Senate alone.[38]

Increasingly, debate about Senate reform has less to do with maintaining the tapestry of federalism (the focus of reform activity in the last quarter of the last century) than it has with an evolving sense of constitutionalism that, as the SCC opinion of 1980 demonstrates, preceded the adoption of the Canadian Charter of Rights and Freedoms but that has been reinforced by it. Proponents of term limits for senators or of advisory elections to determine nominees for appointment find the resulting debate conducted at a level of constitutional abstraction distant from the object they seek.

In part, the conundrum of Senate reform is that it has had more popular competitors, as witness the contents of the Constitution Act, 1982. More fundamental still is that reform of the Senate in terms of the selection of its members, or in the redistribution of their number among the provinces, according to some standard of equity, has immediate implications for the other two parts of Parliament – the senatorial floor to provincial representation in the Commons and the prerogative power of appointment possessed by the Crown. The unity of the Crown-in-Parliament and the theory that sustains it – that there is no constituent power outside of that tripartite institution – acts as an original and powerful disincentive to articulating and initiating reform of the Senate and then carrying it through to a successful conclusion.

## House of Commons

Notwithstanding the constitutional order of precedence, the premier institution of Parliament is the House of Commons. In the United Kingdom the Reform Act of 1832 expanded the franchise for the first time and in so doing statutorily acknowledged the transfer of power from Lords to Commons already in progress. As a result of this chronology, the lower houses (the legislative assemblies) of the colonies of British North America quickly became, as they have remained, the dominant political institutions of their respective jurisdictions. Unlike the Senate of Canada, which was purpose-built by the Fathers of Confederation to make federal union a reality, the assemblies and later the Commons were derivative bodies modelled in practice and procedure on the Commons at Westminster.

Besides initiating a broadening of the franchise that took nearly a century to complete, the 1832 Act introduced, but fell far short of realizing, the principle of representation by population. The reason for this digression into political history is to recall that more than four decades later, at the time of Confederation and the same year as the second expansion of the British electorate, the object of rep-by-pop was by now established in the constitution to which Canada's was to be 'similar in Principle.' Rep-by-pop was as important an imperative as any that drove the politicians of Canada West to break out of the institutional confines of United Canada. The Union Act of 1840, for instance, had required that two-thirds of the members of each chamber assent to a bill affecting representation before it might pass. After 1867, fixed representation of sixty-five members in the lower house from each of Canada East and Canada West would be a shackle from the past, though one with an echo: in the new federal House of Commons, Quebec would have sixty-five seats *and* the ratio of Quebec's population per member would determine the number of members each province would have in the new chamber. (A similar numerical lineage could be seen in the

Senate: each part of United Canada had had twenty-four councillors in the colony's upper chamber; after 1867, Ontario and Quebec and the Maritime provinces each had twenty-four senators.)

The historical derivation and the continuity of numbers – no province shall have fewer members of the House of Commons than it has senators (Constitution Act, 1915), as well as a grandfather clause that 'ensures that no province will receive fewer seats than it had at the 1976 redistribution or in the 33rd Parliament (1984–8), whichever is less' – had the effect, says John Courtney, 'in the redistribution of the 1990s of granting seven provinces a total of twenty seats more than to which their population entitled them.'[39] The eccentricities of history and political bargaining throw in doubt the accuracy of the term 'formula' when it is applied to the act of redistribution. Bill C-56, 'An Act to Amend the Constitution Act, 1867 (Democratic representation) (2007),' sought, in the federal government's own words, to 'restore [by the addition of new seats] representation by population in British Columbia and Alberta and ... significantly improve the representation of Ontario.'[40] As originally proposed, British Columbia was to receive seven additional seats, Alberta five, and Ontario ten. A year later, following a provincial campaign that argued discrimination because a different formula was being used to calculate its seat allocation, Ontario's number was reported (by the Ontario premier) to more than double.[41] The validity of that assertion is beyond this discussion. What stands out is that new seats are distributed and old seats retained. No one actually loses seats. According to the federal government, among the 'benefits of the new formula' is the following: 'Representation by population for these provinces recognises the significant contributions that British Columbians and Albertans have to make to the country and the national legislative process.' It would be hard to improve upon this statement if one were searching for an example of how far rep-by-pop has travelled from its root idea of popular as opposed to provincial representation. Some of the same tone of argument is heard from proponents of proportional representation for federal general elections – not as a pure system of PR but as a 'topping up' variant that would provide MPs for parliamentary caucuses from provinces where the plurality system denies them success. These comments testify to the identification of the Commons as a federal body or, perhaps more precisely, as a body that must accommodate federalism. A provincialized House of Commons would seem to be an oxymoron, though one substantiated through research: 'An increasing focus on regional concerns during members' statements mirrors the increasingly regional nature of the House of Commons.'[42] Then again, maybe it is a product of the same forces that have given Canada such an unusually rich history of third parties. In any case, as the proponents of Senate reform would doubtlessly say: 'This is what happens in a federation when the structure of its upper chamber is incongruent with the country's geography and demography.'

Federal politicians after the Confederation era did not view the ranks of backbench members through a lens quite so provincial. The distinction is subtle, of course. As W.P.M. Kennedy wrote many years ago: 'The federal idea [in Canada] has sought from, and has been granted by, political parties a place in the other organs of government.'[43] This was true whether the subject was cultural or territorial federalism. As long as there were two parties that thought of themselves as national, and no party like the Bloc Québécois intent on winning seats in Quebec, the formula for success in federal elections was to win strongly there – since the convention was that 'you cannot govern Canada without Quebec on your side' – split, if you could not sweep, Ontario's seats, and take at least one or two provinces in the West and the Maritime provinces. This was Jimmy Gardiner's strategy when Saskatchewan had the third-largest number of Commons seats (between the censuses of 1921 and 1961). The added value of this calculation was that it made Saskatchewan the kingmaker. Until late in the last century, Quebec's seats were essential to any party anticipating a sustained period in government.

If party organization was crucial in Quebec, it was just as necessary in the other provinces, and for the same reason – to guarantee a majority of seats in Parliament. Governments secured their national majorities by winning locally and provincially. This is why political parties were the essential agency of federalism. Would matters have been different if the Senate of Canada had been organized in a more overt federal way? Will matters be different if the Senate becomes an elected body? The answers to these questions are at best suppositions. What is neither equivocal nor ambivalent is the nub of another of Kennedy's succinct remarks: 'The common statement that we are the first to succeed in combining federalism and parliamentary government has only been proved true because we have been forced to federalize the national Cabinet.'[44]

The reference to a federalized cabinet is not original: Macdonald defended the size of his first cabinet on the grounds that a range of voices had to be heard – and not just geographic. There are multiple levels of federalism within the cabinet – language, region, religion, and, more recently, gender and sometimes race. 'It seemed necessary that all the Provinces which composed the Union should be adequately represented in the Government ... No one individual whatever might be his ability ... could be held to be a sufficient representation of that Province.'[45] To those who pointed to the high cost and liberal representation such a policy entailed, Macdonald proclaimed it 'the duty of every lover of the [Canadian] Union to see that no false economy was exercised.' Published literature on the federalized cabinet is not as extensive as might be expected given its central location in the order of government. One reason for the gap is the paucity of ministerial autobiographies; another is that even where these have appeared, the subject of cabinet's role in integrating the nation is not one that an individual minister is apt to perceive as central to his or her own account of cabinet life. More recently, Donald Savoie's description of cabinet as a 'focus group' suggests a passivity on the part of its members that is not conducive to memoir writing.[46]

In the classic federalized cabinet, as described by Reginald Whitaker in *The Government Party* (1977), ministers have responsibilities not only for their own portfolio but also for the party organization in their home province. They are the crucial link between the centre and the periphery. The 'focus group' analogy is so static an image as to raise the question whether ministers do more than listen. A different metaphor, this time from a former cabinet minister in the United States, Willard Wirtz (Secretary of Labor in the Kennedy and Johnson administrations), describes cabinet and ministers as being involved in the democratic equivalent of a stylized 'Kabuki drama and dance.'[47] Paradoxically, that comment, originating in a system that does not have responsible government as understood in Canada and therefore one that distances the minister from the legislature in a manner comparable to Savoie's focus-group analogy, communicates the dynamic element of cabinet government in a parliamentary federation, even if members of cabinet may no longer exert the 'ministerialist' authority that Whitaker chronicled so thoroughly.

At the end of the first decade of the twenty-first century, no party in Parliament can claim to draw support from all regions of the country. Certainly not to the extent seen a decade or so ago. It is unlikely that a public inquiry today would speak with impressive certainty, as the Macdonald Commission did in 1985, about the fundamental need for 'cohesive disciplined political parties' and of 'the ideal of a national government which is responsive to national constituencies and which pursues comprehensive national goals.'[48] The traditional view of political parties as organizations whose duty it is to 'forge internal consensus across regional, linguistic and social lines in order to promote the interests of the country as a whole' possessed official sanction into the 1990s, as witness the federal government's background paper on 'Responsive Institutions for a Modern Canada' (1991).[49]

The rise of regionally based political parties in the West and in Quebec, the consequent fragmentation of the national two-party system, the failure of the mega-constitutional proposals of the 1990s, the near victory of those seeking Quebec sovereignty in the provincial referendum in 1995, the divisions in the Liberal Party of Canada over how faithfully it should adhere to the Trudeau legacy in the matter of Quebec – a decade or more of these disruptions have transformed the 'tradition' of national political parties into a memory. A succession of minority governments – 2004 (Liberal), 2006, and 2008 (Conservative) – suggests that no longer is there, nor is there a likelihood of being, a national party with a national purpose. As serious as that weakness may be for Canadian politics, for the present discussion the issue is what the transformation in the party system means for parliamentary federalism.

In one respect the attenuation of political parties as the ligaments of the federation is nothing new. For at least fifty years, party organizations and party supporters have been compartmentalizing themselves so that in several provinces there are, for example, two Liberal parties: one for federal elections and one for provincial elections. One explanation for the change lies in the heightened political capacity and proliferating objectives of provinces in the years after 1945. As this occurred, there was more occasion for divergence in allegiances within parties. In another respect, the disappearance of national political parties, as evidenced in the inability of either of the old political parties to form a majority government, is new. New, and a challenge for the operation of parliamentary federalism, as it is also a challenge for the practice of responsible government. On this last point, it deserves mention that more has been written recently about the confidence convention than for some decades.[50]

The disentanglement of federal and provincial politics is not a new concern, either. In fact, between 1867 and 1873 members of provincial legislatures (where provincial law allowed) were permitted to sit in the House of Commons. Indeed, in a bizarre twist on the later intrastate federalism model, 'a majority of the provincial Cabinet [of Ontario and Quebec] held federal seats' in the first House of Commons.[51] It is no surprise that Conservatives favoured the dual mandate and that Liberals opposed it. What is surprising from the perspective of this study is that the six-year debate to eliminate the practice focused not on its inappropriateness in a federal system, but rather on its threat to the independence of Parliament and the provincial legislatures. When it came to electors, as opposed to the elected, another issue that ebbed and flowed, depending upon the party in office, concerned the franchise. After acrimonious debate, the Conservatives introduced a federal franchise in 1885; up to then the qualifications to vote provincially had determined who voted federally. Liberals thought a federal franchise itself unfederal – since in their mind it trespassed on provincial rights – and they abandoned it in 1898. The issue was resolved at last in favour of a federal franchise in 1917, though at the time this was presented as a wartime measure.

A central theme of the next chapter, 'The Practice of Federalism,' is the growth and extent of extraconstitutional practices and arrangements that facilitate the conduct of government in Canada. An obvious example is first ministers' meetings. One explanation for this development is said to be the unresponsive institutions of parliamentary federalism. The indictment of the Senate and the House of Commons on this score has two parts: one concerns structure, the other process. Enough has been said about the variation among senatorial divisions to suggest the terms of the first part of the indictment. The Commons is another matter, since seats there are allocated among the provinces, and MPs do caucus to a degree on the basis of regions not all that dissimilar from the senatorial divisions. But there is a barrier between this kind of shadow federalism and the interpenetration of federal and provincial politics that advocates of intrastate federalism seek and that critics of parliamentary federalism say is absent from the current institutional arrangement. That barrier – the process part of the indictment, under its more familiar name party discipline – has long been cited as an enemy of true federalism. The party whips, not the interests of constituency, province, or region, determine how MPs vote, and in so doing make them little more than automatons.

The substance of this argument was well rehearsed in the 1920s by the Progressives, disappeared for some decades in the postwar period, and then made a return appearance almost in tandem with the movement in favour of an elected Senate.[52] Most recently, the party discipline critique has been advanced in company with a critique of the single-member-district–simple-plurality-vote system of election. There is a pattern to this clustering of reform initiatives, one seen after the First World War in Europe, when proportional representation systems were first introduced and when debate about upper chamber reform was popular. As John English illustrated in his book *The Decline of Politics*, there was an echo of similar sentiment in Canada.[53]

All of this is secondary to the matter of first concern, which is, that the House of Commons serves federalism scarcely more effectively than does the Senate. Only through the national political parties, which animate the structures of Parliament, are the multiple and conflicting interests that comprise the federation given expression. The apotheosis of this partisan-based federalism finds expression in the cabinet. As a consequence, the 'reality of Canadian governance,' said the SCC (1999), is that 'except in certain rare cases, the executive frequently and *de facto* controls the legislature.'[54] Because the strain inherent in the concept of parliamentary federalism is less assuaged by national political parties now than in the past, and because it is not relieved by a 'federal' upper chamber, federalism is moving away from Parliament. Once within the constitution, accommodative mechanisms essential to the good health of the federal system are found increasingly outside, in extraconstitutional arrangements such as the Council of the Federation, that is, the annual meeting of the provincial premiers.

With one important exception: in cultural federalism, Parliament plays not just an accommodative but a declarative role. Examples would be parliamentary resolutions proclaiming Quebec 'a nation within a united Canada' (2006) or supporting legislated bilingualism in Manitoba (1984). In addition, through its Standing Orders and by convention, the House offered a model of bilingualism long before enactment of the Official Languages Act in 1969. In the Constitution Act, 1867 (Section 133), French and English are treated equally: nowhere does reference to one language appear without reference to the other. Still, in practice, the use of French in debate and in committee, as well as the quality of translation (verbally and in reports), improved with the passage of the Official Languages Act, 1969, and, markedly so with the arrival of the Bloc Québécois two decades later.[55]

Parliamentary federalism, as it operates in Canada, is complex and less than universally applauded. This has been especially the case in the last forty years, as the tensions associated with reconciling cultural versus territorial federalism have increased and the critics of each have multiplied. There was once a time when the parliamentary – Westminster – model was deemed perfection. Here is Sir Wilfrid Laurier in 1908 in one of the episodic debates on Senate reform: 'There is no absolute power under the British system ... The Crown is not absolute because the Commons can refuse supply. The Commons are not absolute because the Commons can be dissolved. The Lords are not absolute because the Lords can have their membership increased, and thereby their power can be destroyed.'[56] This assessment predated the Parliament Act of 1911, which gave the Lords a suspensive veto and in so doing made Westminster in the eyes of some critics a unitary parliament for all practical purposes.

The point of Laurier's encomium was to draw a contrast between the flexibility inherent in the mother of Parliaments and the rigidity that characterized her Canadian offspring. To be precise, the fixed upper limit on the size of the Senate of Canada made that body – in theory – absolute. In fact, the Senate did not exercise its latent powers because even in the early twentieth century, parliamentary democracy dictated that the Commons, where the government sat and from which it was overwhelmingly drawn, was the pre-eminent legislative body. It also did not exercise its powers because its members were selected on the basis of partisan loyalty; they had to be so selected if the upper chamber was not to pose a threat to the life of the government.

The fixed upper limit on the number of senators and their unequal distribution among provinces through the means of senatorial divisions was the sine qua non of the federal agreement preceding Confederation. The principal consequence of this essential condition, in addition to making change to its own terms to date impossible, was to guarantee that intense partisanship would pervade all aspects of Canadian government, both at the centre and in the provinces. As W.P.M. Kennedy said decades ago, the political parties were the practical instruments of Canadian federalism – on their health depended the health of Parliament, and on Parliament's well-being the soundness of the federation.

# 5 The Practice of Federalism

'"Canadian federalism is incomplete because the Canadian constitution is inadequate": Discuss.' Some variant of this statement is to be found on the final examination of most courses in Canadian politics today. This is true whether the subject is the absence of intrastate mechanisms: 'the apparent ineffectiveness of ... federal institutions ... to accommodate and reconcile ... regional interests' (Smiley and Watts)[1]; or the proposition that because of the 'failure' of the Meech Lake Accord 'the Canadian federal regime of 1867 ... is now bankrupt in Quebec' (Laforest)[2]; or the public's rejection of 'elite' politicians ('eleven men in suits') who negotiated the mega-constitutional agreements of the 1980s and 1990s[3]; or, perhaps, even, the lack of self-worth on the part of Canadians, who 'fail[ed] the [direct democracy] test set by their leaders'(Johnston et al.).[4] Nor does this list exhaust illustrations of the sense of disconnection that pervades much writing on Canadian federalism. Consider, for instance, the lament that the federal government's superior power to spend, through shared-cost programs with the provinces, 'trespasses' on areas of provincial jurisdiction (Telford).[5] None of these concerns is trivial, as the substantial literature on Canadian federalism testifies. Yet the point at which federalism and the constitution intersect in Canada is not quite the wasteland this depiction of unfulfilled expectations might lead some to conclude.

As the previous chapters have demonstrated, Canada has asymmetrical federalism but it does not have an asymmetrical Parliament. A federalized cabinet helps but highly disciplined political parties hinder the expression of multiple interests. The structure of the Senate of Canada and the selection of its members blunt rather than sharpen geographically based opinion. This is why Canadian federalism is to be found in the country's parts (the provinces) and not at its centre (Parliament), and it is this separation that concerns the critics.

In Canada, intergovernmental relations have become the substitute for engagement through Parliament. Governments at the centre and in the provinces dominate this relationship, and because they do, the public and the legislatures are excluded. As a consequence, attention is paid at least as much to practitioners – first ministers and bureaucrats – as it is to the practice of federalism. Here is the skeleton of the argument that, when elaborated, leads to the thesis that Canadian federalism is at its core a matter of federal–provincial diplomacy.[6]

The absent presence in this discussion is representation, a subject of modest scholarly lineage in the study of politics in Canada, certainly when compared to either the United States or Australia. Yet this astigmatism is lessening for reasons that do not at first brush appear to touch on intergovernmental relations, but, it will be argued, do, because they elevate individual interests over government in a manner hitherto unprecedented. Three examples illustrate sources for this claim of new interest in representation: first, recognition of (and guilt about) Canada's ignoble record in withholding the franchise from selected categories of residents, such as First Nations and those of Oriental descent; second, cumulative changes to the regime that governs the election of members of Parliament: independent boundaries commissions, a continuing register of voters rather a list compiled through enumeration, public funding for political parties and candidates; and third, criticism of the plurality electoral system for the distortion it produces between the percentage of votes a party receives and the number of seats it wins. What these matters and the proponents of intrastate federalism share is a concern about exclusion, a sensitivity that the Canadian Charter of Rights and Freedoms, with its guarantees of democratic equality, and legal rights, reinforces.

Still, and notwithstanding the academics' indictment communicated in the publications of the Royal Commission on the Economic Union and Development Prospects for Canada (1985) and the Royal Commission on Electoral Reform and Party Financing (1991), federalism in Canada has always been more about jurisdiction than representation.[7] Again, judicial interpretation of Sections 91 and 92 of the Constitution Act, 1867, is a well-explored field of study. The idea behind this chapter is to examine not rivalry but the ramifications of jurisdiction. In Harold Lasswell's language, its interest lies not in who gets what but rather in what they do with what they get.[8] After examining the practice of federalism the chapter turns to its practitioners, and then to policies that are of federal and constitutional import.

There is no doubt that governments are dominant actors in the Canadian federal system. Whether they are also in a position to determine the practice of federalism is another matter with a less emphatic answer, if only because governments, like individuals, are limited in their freedom to act by the long reach of history. Consider, for instance, Canada's financial system. Section 91 of the Constitution Act, 1867, conferred on the central government powers over banking, the incorporation of banks, and the issue of paper money; the regulation of trade and commerce; currency and coinage; savings banks; bills of exchange and promissory notes; and interest and legal tender. Economic centralization would appear to have been the Fathers' intent. Yet as E.P. Neufeld has shown in *The Financial System of Canada: Its Growth and Development*, such categorization is incomplete in the story it tells:

> Most of the trust companies [in the nineteenth century] operated under provincial charters and, contrary to the case of the banks and life insurance companies, a significant portion of the industry has always been composed of provincially incorporated companies. Since the trust companies began by emphasizing their 'estates, trusts and agencies' business, provincial incorporation is not surprising. Such business falls in the provincial sphere under the 'property and civil rights' clause of the [Constitution] Act.

Nonetheless, once their operations crossed provincial boundaries, they did not seek out federal incorporation.

Or, to take another 'economic' example from the same author: Alphonse Desjardins, the 'father' of Canadian credit unions, 'attempted to obtain federal credit union legislation in 1907, and a bill passed the House of Commons but was defeated by one vote in the Senate after both the Banking and Commerce Committee and the Justice Department reported the opinion that it was outside federal jurisdiction.' Before the First World War, several bills on cooperative credit societies were introduced but failed to pass the Commons. During the same period, the government of Saskatchewan took the initiative to establish agricultural credit in that province.[9] In 1923 the federal Minister of Finance authorized H.M. Tory, president of the University of Alberta (and after 1928 first president of the National Research Council) to inquire into provincial systems of agricultural credit. In his report of

1925, Tory said that 'the organization and control of this type of credit should be left to the provinces. Dominion supervision would be difficult and expensive.' Neufeld notes that 'in accepting this opinion the federal government missed the opportunity to become an influential force in the regulation of what was later to become an important type of financial intermediary.'[10]

A very big opportunity indeed, if one considers the ambit of the subject and the capacity of its boundaries to expand. A year after Saskatchewan introduced a program of agricultural credit the provincial legislature passed the General Cooperative Associations Act (1914), whereby producers might register their new cooperatives with the government. In time, co-op trusts, co-op retailers, and co-op manufacturers followed. Later still, co-ops in different western provinces merged, as in the case of Federated Cooperatives Limited, which in time became the largest non-financial cooperative in Canada.

More than business was at stake in these matters: cooperatives, credit unions, and *caisses populaires* provided visible and demanding training experience for individuals who later became community, provincial, and national leaders. (This was the thrust of Seymour Martin Lipset's thesis in *Agrarian Socialism* on the rise of the CCF: highly participatory politics laid the foundations for a 'socialism that spoke in the tones of the cooperative movement.'[11]) In the distant past (1916), Charles Dunning moved from the position of general manager of the Saskatchewan Cooperative Elevator Company (at that time the world's largest grain handling organization), to be provincial premier, and then finance minister in a government of Mackenzie King. In the much more recent past, Janice MacKinnon, once president of the Saskatoon Co-op, entered provincial politics, later becoming a Saskatchewan Minister of Finance and, after leaving electoral politics, chair of the board of directors of the Institute of Public Policy.[12] Examples are invidious, or at the very least selective. The point of citing these individuals is to draw attention to a feature of Canadian provincial politics that receives inadequate attention: when federalism and the constitution intersect, especially in economic matters, it results in activity that is often non-partisan in the first instance. Arguably, partisan neutrality appears to be a condition for the early success of individuals as well as movements. Consider the careers of Aaron Sapiro, 'the apostle of cooperation' and organizer of the Wheat Pool; Henry Wise Wood, 'the uncrowned king of Alberta'; 'honest' John Bracken; or E.C. Drury, 'farmer premier' of Ontario. But more is obviously required, as the history of the Maritime Rights Movement, which received strong cooperative allegiance but failed as an electoral force, bears witness.[13]

While the perverse effect of judicial review upon the course of Canadian federalism – that is, producing stronger provinces than the Fathers of Confederation intended – is a traditional topic in the study of Canadian politics, the discussion up to this point has had little to do with the work of judges. Of course, judicial interpretation may exert a strong influence over provincial politics, as demonstrated following the decision in *Toronto Electric Commissioners v. Snider* (1925). Here the JCPC found a federal statute, the Industrial Disputes Investigation Act (1907), which was intended 'to aid in the prevention and settlement of strikes and lock-outs in mines and industries connected with public utilities,' beyond Parliament's power to enact in other than an emergency situation. In other words, federal authorities were powerless in peacetime to conciliate labour disputes unless these involved interprovincial undertakings such as railways.[14]

As a result of *Snider*, labour became for most purposes a provincial matter. Provinces established minimum wages and passed labour legislation, which, in the case of Saskatchewan's Trade Union Act of 1944, gave labour, including public servants, for the first time in Canada, the right to associate freely and bargain collectively. Among other innovations, it also established a quasi-judicial Labour Relations Board.[15] The suppressing effect of *Snider* on the development of a strong national labour movement and, electorally, on a successful national labour party may readily be surmised, especially when the constraints associated with the history of labour in Quebec, or Newfoundland and Labrador or other provinces, are introduced as backdrop for that assessment. It remains unclear whether, and to what extent, the Agreement on Internal Trade, reached by first ministers in 2009 and aimed at eliminating trade barriers and enhancing labour mobility, will in time alter this provincial-centric tradition.[16]

The aim of the current discussion is to underscore the impact that comes with jurisdictional competency. Vernon Fowke's *The National Policy and the Wheat Economy* (1957), one of the ten volumes in the Social Credit series, has been described as a study that emphasizes 'the economic base of western protest.'[17] And it is, though in a manner that gives more attention to originating cause than to subsequent effect. Fowke's concern had less to do with the farmers' response to Ottawa than with the central government's tariff and monetary policies that occasioned that response. In fact, Fowke reversed his analytical perspective in the course of writing the book. In a letter to S.D. Clark, sociologist in the Department of Political Economy at the University of Toronto, general editor of the Social Credit series, and the individual who secured the Rockefeller Foundation grant to bring the ten volumes to publication, Fowke said (a year after his initial proposal) that he was changing his title from 'Farmers' Commercial Organization and the National Economy' to 'The National Policy and the Wheat Economy.' 'This change implies,' he wrote, 'more emphasis on government policy and less on agricultural organization ... In short, I am preparing an analysis of the development of the national policy as it affected, and was in turn affected by, the economic development of the Prairie Provinces.'[18] The dynamic of reciprocating influence embedded in a federation characterized by strong jurisdictions has seldom been so succinctly stated.

While not all volumes in the Social Credit series focus on the influence of centre on periphery, another that did was James Mallory's *Social Credit and the Federal Power* (1954). In rather similar fashion to Fowke, Mallory felt compelled to change the title of his proposed study, which he had originally called 'Social Credit in Alberta and the Constitutional Issue.' The reason became obvious: the book was far less a study of the rise of Social Credit than an explanation for why federal authorities employed the (by then) little-used powers of reservation and disallowance to thwart its program. Nor, most important, as Mallory conceded, was the consequence of federal action at all provincial in its ramifications: 'The Social Credit party in Alberta not only helped to shift the weight of legal pressure against the provinces, but also ensured the success of that pressure by the nature of its programme. The Aberhart programme provided the *reductio ad absurdum* which was required to demonstrate the unsuitability of the provinces as agencies of major fiscal and economic policy.'[19]

The indecisiveness that these particular authors experienced as they wrote their books signalled a larger want of direction to the series itself. Clark, a graduate of the University of Saskatchewan, with degrees in history and political science, and in 1958 – the time the series was well under way – president of the Canadian Political Science Association, is acknowledged as a seminal figure in the development of the discipline of sociology in Canada. The 'Social Credit Study,' he told two Columbia University professors (R.S. Lynd of the Department of Sociology and J.B. Brebner of the Department of History), was intended to illustrate a more general thesis about 'revolution and counter revolution in Canada.' It would be 'an attempt to show how successive revolutionary movements have grown up in Canada but been beaten down by coun-terrevolutionary forces.'[20] In fact, this synoptic framework remained uncompleted, though the subject continued to interest him.[21] The gap is unfortunate since the series – to date still the largest collaborative research project to examine a Canadian political party – lacks an ana-lytical dimension of general applicability to Canadian politics.

Contrary to Clark's ambition, the ten volumes seem to affirm what he set out to dispute – that Alberta politics was distinct from rather than a variant of Canadian politics. More unfortunate still is the fail-ure to explore the revolutionary–counter-revolutionary tension that Clark perceived in Social Credit in Alberta – a tension that (it may be argued) manifested itself in the hostility the Roman Catholic Church showed for the CCF in Saskatchewan and for trade unions in Quebec and throughout Canada; and in the religious and social cleavage that underlay partisan politics in a number of provinces. It is worth remark-ing that almost to a man, the leaders of western protest parties were not native-born Canadians. Almost without exception, they came from the British Isles, Europe, or the United States.

To use the language of Pepin-Robarts forty years later, 'remnants' of the original constitution contributed to a renaissance of federal power that would continue through war and for the next twenty years. In the context of Mallory's thesis, it is notable that the Royal Commission on Dominion-Provincial Relations (Rowell-Sirois), appointed the same year as three Social Credit bills were reserved by the Lieutenant Gover-nor of Alberta (on the advice of the federal Minister of Justice), restrict-ed its analysis, and later recommendations, to matters of federalism while avoiding matters of the constitution. The reason for maintaining the distinction lay with the formation of a second inquiry, appointed as a result of a motion by then senator Arthur Meighen and chaired by W.F. O'Connor, Parliamentary Counsel of the Senate. According to Alex Skelton, secretary of the Rowell-Sirois Commission, the 'purpose [of the O'Connor inquiry] was to show how much more simply and cheaply a (better) report could be prepared by Mr. O'Connor than by the Commission.'[22]

Skelton's comments on the provenance of the two inquiries, each of which was to influence scholarly conceptions of federalism and the constitution in Canada, deserve extensive quotation. Writing to R.A. MacKay, the 'Maritime member' of the commission, Skelton empha-sized the following distinction:

It is of course a mistake to consider O'Connor's inquiry as a rival Commission, as is done in some quarters. Our Commission has only to report on what would be the best distribution of Dominion–provincial [sic] powers in relation to the economy as it exists today, and not on the means of attaining such a distribution. As I understood the position ... at the first meeting of the Commission ... it is definitely not within the province of the Commission to consider ways and means of amending the constitution. As a corollary I assume that we do not have to consider possible objections to amendment, such as implied in the contract theory. Neither would I think that the specific problem given O'Connor to report on – the intentions of the Fathers – is relevant to the Commission's work. I thought that the Commission's terms of reference had made every effort to exclude such a legal investigation of the original Act, and of Privy Council interpretations, in order to determine whether the original intentions were being carried out, and directed only an examination of the basic economic and public finance situation with a view to determining what would be the most efficient and economical distribution of governmental powers today. I hope you will pardon my lengthy effusion, for the point is a fundamental one.

O'Connor was given the task of determining why the Constitution Act, 1867, had 'failed,' that is, why the intent of the Fathers of Confederation to achieve a strong central government had not been realized. He concluded that 'failure' lay not with the work of the 'Fathers' but with the interpretation given it by the JCPC. To those in 1940 who said that cooperative federalism was the answer to Canada's problems, he replied that 'the Dominion was founded upon failure in fact to achieve cooperation.' The distribution of legislative powers under the Act, properly applied, was 'so flexible ... that those who framed it might justifiably have hoped that such a simple and efficient scheme ... could not be misunderstood.'[23]

At the outset of their work, the Rowell-Sirois commissioners had decided to collect 'documentary materials on Confederation,' such as Orders in Council, quotations from the Fathers of Confederation, debates of the period, and newspaper accounts. Later these were transferred to O'Connor in the hope that 'he could be encouraged to answer the contract theory instead of us.' (Mackay speculated that this 'might easily be done since Dean [Vincent] MacDonald of the Dalhousie Law School is his son-in-law and has considerable influence with him.'[24])

This proved both a successful strategy (Annexes 4 and 5 of O'Connor's report, 180 pages in total, are devoted to documents), and prescient, too, for despite Mackenzie King's assurance – to the Dominion–provincial conference called in January 1941 to consider the commission's report – that 'there has been no attempt [in the report] to upset our typical Canadian form of federation,' the premier of Quebec, Maurice Duplessis, continued to protest that Confederation was in 'the nature of a contract [and] cannot be amended ... except with the unanimous consent of all Provinces which were responsible for its enactment.'[25]

Duplessis was not alone in objecting to the prospect of greater activity by the central government. William Aberhart of Alberta articulated the same sentiment but in a distinctive language that E.C. Manning, his successor in office, would repeat at subsequent Dominion–provincial conferences: 'Centralization of power is diametrically opposed to the grand old British ideal of good government under which the Empire has been built.' Still, they did not speak for everyone; certainly Aberhart did not speak for the other two prairie premiers, who, as Bracken said, had 'lost a great deal of our enthusiasm for this [theoretical] autonomy' secured ten years before with the transfer of natural resources. What they wanted, and what Confederation had been 'designed to achieve [was] a single national economy, as distinguished from a number of provincial economies.'[26]

Despite its later stature as itself a foundational document in the history of Canadian federalism, the report says little directly on the topic of federalism. Its principal recommendations call for (1) the federal government to assume full responsibility for unemployment insurance, for the operating-cost relief of primary industries – particularly agriculture, and for the net debt-service charge of the provinces; (2) the provinces to renounce their existing right to personal and corporate income taxes, to other corporation taxes excepting bona fide licence fees, to succession duties, and to existing annual Dominion subsidies; and (3) the Dominion government to pay annually to each province a 'national adjustment grant.'

In May 1938, in a list of subjects he compiled requiring study, which included problems of taxation, debt adjustment, and subsidies, MacKay observed, with evident surprise, that 'we seem to have completely overlooked any studies of the technique of cooperation between the Dominion and the Provinces ... A study should be made on the methods of cooperation ... especially Dominion–Provincial Conferences and conferences of department officials.'[27] Yet in the report's more than seven hundred pages, only four deal with these matters. That paucity of attention to structures, when linked to what already has been said about the nemesis of the compact theory to achieving institutional change, and keeping in mind the (then) apparently hopeless task of agreeing on a domestic amending formula for the Constitution Act, 1867 – a quest begun at the Dominion–provincial conference in 1927 – explain the strong concentration in the report on monetary and tariff policies.

Additional reasons for the economic focus of the report are still to be accounted for. First, the centre's control over the periphery's public lands and natural resources needs to be recalled. It was because of this patrimony that Parliament passed the Dominion Lands Act, 1872, thus permitting homesteading and settlement of the West, as well as providing the massive land grants to finance construction of the CPR. Historically, and even in the present century, a large portion of Canada is federal territory. The central government has had a direct role in the development of resources, on the prairies before 1930 and North of 60 today. Second, monetary policy may be designed to, and may in fact, benefit the whole country but not necessarily its component parts equally. This was a long-standing complaint coming from western Canada and is a central theme of the Rowell-Sirois Report. One reason for this differential regional effect is that the provinces possess uneven resource endowments, perhaps most notably in the matter of oil and gas. The National Energy Policy (NEP), introduced by the government of Pierre Trudeau in 1980, was one attempt by a central government to moderate the price of energy for the majority of Canadians, but at high financial cost in the form of forgone revenues to the producing provinces of Alberta and Saskatchewan and at great political expense to the Liberal Party.

In the eyes of westerners, the federal government's retention of the natural resources of the prairie provinces violated their right to full self-government, a grievance the preamble of each of the Natural Resources Transfer Agreements of 1929 (legislated in 1930) acknowledged: 'Whereas it is desirable that the province[s] should be placed in a position of equality with the other provinces of Confederation ...' And so it continues to frame western interpretations of federal government actions and policies. Consider the speech in 2007 to the Canadian Bar Association by former Alberta premier Peter Lougheed, in which he stated that federal environmental and provincial resource development policies were on a collision course (the issue was development of the Alberta Tar Sands) and that the discord would be 'ten times greater' than in the past.[28] On this issue time stands still and the roles of perpetrator and victim are indelibly cast.

Disparities in fiscal capacity among provinces lead either to widely disparate tax levels or to disparate public services among provinces. The subsidies set out in Section 118 of the Constitution Act, 1867, have been repealed, and replaced again over the years. By the time of Rowell-Sirois the financial arrangements then in place were universally labelled as inadequate. Here is the source for the recommendation to introduce 'national adjustment grants,' which, for the purposes of this discussion, may be treated as a harbinger of the scheme of equalization grants that appeared in 1957.[29] The purpose of the grants is to equalize the fiscal capacity of provinces based on a formula of a range of taxation sources. Mackenzie King's biographer, Blair Neatby, credits the federal Royal Commission on Maritime Claims, chaired by Sir Andrew Duncan (1926), appointed to investigate the grievances of Maritimers and to suggest remedies, with introducing the idea that 'the federal government should provide a minimum standard of living throughout the Dominion.'[30] He adds that 'the far-reaching implications of this assumption were ignored.'

And far-reaching they were. Fifty-six years later, in Section 36(2) of the Constitution Act, 1982, equalization became constitutionalized: 'Parliament and the government of Canada are committed to the principle of making equalization payments to ensure that provincial governments have sufficient revenues to provide reasonably comparable levels of public services at reasonably comparable levels of taxation.' In its journey from inchoate idea spawned by regional dissatisfaction to the status of a constitutionally entrenched right available to all, equalization mimics Section 41(b), the provision (mentioned in an earlier chapter) that a province shall have no fewer members of the House of Commons than it has senators, and which for its amendment requires unanimous approval of the two houses of Parliament and the legislative assembly of each province.

Constitutional protection from the vagaries of *territorial* federalism, with little concern for *cultural* federalism – that would seem to be the view held by residents in some parts of Canada:

The configuration of Canada as a bilingual and bicultural nation – which has weak notions of regionalism implicit in it – is a more central theme. Canada has a regional Senate, a grandfathered Commons representation, a central-Canada-weighted cabinet, a Supreme Court with two-thirds of its members from the two central provinces and other federal courts with Central Canadian-biased selection rules, a language- based criterion for part of its bureaucracy, and a host of other arrangements because of a simple fact: Canada was founded with special attention to the linguistic and cultural needs of Quebec and this needs to be fostered and creatively renewed from era to era. It is in this context ... that Newfoundland and Labrador's representational concerns must be addressed. The road is all uphill.[31]

The validity of Newfoundland and Labrador's complaint is not at issue here, nor is the strength of sentiment behind it. Fifty years earlier, at the 1950 Federal–Provincial Conference, Joseph Smallwood alluded to the then Dominion of Newfoundland's economic collapse in the 1930s. That disaster, much like the twin calamities of depression and drought on the prairies of the same decade, marked its people thereafter: 'It is quite easy,' he told his fellow premiers, 'to picture a situation in which self-government in Newfoundland would become quite intenable [sic]. That is the alternative to economic development.'[32]

The hold of memory on Smallwood at mid-century and the fear it engendered for the future are worth reflecting upon in a study of federalism and the Constitution of Canada – if only because the past exerts a strong hold on the present in Canadian politics. Hugh John Flemming, at the time premier of New Brunswick, noted that the 1955 federal–provincial conference was the first time the premiers had met in circumstances not 'dictated by national emergencies [or] beclouded by controversies of perhaps dangerous urgency.' Such considerations, he believed, had prevented the first ministers from 'seeking longer term solutions and establishing principles.'[33]

The sense of vulnerability, of being powerless to affect economic outcomes because of dependency on factors over which there is no control – oil prices, cod stocks, softwood lumber embargoes, and outsourcing are examples – affects all provinces but distinguishes 'the nine' from Quebec, where the concern for nearly half a century has been cultural and linguistic as well as economic security. It is that difference that sets Quebec apart from the others and that explains, in part, the singling out of the province, as in the quotation about Newfoundland and Labrador's concerns noted above. But only in part, because another – governmental – dimension has emerged in the last four decades to transform federal–provincial relations.

Since, and largely as a consequence of, the Report of the Royal Commission on Governmental Organization (Glassco Commission) in 1962, in conjunction with the acceptance of official bilingualism, a new 'policy' orientation to government has appeared.[34] In 1922, R. MacGregor Dawson published his PhD dissertation, completed under the supervision of Graham Wallas at the University of London. Its title was *The Principle of Official Independence: With Particular Reference to the Political History of Canada;* its theme, the 'abandonment of [political] control of the technical specialist.'[35] Before Glassco there was a long tradition in Canada of letting the expert get on with his or her expertise unencumbered by government. After Glassco, and in the phrase most often associated with that Royal Commission, the guiding rule became 'let the managers manage.' Several examples of the earlier perspective particularly in the fields of science and culture might be cited. One that is extensively documented is the Geological Survey of Canada. Founded in 1842, under Royal patronage, the survey trained scientists and engineers, whose work assisted some of Canada's premier industries, and who, through its Topographical Division, surveyed and mapped the country's vast terrain. In addition, it established close research ties to university departments of geological and engineering sciences across the country.[36] At the Dominion–Provincial Conference after the Second World War, at which the provinces responded to the central government's proposals on reconstruction, Saskatchewan acknowledged that the province was 'almost wholly dependent on the Canadian Geological Survey for systematic geological mapping of the province.'[37]

The aim of this discussion of the survey, as would be equally true of a discussion of the National Research Council (NRC) – which began its life in 1916 as the Honorary Advisory Council on Scientific and Industrial Research – or, for that matter, of the Canada Council, is to underscore the independence these bodies enjoyed at their creation. In the view of one critic: 'The early NRC was in a genuine sense a national body developing science in the national interest as distinct from the governmental interest.'[38] The same language was heard in 1927, when the first president of the NRC, Henry Marshall Tory, spoke of establishing 'a central organization [which would] save the nation in productive wealth.'[39] The change in attitude arrived in the late 1960s, 'when the Glassco Report and the later Lamontagne report ['A Science Policy for Canada: Report of the Senate Special Committee on Science Policy,' whose chairman was Senator Maurice Lamontagne] condemned the NRC's performance in past history and proposed that the government could and should ... both define the national interest in knowledge and pursue it more efficiently than could any "Honorary Advisory Council" lacking public service controls and methods.' In short, 'government captured ... monopoly control of competence to define the national interest.'[40]

The move toward a governmentally defined national science policy touches federalism and the Constitution of Canada in a number of ways. Science, like culture, is a generic term that has no clear allocation under the divided jurisdictions of a federal constitution. In recent decades, however, science, unlike culture, has been viewed as of national and international significance and thus in need of strategic goals, multidisciplinary partners, and a mission orientation. Energy, health, and the environment are subjects where central governments believe national policies are required. Yet in a federation like Canada's, where natural resources fall under provincial jurisdiction and where medicare arose because of the commitment of a determined provincial government, that opinion is not unquestioningly shared. Science policy leads over time to such interventions as Canada Millennium Scholarships and Canada Research Chairs; federal financing of health care leads to the Canada Health Act, which imposes 'a code of conduct on the provinces to qualify for federal medical support.'[41]

At the federal–provincial conference in 1966, Lester Pearson, then prime minister, rejected the argument that because provinces had jurisdiction over education 'in and for a province,' the federal government was excluded from activity in cultural affairs or from concerning itself with research. Nor was his refutation simply the spending-power argument redux: 'In our view, research, as the means by which we expand the frontier of knowledge, is today one of the most important factors in the economic and social growth of any modern political society. The restriction of federal aid to research to subject matters that are within federal legislative jurisdiction would frustrate the purposes of the scientific spirit.'[42] (In his linkage of government and science there is a trace of C.P. Snow's then much discussed but now generally accepted thesis of 'The Two Cultures and the Scientific Revolution,' the title of his Rede Lecture delivered at Cambridge University in 1959.)[43]

Frustrated or not, aid to research without regard to jurisdiction does on occasion lay bare Canada's double federalism. Despite the vast literature devoted to the subject of Canadian federalism and despite the memorable image, coined by the JCPC, of its 'watertight compartments,' there is still evidence that for many Canadians federalism remains not a principled but a convenient arrangement of power. That is the conclusion Canadian philosopher Will Kymlicka draws about English-Canadian attitudes toward federalism. While working for the Royal Commission on New Reproductive Technologies, he discovered that most groups that made submissions – be they pro-life, pro-choice, medical associations, or other – assumed that the federal government should set the basic rules. Most groups, that is, except for those in Quebec; there it was 'assumed that provincial governments should set the basic rules.' For English-speaking Canadians 'the idea that the federal government might be constitutionally prohibited from establishing such a scheme was never even considered.' On the contrary, any question deemed sufficiently important was 'assumed' to confer on the federal government 'a kind of ultimate authority.'[44]

Dawson's thesis of 'the principle of official independence,' tamed, so to speak, by Glassco forty years later in the interests of imposing standardized administrative methods, has in the eyes of some twenty-first-century scholars now come full circle. As Canada's publicly funded health care program has developed, the role of the federal government has 'thickened,' but not by means of overt jurisdictional trespass. In evaluating the recommendations of the Commission on the Future of Health Care in Canada (chaired by Roy Romanow), Peter Graefe and Andrew Bourns conclude that the commission's 'proposal [in 2003] to create new institutions, including a Health Covenant and a Health Council, further erodes the basis of provincial autonomy, by taking decision-making out of intergovernmental relations, and placing it within "expert" and "neutral" institutions that are pan-Canadian in their outlook and orientation.'[45] Is 'defederalization' the product of a constitution that makes inadequate provision for accommodating the tensions inherent in a federal system? Would the result be different if, say, there were a second chamber to Parliament with powers approximating those of the United States Senate? As noted in an earlier chapter, political parties were, and remain, the building blocks of the federation. To the extent that partisanship in Canada is moderated, deliberately or in response to changes such as electoral finance reforms, federalism is weakened. But significantly, the incidence of that outcome is in one direction only – a more dominant centre at the expense of the provinces. Professionalism, it appears, is the enemy of the provinces, unless the provinces are able to become more professional than the centre. Here is the story, aphoristically, of such local successes as the CCF in

Saskatchewan, the Parti Québécois in Quebec, and the Liberals under Louis Robichaud in New Brunswick.

If, as this argument maintains, the practice of federalism in Canada is consigned to the periphery because the constitution makes inadequate provision for its representation at the centre, then intergovernmental relations necessarily assume an extraconstitutional guise. Indeed, that attribution is a recurring theme in the literature of Canadian politics. Illustrative of the genre is the following analysis by Donald Smiley, the dean of political scientists writing about Canadian federalism in the 1960s and 1970s: 'Federal-provincial relations absorb a relatively small amount of time in the debates of Parliament and provincial legislatures and under many circumstances these bodies have no real alternatives to ratifying decisions reached in intergovernmental negotiations.'[46] The separation between federalism and the constitution has grown as the political parties that fill the House of Commons, comprise the government, and bind constituencies to the centre fragment and prove incapable of rallying popular support to the degree they once did.

At one time the practitioners of federalism, whether federal or provincial politicians, operated within one of two national political parties. The exception to that generalization was Alberta, the overwhelming majority of whose MPs between 1921 and 1958 came from the Progressive and then Social Credit parties. Federal–provincial relations were the preserve of intraparty or at least intra-Parliamentary negotiations. It was for this reason that Dominion– (later federal–) provincial conferences played only a peripheral role in the practice of federalism. In the words of Mackenzie King to just such a conference in 1935: 'We are not a parliament ... I assume that we are not adopting the attitude that ... it is for us to determine what is to be done with respect to the matters mentioned in the several reports which have just been read ... I imagine that all of us will recognize that in these matters the legislatures and the parliament of Canada have very special responsibilities of their own.'[47] King liked to draw a parallel between the conduct of intergovernmental meetings in Canada and the practice and proceedings of Imperial Conferences.[48] That subsidiary role reinforced in the public's mind the seemingly permanent failure of the conferences to reach agreement on a domestic amending formula for the constitution. In and of itself, lack of agreement was of minor practical importance since the United Kingdom Parliament amended the Constitution Act, 1867, without dispute and at the request of the Canadian Parliament. Symbolically, however, Canada appeared less than a fully independent country; symbolically, too, absence of agreement among the country's governments on a way out of the impasse signalled a failure of existing extraconstitutional mechanisms.

Attitudes changed beginning in the mid-1960s with the arrival of first ministers' conferences addressing ambitious constitutional agendas and, most important, with the presence of television. For the first time in Canadian history – and at the very moment when the Quiet Revolution in Quebec and the federal Royal Commission on Bilingualism and Biculturalism were attracting public attention – federal–provincial issues and federal–provincial politicians were seen and heard in individual Canadians' living rooms. The practice of federalism was now made accessible to citizens in an unprecedented manner. One long-time participant in these meetings has commented both retrospectively and prospectively:

> I am very much of the view that we've got to come back to the pressure on the federal government to have annual First Ministers conferences that are set at a particular time of year. People work and plan and then you go to them and they're not just back in 24 Sussex Drive, but they are out in the middle of the public arena, in which the public can watch and observe it. My sense is that … we had more public awareness of issues there than we've ever had since. Because we would debate them in the public arena of the federal-provincial conference in Ottawa.[49]

The comparative decline of political parties as instruments of federalism on the one hand and the rise of federal–provincial conferences on the other has resulted in an unanticipated development – a redefinition of regionalism, at least in western Canada. Despite their individual histories, the three prairie provinces were for a long time treated as a unit or region. Common topography, settlement, and constitutional origin was one explanation, but almost as determining was the practice by Statistics Canada and its predecessor organization of collecting and reporting data by 'prairie region.' Because of the rapid influx of population into the prairies after 1900, the federal government agreed to introduce in 1906 the first (of what was to last for half a century) quinquennial census. As well, the prairie provinces became a statistical unit for other than government agencies, as witness reports of polling data, for example, from the middle decades of the last century; societal and commercial patterns reflected this orientation too. This was the era when Winnipeg was the undisputed capital of the region.

All of this changed after the war. The rise of oil and natural gas industries in Saskatchewan and Alberta, and the emergence of the CCF in the former province, with its distinctive social and economic planning philosophy, set the two westernmost provinces apart from Manitoba. Indeed, it was possible to say that over time those two provinces became a common labour market, with people from Saskatchewan migrating to Alberta in search of work. (Saskatchewan's prosperity in the twenty-first century has caused that westward flow to reverse.) Throughout this period British Columbia was treated as a region unto itself.[50] Significantly, change in this bifocal perspective on the West came as a result of federal government initiative. Following the federal general election of 1972, no Liberal was elected west of Manitoba. To fulfil the convention that the cabinet should be federalized with, in this instance, ministers from the three westernmost provinces, the prime minister selected senators from each of the provinces to sit in cabinet.

In 1973 the prime minister, Pierre Trudeau, invited the four western premiers to meet with him in Calgary at what was christened the Western Economic Opportunities Conference (WEOC). That conference considered in some detail the West's (not just the prairies') economic grievances against the federal government. As with first ministers' meetings of the period, its proceedings were televised. Attended by NDP premiers from all but Alberta (represented by Progressive Conservative Peter Lougheed), WEOC provided a catalyst for western provincial cooperation that continues to the present, thanks in part to the close personal friendship forged at the conference between Allan Blakeney, premier of Saskatchewan, 1971–82, and Peter Lougheed, premier of Alberta, 1971–85: 'While the WEOC was a one-time event, the Western Premiers' Conference can trace its origins to that meeting and is now a well-established institution ... [Cooperation] goes beyond developing a common front for federal-provincial questions and extends as well to matters of interprovincial co-operation, one example being internal trade.'[51] In the words of Janice MacKinnon, the annual western premiers conference 'provides a glimpse into the unique regional mindset.'[52]

Like the legendary Royal Commission on Dominion–Provincial Relations of the late 1930s, with whose report modern conceptions of fiscal and jurisdictional federalism in Canada begin, WEOC demonstrated the reality that federalism cannot abide great discrepancies in standards. This is the case whether the issue is health or employment, debt or taxation. Regional disparities are a threat to national unity. As such, they necessitate a response from the centre. The reason for this is that for at least seventy years the belief has been growing that people matter more than their provincial governments – a sentiment the Charter solidifies and promotes.

The heart of Canadian federalism is the question of jurisdiction – which order of government has which powers? It is not about representation, or the failure of institutions of representation, at the centre. There is a simple enough reason for this priority: all of the provinces of Canada, with the exception of Manitoba and British Columbia, had before Confederation experienced self-government. Indeed, the political momentum of that part of the North-West Territories that became the provinces of Saskatchewan and Alberta in 1905 had been driven by an imperative for self-government. In Atlantic Canada and in central Canada more than a quarter-century had been spent (before 1867) achieving and securing responsible self-government. This is another way of saying what has been stated earlier in this book: the provinces preceded the nation in political maturity. In the United States, the constitutions of state and nation were almost coterminous. Not so in Canada, where constitutional development was (and is) linear, beginning, it should not be forgotten, in England long before there was a Canada.

Chapter 6, 'Courts and Charter: Constitution and Federalism,' will examine judicial interpretation and its influence on the course of Canadian federalism – in a modest way, since that subject is one of the most thoroughly studied in Canadian politics, history, and law. Conflict and conflict management are topics that predictably appear when the subject is courts and judicial interpretation. Perhaps they appear too predictably, since they project, excessively one might say, the adversarial character of the Anglo-American legal tradition into considerations of federalism. Yet as this chapter maintains, much of what happens under the rubric of federalism is no more (and perhaps even less) conflictual in character than when the subject of discussion is, for example, collective bargaining or faculty–administration relations in a university. The key matter in the study of a federation like Canada is what sustains the arrangement rather than what threatens it.

In a recent assessment of writing on federal theory, William H. Riker's *Federalism: Origin, Operation, Significance* (1964) receives top marks as 'the *only* theoretical perspective on the subject worthy of that name.'[53] All other writing is judged partial in its ambition and descriptive or prescriptive in its execution. Riker's is celebrated for its perspective, which is described as general, rather than an analysis of a particular system; and for its approach, which accounts for rather than describes what occurs. On the matter of the system's prevailing through time, Riker's conclusion is that 'federalism continues because local leaders who strive to maximize their power are able to embody this compromise in the political party system, while national leaders with the same motivation acquiesce in exchange for support from these local leaders.'[54] Though neither K.C. Wheare nor William Livingston are mentioned in this celebration of Riker, the inference to be drawn is that the scrupulous definitions, categories, and classifications they offer are restrictive and uninformative when it comes to explaining the actual practice of federalism.

The emphasis on the centrality of political parties raises momentary doubt as to Riker's applicability to the Canadian case, since national parties are as weak now as they have ever been in the country's history. Nonetheless, the attraction of Riker lies in his theory's being general – it does not depend upon the congruence or continuation of a set of facts. Whether Canadian federalism today is more decentralized than in the past – whether indeed it is the world's most decentralized federation; whether Canadian federalism may rightly be described as 'collaborative,' or 'cooperative,' or 'constructive,' or any other adjectival-noun combination, is not so much irrelevant as secondary to understanding its practice over time.[55]

On the basis of recent history, the iron-cold answer to the subtitle of Peter Russell's book *Constitutional Odyssey: Can Canadians Become a Sovereign People?* seems to be 'no.'[56] This is why Canada will never become a republic. Yet in the everyday practical world, Canadian federalism is far from paralysed. It performs, and to the degree that it does, it demonstrates that what matters is what governments choose to do rather than what the division of powers they inherit says they may do.

# 6 Courts and Charter: Constitution and Federalism

Notwithstanding Riker and his theory of the political bargain, judicial interpretation of the constitution occupies an entrenched place in the study and practice of federalism. K.C. Wheare explains why: 'While it is the duty of every institution established under the authority of a constitution and exercising powers granted by a constitution to keep within the limits of these powers, it is the duty of the courts, from the nature of their function, to say what these limits are. And that is why courts come to exercise this function in a federal government.'[1] Indeed, in Canada, fascination with interpretation of the Constitution Act, 1867, by the courts, and especially by the Judicial Committee of the Privy Council, which acted as Canada's final court of appeal, dominated all other analysis of Canadian federalism until at least a decade after appeals to London ended in 1949. Even then, the lure of what had gone before continued to exert scholarly attraction in the form of posing either one of two questions: To what extent did the Supreme Court of Canada deviate in its later judgments from the opinions of the JCPC? Or how does one explain the JCPC's own deviation from the intent of the Fathers of Confederation?

Important as answers to these questions are, they are not the central undertaking of this chapter. That object is to analyse the interrelationship of judicial interpretation of the constitution and federalism, and to weigh the implications of an entrenched Charter of Rights and Freedoms on that existing relationship in the last quarter-century. Still, it needs to be said, because it is fundamental to comprehending the course of modern Canadian federalism, that within a quarter-century of the ending of appeals to London, 'the unanimous verdict [of academics and politicians] was that the cumulative result of [the Supreme

Court of Canada's] decisions had been favourable to the federal government. Stealing a line from Maurice Duplessis, René Lévesque put it best: "Comme la Tour de Pise, la Cour penche toujours du même bord."'[2] In addition, according to legal scholar Jean Leclair, patriation of the constitution a decade after that reinforced this orientation. Furthermore, he argues, 'in recognizing very extensive powers to the Federal Parliament in matters such as the protection of health and the protection of the environment, on the basis of the criminal law power, the Court participates in a process of legitimation of the Canadian state and in the construction of a national identity.'[3]

Interpretation of the Court's influence on Canadian federalism in the sixty years since the end of appeals to the JCPC may not be shared by all scholars; or they may not view the influence as quite so uniformly exerted. This chapter will examine the subject of the SCC and federalism in more detail later, for several reasons, including one that Leclair alludes to in his reference to health and the environment, and that the constitutional scholar Geoffrey Marshall precisely anatomizes: 'Any branch of the law, whether it deals prima facie with finance, or crime or local government, may throw up constitutional questions. Like policy, they are bred in the interstices of administration.'[4] As with the practice of federalism, so too with its adjudication: knowledge of the constitutional division of powers is a necessary but insufficient condition for understanding the development of federalism.

Thus, in the last half of the twentieth century, the Court proved to be no captive of the JCPC's priorities or, if one took a critical stance, of its prejudices. And many Canadians did see the JCPC as prejudiced, or biased, or hostile to the project of the Fathers of Confederation. Particularly aggrieved were English-speaking Canadian nationalists after the First World War, who saw the road to Dominion autonomy littered with jurisdictional obstacles erected by the JCPC. That committee declared as *ultra vires* bills introduced by the federal government in the 1930s to improve conditions of work nationwide.[5] Similarly, when the federal government signed international conventions with goals similar to those of the ill-fated domestic legislation, these too were declared to be beyond Parliament's power.[6] These events are extensively documented and require no rehearsing here. It is well understood that, whereas in federations such as the United States and Australia treaty obligations incurred by the federal government in the exercise of its external affairs power confer on that government authority to legislate in fields of jurisdiction that otherwise fall to the states, this is not true in Canada. While only the federal government possesses the international personality to conclude a treaty, of whatever subject matter, legislation to implement the accompanying obligations is shared by both federal and provincial governments depending upon whether the subject matter lies in one or the other's jurisdiction.

If, in the half-century between the mid-1880s and the 1930s, the opinions of the JCPC transformed Canada from the centralized federation envisioned by the politicians who met at Charlottetown and Quebec into an approximation of a classical (Whearean) arrangement of coordinated and independent spheres, it did something else quite different. It fuelled English-Canadian nationalism, not by itself, of course, since Canada's participation and sacrifice in the war and the accelerating movement toward Dominion autonomy afterward had ignited the transformation; but the JCPC's opinions – indeed, its very existence – represented a rebuke to nationalists' ambitions. Viscount Haldane, Lord Chancellor from 1912 to 1928, was subject to particular scorn, a Chief Justice of the Supreme Court of Canada describing him as having '"fashioned the procrustean bed" in which the British North America Act was to lie.'[7] An illustration of the tone of that sentiment can be found in Frank Scott's chapter 'The Privy Council and Mr. Bennett's "New Deal" Legislation,' printed in his book *Essays on the Constitution* (1977) but drawn from two articles he published in 1937.[8] According to Paul Romney, Scott had 'presented his first sketch of the travails of Canadian federalism under the baneful aegis of the Privy Council' at the 1931 annual meeting of the Canadian Political Science Association, the same meeting at which Norman Rogers 'demolished the compact theory.'[9]

Nor was Scott's a lone voice in the academy. F.C. Cronkite, dean of law at the University of Saskatchewan and co-author of Saskatchewan's brief to the Rowell-Sirois Commission, echoed – and embellished – that sentiment:

Have their Lordships done this [rejection of legislation] deliberately in order to fasten a colonial status upon the Dominion? I am inclined to think that two or three of them have. In the main, however, the result can be explained by an ignorance of Canadian and colonial history ...

[I] wish to insist that the fathers [*sic*] of Confederation envisaged a Canadian citizenship as did the text of the British North America Act. Now true citizenship must involve a good deal especially when we reflect that our Confederation was born in the full flood of British liberty ... I

would say that [citizenship] must ... guarantee free movement within the
Dominion ... that the citizen who moves from one province to the another
will feel reasonably at home ... It must involve complete freedom of religion and toleration for minorities ... Otherwise Canadian citizenship is
a meaningless term. I believe, therefore, that all these matters should be
committed to the central government. I believe they were – but apparently
the central authority has lost its control. I would much prefer this solution
to a guarantee of these liberties through the insertion in a bill of rights.[10]

The JCPC gave federalism a bad name. That at least was the conclusion that audiences who heard the English-speaking nationalist
critics of the 1930s might reasonably draw. In the speech just quoted,
for instance, Cronkite expressed the view that 'if we have a genuine
democracy we need not fear the legislative supremacy of a central Parliament. After all Great Britain is referred to as a model of liberty, but
there we find a theory of Parliamentary absolutism.' This 'genius of the
Constitution' argument was still being invoked, if not necessarily with
blanket approval, two decades later by prominent academics.[11] Still, by
the late 1950s (a decade after it had ceased to be Canada's final court
of appeal), the earlier labours of the JCPC elicited commendation for
creating 'authentic federalism.' That phrase appeared in the Report of
the Royal Commission of Inquiry on Constitutional Problems (a Quebec Royal Commission, appointed in 1953, and popularly referred to
as the Tremblay Commission after the surname of its chairman).[12] The
provenance of the comment is hardly surprising in view of Quebec's
long-held concern, in a country whose population was otherwise overwhelmingly English-speaking and Protestant, to protect its cultural distinctiveness. Yet the comment was different from what had gone before.
'Authentic federalism' is not a synonym for the compact theory, though
the latter might be considered an element of the former.
    Tremblay's report went further: 'The federative principle require[s] ...
a division between two orders of government, co-ordinate with each
other, and with each of them enjoying supreme authority in the sphere
of activity assigned to it by the Constitution.'[13] The same report cited a
1921 opinion of the JCPC that employed similar terminology: 'Within
the spheres allotted to them by the Act, the Dominion and the Provinces are rendered on general principle co-ordinate governments.'[14] Yet
the phrases are sufficiently different to indicate the arrival of classifica-
tory rigour in the form of Wheare's *Federal Government*, published a
decade previous to the Tremblay Report and cited numerous times in

its notes. This reference is no slight on the distinctiveness of that report – far from it, for Tremblay stands as a unique document on the subject of federalism in Canada. The contrast that Jean-Charles Falardeau drew at about the same time between English- and French-Canadian novels, the first a 'description of a social situation,' where tension lies between individuals, the second 'a plunging into the depths of an individual soul,' where tension exists between 'individuals and their [own] destinies' – finds support as well in a comparison of federal and Quebec Royal Commissions.[15] Jacques Maritain, Arthur Koestler, and natural law, cited in Tremblay's exegesis of federalism, find no sanctuary in the social science language of Rowell-Sirois, or Macdonald, or any other federal inquiry.

Scott and Rogers used the occasion of the annual meeting of the Canadian Political Science Association in 1931 to launch their broadsides on the JCPC. Significant too was the fact that both of them published articles on the themes of their addresses in the *Canadian Bar Review*. One reason for that venue was that the *Canadian Journal of Economics and Political Science* did not begin publication until 1935; another was the close association between law and political science in this period. For the profession and the discipline, the domestication of the constitution and the achievement of an acknowledged international personality for Canada were subjects of major scholarly interest. The CPSA annual meeting was just one of many forums in this period available to advocates of these issues. According to Brooke Claxton, later a federal cabinet minister and later still the first chair of the Canada Council, 'there were four organizations which especially had a considerable influence on the development of Canadian thinking and policy. These were the Association of Canadian Clubs, the Canadian League, the Canadian Institute of International Affairs (CIIA) and the League of Nations Society of Canada ... They had "interlocking directorates."' Graham Spry, co-founder with Alan Plaunt of the Canadian Radio League, made a comparable observation about 'the quite extraordinary pattern or web of personal relationships and friendships extending from coast to coast.'[16]

These and other 'nationalist organizations,' like the Canadian Radio League, were based on individual friendships formed 'through university and wartime associations,' 'business and professional relationships,' and 'the new associations themselves,' whose goal of creating national unity was promoted 'in their annual conventions and the travels of their officers.'[17] Of this last an exceptional case in point was Escott Reid, from the mid-1940s to the mid-1960s a prominent Canadian diplomat, but between 1932 and 1938, national secretary of CIIA. In this position he travelled extensively across Canada interviewing nearly every prominent political and public figure of the day.[18] From the point of view of this study, there were three striking features to the development of these associations: a predominantly urban milieu, a focus on elites rather than on a mass base, and an imperviousness to regional distinctions – in other words, to federalism. Notwithstanding strong affection for 'the British tradition' on the part of most of the associations – though there was, in the words of Norman Rogers, 'no enthusiasm for European entanglements and an inclin[ation] more and more to accept the full implications of our North American situation' – the volunteerism of the postwar period could be interpreted as one counterweight to the perceived provincial thrust of the JCPC's interpretation of the constitution.[19]

In these events there was a still more striking juxtaposition to note. The nationalist orientation evident in the activities of broadcasting, adult education, and patriotic groups in Canada ran counter to the 'federalistic feeling [then] curiously widespread in Britain.'[20] Counter, because at that time federalism on the other side of the Atlantic Ocean was treated as tantamount to pluralism. Writing in 1921, Harold Laski observed that in the individual 'a thousand associations converge ... We are all a bundle of hyphens.'[21] Arguably then, the virtue of federalism lay in its capacity to channel those sentiments and interests so as to strengthen local community rather than national centre. Evaluation of that claim is better left for examination in the following chapter, 'The Habit of Federalism.' The reason for introducing it now is to suggest a parallel with the reasoning of the JCPC when it came to interpreting the Canadian constitution. As said in an earlier chapter, there are two reasons for adopting a federal form of government: one outward in ambition – to expand; and one inward – to recognize difference. The Canadian federation embraces both objects. 'Laski's federalism,' which in the first decades of the last century was a well-publicized view of the subject in Great Britain, 'resulted not in the joining of smaller states into larger ones ... but in the disaggregation of larger states into smaller territorial and functional groups in which powers of self-government were given recognition.'[22] Fissiparous federalism, one might almost call it.

Not representation but self-government was the core value espoused. Canadian understanding of the reasoning of the JCPC is altered when the decentralization that Laski so prolifically championed is taken into account. A majority of the provinces were self-governing entities when they entered Confederation. Retention of that status in face of the central government's superior powers of, among others, taxation, appointment, and reservation and disallowance, and in company with long-standing suspicion of institutional reforms that might compromise provincial autonomy, including the Trojan Horse of intrastate mechanisms, explains Canada's tradition of combative, even demagogic, premiers – Hepburn, Aberhart, and Pattullo, from the past, Ralph Klein and Danny Williams, more recently. It is difficult to imagine that elected senators from those provinces, then or now, would have more effectively articulated their province's case than these, or other premiers, have done. Certainly, they would not have been in the position to challenge legally, politically, or economically federal government policies.

The imperative to provincial self-government was driven by another feature of the Canadian constitution, one of great relevance for judicial interpretation and for federalism. The constitutions of the other federations with which Canada has most in common, the United States and Australia, enumerate specific subjects under which the central government may make law. All other 'heads of power,' that is, the residuary powers of the constitution, rest with the states. The distribution is more complicated than that bare statement implies, but the central point remains that there is only one list of powers in these constitutions – that which applies to the national government. Canada's Constitution Act, 1867, is unusual in having two lists (Sections 91 and 92). Yet even here, there still had to be provision for residuary power. One of the principal controversies surrounding the interpretations rendered by the JCPC turned on whether that committee had substituted Section 92(13), 'Property and Civil Rights,' for the preambular phrase in Section 91, 'Peace, Order and Good Government' as the location of the constitution's residuary power. Much of the literature that examines the JCPC's work as it affected Canada is devoted to answering that question.

The answer, however, is not relevant to this discussion. What *is* relevant, and provides one explanation for the approach adopted by the JCPC, is the distinction that follows from this difference between Canada and the other federations. Geoffrey Sawer, Australian legal scholar and scholar of comparative federalism, articulated the difference most clearly – almost at the same time as Wheare, another Australian, was writing *Federal Government:* 'It can be said of the British North America Act that its "object" is the "maintenance" of Dominion and provincial powers, since both are set out as exclusive powers with cross-residues, but apart from the specific "maintenance" of certain State powers ... the Australian Constitution does not itself "maintain" State powers. They are "maintained" by the State Constitutions.'[23] Coincidently, and at almost the same time, Sawer's perception of the Canadian constitution as a 'maintaining' document was being echoed, in different words, by T.C. Douglas, premier of Saskatchewan at a federal–provincial conference: 'When we use the phrase "constitution of Canada" we are using language descriptive not only of the dominion parliament, but also of the provinces of which Canada is composed. The word "federal" likewise has a double use. It is used not only to describe dominion power, but also a type of union which necessarily embraces provinces, possessed of original powers, as well as a central government.'[24]

Canadian provinces do not have 'constitutions' in the sense that Americans and Australians use that term when discussing the units of their federal systems. For that reason, there are no publications here comparable to Anne Twomey's nine-hundred-page work, *The Constitution of New South Wales*.[25] While extraneous to the present discussion, it is pertinent to note that state – indeed, colonial – constitutions are a source of an important contrast between Canada and Australia, one that explains Australia's tradition of strong bicameralism with powerful upper houses, an early sense of a higher law (that is, higher than Parliament) that required governments to justify their actions, and a strong (certainly when compared with Canada) republican sentiment.[26]

Though frequently commented upon for its asymmetry, it should come as no surprise that the court system of Canada does not mirror the spheres of the federation. Rather than a balance of judiciaries – federal and provincial – as found (with the appropriate name change) in the United States, in Canada the court structures are telescoped. (Asymmetry in the matter of the courts is but an echo of legislative asymmetry: bicameralism is a feature of Parliament alone, and not of the provincial legislatures. Once again, the student of Canadian politics is reminded that Canada is no formulaic federal system, but distinct in and of itself.) The judiciary is not normally thought of as a part of government; *independent* is the adjective most often used to denote its separate status. This is the case even though under Section 96 of the Constitution Act, 1867, Justices of the Supreme Court of Canada and judges of district, county, and superior courts of the provinces are appointed (and may be removed) by the Governor General, while the constitution, maintenance, and organization of provincial courts rests with the provinces (Section 92(14)), and similar responsibility for the SCC (and any other additional courts established by Parliament) lies with the central authorities.

Among federations, Canada's court system may be unusual; it would be an exaggeration, however, to say that because of its unified structure it is inferior. Arguably, a contrary view, in this instance by Richard Risk, may be taken: 'The comprehensive jurisdiction of the Supreme Court is one of the few unifying institutions to survive the late-nineteenth-century onslaught of provincial rights, and it is one of Macdonald's few triumphs on the battleground of law and the constitution.'[27] An essential aspect of the Court's unifying function lies in its composition – a statement that does not apply to the Supreme Courts of Australia or the United States. By law, three of the Justices of the Supreme Court of Canada must be trained in the civil law and come from Quebec; by custom, three come from Ontario; and of the remaining three, two come from the four western provinces and one from Atlantic Canada. By contrast, the members of the High Court of Australia come overwhelmingly from the Sydney and Melbourne bars, while in the United States, the rigid regionalism of the Canadian bench (and cabinet) has no equal. The explanation for Canada's distinctiveness lies, as is so often the case, in the presence of Quebec, but here, more particularly, in Canada's having both common law and civil law systems. How the practice of legal dualism – in two official languages – affects comprehension of the constitution is yet another understudied topic in Canadian politics. The composition of the SCC is a subject of long-standing interest, though from the perspective of judicial interpretation of the constitution, perhaps one given exaggerated importance. That would be one conclusion to draw from Wheare's statement that 'in spite of the formal dependence of the supreme courts on the executive and legislature of the general government, they have exhibited a considerable impartiality in the exercise of their function as interpreters of the division of powers. In Anglo-Saxon countries, the traditions of the bar and the bench tend strongly to safeguard the integrity and independence of the judges.'[28]

The principle of an independent judiciary owes nothing to the grant of responsible government. Recognized in British North America well before the 1840s, that principle had received statutory sanction in England more than a century earlier in the Act of Settlement, 1701. It needs to be remembered that with the significant exception of the Dominion courts (the SCC being the obvious example), the administration of justice went largely untouched by Confederation. The signal characteristic of the judiciary after 1867 was its continuity with the past.

The relevance of Canada's court structure to the subject of federalism and the Constitution of Canada lies in the manner of selection of the judiciary. All non-provincial court judges are federally appointed. Thus, by whatever name they may bear, all trial and appellate judges in the provinces are appointed by the Crown in right of Canada but on the advice of the government of the day. With this arrangement a continuing band of critics finds two faults: one, appointments are patronage based since they are controlled in the last analysis by a partisan government; and two, appointments controlled at the centre are insufficiently 'sensitive to the importance of guarding provincial autonomy.'[29] The first is only a tangential concern of this book, though the different practices and patterns of patronage across the country, even when the subject is federal appointments, suggest a topic for a study yet to be written. The second goes to its heart, since the core of the argument is that the provinces do not receive a fair hearing from the courts:

> Ces décisions judiciaries, qui assujettissent les gouvernements provinciaux à la volonté d'Ottawa, ne devraient surprendre personne, puisque le système judiciaire canadien est l'un des plus centralisés au monde. Contrairement aux fédérations suisse et americaine, par exemple, le système judicaire canadien est parfaitment unifié, la Cour suprême agissant comme tribunal de dernière instance pour le droit tant fédéral que provincial.[30]

The fact that the preceding quotation is in French might suggest that the opinion it expresses is limited to residents of Quebec. That would be false. During the dispute between the western provinces and Ottawa of the 1970s, with regard to provincial powers over natural resources (which ultimately led to the insertion of Section 92A in the Constitution Act, 1982), Allan Blakeney, then premier of Saskatchewan, expressed the same concern to then prime minister Pierre Trudeau:

> The time has come to make such changes as are necessary to ensure that the Supreme Court of Canada is seen to be independent and not unduly reflective of federal views in constitutional cases. I am not questioning the integrity of those who serve on the present Court, nor am I questioning their ability. But I do question the wisdom of having the members of our Supreme Court, the final arbiter of constitutional disputes, appointed by the executive branch of one level of government, and largely representa-

tive of one or two regions of the country – without intervention or voice of the executive branch of provincial governments, by provincial legislatures, or by Parliament.[31]

Three months later, in its report titled *A Future Together*, the Task Force on Canadian Unity offered an extreme variation on this proposal: 'The Supreme Court should be composed of eleven judges, five of whom are to chosen from among civil law judges, and six from among common law judges and lawyers, having regard, in the latter case, to regional distribution.' Appointments of the first division would be made subject to consultation with the attorney general of Quebec, and of the second division following consultation with the attorneys general of all other provinces. 'Appropriate committees' of the reformed Senate, now called the Council of the Federation, would 'ratify' the nominations. In addition, the Task Force recommended that the 'chief justice of the Supreme Court should be chosen by the governor in council, for a nonrenewable term, from among the members of the Court, in alternation between a common law judge and a civil law judge.'[32]

Here is a striking exposition of the multiple dimensions of Canadian federalism. What geometric – let alone recognized federal – construct might grant coordinate status to central, provincial, and Quebec jurisdictions? Or, rephrased, how might vertical (cultural) and horizontal (territorial) federalisms be joined in a manner that acknowledged each as equal and neither as subordinate? Or, again, was such an equation impossible to achieve, as one might conclude from reading the recommendations of the Task Force? That appears to be the conclusion the Supreme Court itself reached in the so-called 'Quebec Constitutional Veto' appeal – in which the province argued that it possessed a unique conventional right of veto – when it upheld the following opinion of Court of Appeal of Quebec: '[A]t law, all the provinces are fundamentally equal and the Attorney General of Quebec ha[s] failed to establish that either the Government of Canada or the other provinces ha[ve] constitutionally recognized in Quebec any special power of veto over constitutional amendment not possessed by the other provinces.'[33] In other words, the principle of equality among the provinces is incompatible with a special power of veto for Quebec.

The view of federalism propounded by the Task Force on Canadian Unity did not find favour with Pierre Trudeau or with the majority of Canadians outside Quebec.[34] Nonetheless, and in retrospect, it has to be seen as opening the final stage of constitutional negotiations, which in 1982, unlike the preceding half-century of discussions, ended in agreement on a domestic amending formula. Within a year of the Task Force's report, the government of Quebec held its first referendum on sovereignty, which it (the leading advocate) lost and the federal government (the leading opponent) won on the promise of introducing major constitutional change. Here was the background to the federal government's move, later the same year, unilaterally to patriate the constitution. Those events, and especially patriation of the constitution 'in amended form over the objections of Quebec,' created a new context for interpreting the relationship between federalism and the constitution.[35] In large part this happened because the Supreme Court set about enunciating constitutional principles for Canada to an unprecedented degree.

These events are well documented. What requires emphasis is the following: achieving the hitherto unachievable – agreement on a domestic amending formula, which for its method of calculation treats all provinces, including Quebec, as equal – came at the cost of disguising the essence of the Canadian federation. At one time the compact theory – that is, Confederation is the product of the uniting provinces, and any change to its terms requires the assent of the same provinces – was a levelling theory (for those who held it) that applied to all provinces, including Quebec. Over the last thirty years a division has arisen that sets Quebec apart from the other provinces.[36] The amendment procedures set down in Part V of the Constitution Act, 1982, make no provision for either a Quebec veto or provincial unanimity, except on five matters itemized in Section 41: the offices of Queen, Governor General, and lieutenant governor of a province; the right of a province to no fewer members of the House of Commons than its number of senators; the use of the English and French languages; the composition of the Supreme Court of Canada; and an amendment to the amending procedures themselves – that is, to Part V of the Constitution Act, 1982. The source of the change lay in the Supreme Court's opinion in the patriation reference. There the Court held that the federal government might in law unilaterally patriate the constitution, but that by convention a 'substantial degree of provincial consent 'was required.'[37] The reason for this rule, the Court said, 'is the federal principle.' Patriation invalidated existing assumptions about constitutional amendment. The new formula subsequently agreed upon by all first ministers, except Quebec's, could not logically revert to a unanimity rule analogous to the old compact theory. Add to this the pan-Canadian force that the

Canadian Charter of Rights and Freedoms (Part 1 of the Constitution Act, 1982) was said to represent, and the result, said Gilles Bourque and Jules Duchastel, 'amen[e] le thème de l'égalité des provinces.'[38]

Yet the government of Quebec refused its assent to the Constitution Act, 1982, despite more than a decade of negotiations surrounding the Meech Lake and Charlottetown accords. A second Quebec referendum on separation was narrowly defeated in 1995. This was followed in a matter of months by Parliament's Act Respecting Constitutional Amendments (S.C. 1996, c. 1). Under its terms, certain amendments to the Constitution must be consented to by a majority of the provinces before they are tabled in Parliament. The majority of the provinces must include Quebec, Ontario, British Columbia, at least two of the Atlantic provinces comprising at least 50 per cent of the region's population, and at least two of the prairie provinces comprising at least 50 per cent of the region's population.

For all practical purposes, the 1996 Act – a consequence of the second referendum – restores the *status quo ante* as regards Quebec and constitutional amendments that prevailed at the time of the first referendum, that is, prior to the constitutional amendment agreement of 1982. On the basis of this comparatively short history, it might be said that amendment procedures, which until 1982 were not codified, exist in uneasy tension with expressions of the popular will obtained through mechanism of the referendum, itself a procedure with shallow roots in Canada.

In 2007 the Constitution Act, 1982, had its silver anniversary, and as is the way with such occasions, there was considerable marking, if not uniform celebration, of that event. The Saskatchewan Institute of Public Policy was one of several bodies in Canada to organize a conference: 'A Living Tree: The Legacy of 1982 in Canada's Political Evolution.'[39] The brochure calling for submission of topics for papers mentioned, as illustrations, 'several pertinent issues, including: an assessment of the political imperatives that led to the success of the 1982 Constitution; the effect of the Constitution Act, 1982 on Canada's shifting definitions of federalism; how the discourse of human rights … has evolved as a result of the Charter of Rights and Freedoms; the current agenda for constitutional reform.' Forty-two detailed proposals for papers were received, and of those, sixteen dealt directly with the Charter. Such specificity contrasted sharply, wrote one of the conference organizers, with the breadth of debate heard in the 1976 to 1982 period:

Here are some of the things that were around: completing national sovereignty, incipient republicanism (or, at least, a highly contested – and expanding – sense of the place of domestic popular consent in changes to basic law), the idea of constituting political values that inhere in individuals and minority groups, a thrust to underscore federal power over market regulation, the idea that federal jurisdictions robbed provinces of essential elements of social and cultural self-determination, the idea that non-renewable resources were a particular form of patrimony that should fall to provincial exploitation and regulation, the sense that horizontal equity between governments – and, hence, possibly, between people – needed to be constituted, notwithstanding incipient republicanism national consent should be constructed governmentally and federally, the cause of feminism warranted constitutional recognition, the claims of Aboriginal peoples required, at the least, rhetorical recognition, and, of course, the need to supplant Quebec nationalism with a newer narrative.[40]

Notwithstanding a range of subjects with the potential to exert infinite influence over constitutional perception and practice, a quarter-century later scholarly interest has focused to an unexpected degree on the Charter (literally Part 1 of five substantive parts of the 1982 Act). Unexpected, in part, because according to some contributors, the Charter was not the primary animating force behind the patriation initiative. On the contrary, patriation was 'largely meant to be a response to the challenge of Canadian duality,' says Marc-Antoine Adam, while Garth Stevenson argues that 'the transfer of amending power from the Parliament at Westminster to Canadians, was originally the main point of the exercise.'[41] A funny thing happened on the way to the silver anniversary celebrations: dazzled by the brilliance of the Charter, Canadians lost sight of both the causes and the effects of the Constitution Act, 1982. More than that, perceptions of federalism and the constitution have become clouded. The most ambitious package of constitutional reforms in the country's history is now either forgotten or viewed as failure.

No one today talks about Section 92A, which states that 'in each province, the legislature may exclusively make laws in relation to exploration ... development, conservation and management of non-renewable natural resources and forestry resources in the province.' (Nor did anyone proposing a paper to the Living Tree conference suggest 92A as a topic.) Yet as three commentators close to the 1982 negotiations note: 'The importance of natural resources [at the time] was underlined by the placement of this item as first on the agenda.'[42] Their evaluation of the constitutional discussions of 1982 does offer one reason for later scholarly silence about the subject of natural resources – it is too complicated for non-participants to understand or, for that matter, to be constitutionally entrenched: 'The interrelatedness of the questions of distribution of revenue, regional aspiration, equalization among provinces, and federal economic strategies suggests that the attempt to achieve reconciliation through constitutional reform is probably unworkable.'[43] Too complicated, yet too important to be placed into law: Is Canada unusual among federations in having reached a stage where some matters vital to its well-being cannot be constitutionalized, but rather depend upon intergovernmental negotiation to reach agreement?

Take, as another example of oversight, the amending formula with its six different procedures: Garth Stevenson says 'its most significant characteristics [are] extreme complexity, extreme rigidity and the absence of any provisions for popular (that is to say, non-governmental) involvement in the amending process.'[44] That is a widely held view – one reinforced by the failure to ratify the post-1982 mega-constitutional efforts represented by the Meech Lake and Charlottetown accords – that possibly explains why there are only two paper proposals on the subject to the 'Living Tree' conference. Still, that assessment is surprising for two reasons: first, the fifty-five-year quest for a domestic amending formula had at last come to a successful conclusion in 1982 and would seem worthy of examination on that ground alone, and second, the subject had been given prominence following the 1980 Quebec referendum. In the words of Romanow, Whyte, and Leeson: 'The result of the referendum was a mandate for patriation of the Constitution with an amending formula and entrenched charter of rights with language provisions.'[45]

Yet as Warren Newman (the author of the other paper on amendment procedures for the SIPP conference in 2007) has shown, Canada is not in such a straightjacket when it comes to amending its constitution, as is sometimes assumed:

> The constitution has been amended at least 10 times since 1982, largely through the so-called 'bilateral' procedure contemplated by section 43 of the Constitution Act, 1982 ... By any reasonable standard, these are not insignificant accomplishments. Moreover, the failure of an amendment proposal to be ratified is not necessarily tantamount to the failure of the amending processes themselves. The multilateral amending procedures

serve a dual purpose: (1) to permit constitutional amendments where the legal requirements of the formulae have been met ...; (2) to protect constitutional provisions and entrenched guarantees from change where the requisite conditions of Part V have not been met.[46]

Contrary to the view that bilateral amendments deal with subjects of local, and therefore of limited, concern, Section 43 amendments have extinguished denominational school rights in Newfoundland and Labrador and in Quebec, as well as having 'provided for the equality of status and equal rights and privileges for the English and French linguistic communities of New Brunswick.'[47]

Significant as these amendments may be, they are of a particular class: they speak to the concerns of cultural, rather than territorial, federalism. Speaking of the conundrum of Senate reform, Donald Dennison, a former deputy minister in New Brunswick and, more recently, vice-president of the Forum of Federations, has signalled the problem that this chronicle of Section 43 successes conceals: 'The difficulty of gaining sufficient consensus on key matters affecting Senate composition and powers has discouraged thoughts of reforming an archaic institution ever since. Outer Canada continues to feel estranged from national decision-making.'[48] In Dennison's observation there is an echo of Dunkin's 'three kingdoms' analogy of nearly a century ago. There is irony, too, since the constitutionally entrenched domestic amending formula Canadians had waited for for so long seems no more, and perhaps less, adequate to the task than the conventions that once governed amendments to the 1867 Act. Premiers Lougheed and Blakeney played central roles in the constitutional discussions leading to agreement on an amending formula in 1982. So too did their ministers, such as Saskatchewan's Roy Romanow, then provincial attorney general. Most of the constitutional issues that roiled Canadian politics for the first seventy or so years of the country's history – resources, the school question, Social Credit – had western origins. The site of this discontent has been discounted in the last half-century – notwithstanding the rise of the Reform Party in the last two decades of the twentieth – as issues involving language and Quebec have bulked larger in Canadian politics. The period since 1982 may be seen to embrace contradictory forces: on the one hand, constitutional movement, as represented by the Charter; on the other hand, federal stasis, as symbolized in the failure of the Meech Lake and Charlottetown accords and in the perceived rigidity of the amending procedures.

Those forces are also said to interact in a manner disadvantageous to federalism. That is the thesis advanced by such scholars as Janet Hiebert: 'The Charter's intersection with federalism tells an important story of significant change arising from the promotion of identities based on "Canadianness" at the expense of "competing regional loyalties"; the homogenization of legislation; and the defederalization of political culture.'[49] A similar, but more Quebec-focused, perspective says that 'la charte est en effet venue institutionnaliser la conception multiculturelle du Canada aux dépens des conceptions biculturelle, dualiste ou provincialiste.'[50] The contradiction between the particularities of federalism and the universality of rights that recognize no internal boundaries has long been understood. It was William Riker who pungently observed that a country that put civil liberties first in its order of values would have to place federalism second. The Canadian penchant for seeking to reconcile the irreconcilable – political scientist Carolyn Tuohy has labelled the practice institutionalized ambivalence – is revealed, she says, in a 'system [that] legitimizes competing principles: it combines an unwritten with a written constitution, a Westminster model of centralized cabinet government with a decentralized federation, and, since 1982, parliamentary supremacy with a constitutional charter of rights.'[51]

The finesse in this last juxtaposition of principles is found in Section 33 of the Constitution Act, 1982 (the better known 'notwithstanding clause'): 'Parliament or the legislature of a province may expressly declare in an Act of Parliament or of the legislature ... that the Act or provision thereof shall operate notwithstanding a provision included in section 2 or sections 7 to 15 of this Charter.' A declaration to this effect is limited to five years but may be re-enacted for another five. Hiebert describes Section 33 as 'the Charter's most obvious concession to federalism. It allows legislatures to dissent from judicial decisions ... thereby accommodating the territorial-based diversity that federalism was intended to accommodate.' But that example of institutionalized ambivalence is itself ambivalently applied – as of 2001, only sixteen times, and most of these early in the life of the Charter.[52] Critics say that the infrequent resort to Section 33 depreciates federalism (though such a comment may, in light of Chapter 7, be viewed as old-fashioned for its habit of seeing federalism as the work of governments alone). That indictment assumes an especially keen edge in Quebec: 'Les partisans du fédéralisme d'ouverture devraient insister sur ce que la clause nonobstant évite de subordonner les droits collectifs des communautés provincials à des droits individuels, dont Ottawa aurait la responsabilité, grâce à une charte qui accorderait un pouvoir absolu à la Cour suprême.'[53]

Measured by the traditional standards of Canadian academic publishing, literature on the Charter is vast. More than that, the Charter holds comparable interest for the disciplines of political science and law. In this convergence of scholarship, inspired by a common interest in assessing the effect of a higher law on a parliamentary federation, there is a parallel with the mutual preoccupation those same disciplines demonstrated in the 1930s in evaluating the work of the JCPC. Of course, the themes of the critiques are different: today, the claim is that the Charter privileges the federal government at the expense of the provinces; then, it was that the JCPC undermined the federal government to the benefit of the provinces. The inversion of the critiques is not quite as symmetrical as the statement implies, because until the Charter, Parliament (or the legislature, if the sphere of jurisdiction were provincial) was the centre of all things. It is Parliament's displacement from its historic pinnacle that explains the attraction the Charter exerts on academic scholarship. That and something else, for if Parliament, comprised as it is of Crown, Senate, and House of Commons, has been displaced, what now stands in its stead?

It cannot be the Charter, for that is the product of intergovernmental agreement in Canada and parliamentary action at Westminster (Canada Act, U.K. 1982, c. 11). In the discussions leading to the Constitution Act, 1982, the Charter was a pre-eminent part of what the federal government called the 'people's package,' and it has remained eminently popular with Canadians, even in Quebec. In a survey conducted in 2007, 53 per cent of respondents said the Charter 'has had a positive, or very positive, impact on Canada over the past 25 years … Respondents from Quebec viewed the Charter in the most positive light, with 61 per cent rating its impact as positive or very positive.'[54] But populism is not a constitutional principle; it can offer no rationale, say, for House of Commons participation in appointments to the Supreme Court. Here is institutional ambivalence with serious repercussions for public understanding of the constitution – in all its many parts. And for federalism, too; for the people of a federation have a double personality. If intrastate mechanisms in Canada are impoverished, as is usually depicted in the political science literature, how much more so are the institutions of representation? Party discipline is the familiar villain and, on occasion, hero: How often have Canadians outside of Quebec been reminded that 73 of Quebec's 75 MPs supported the constitutional agreement of 1982, the same agreement the province's government and legislature, then and later, rejected? What conclusion for the Canadian federation and the constitution is to be drawn from that set of facts? An informed analysis of the question whether Mr Trudeau or Mr Lévesque 'spoke for the people of Quebec' is to be found in Allan Blakeney's autobiography.[55]

One element of the amendment process altered in 1982, and with implications for representation in the federation, was the introduction of a suspensive veto for the Senate in constitutional matters. Before 1982 the Senate had the power, as did the House of Commons, to veto resolutions leading to amendments. After patriation the Senate was limited to enforcing a delay of no more than 180 days (Section 47(1)). This was the first time a suspensive veto had appeared in Canadian politics, though the Parliament Act, 1911, had restricted the House of Lords in a similar but unlimited manner in the United Kingdom. As already noted, the discussions leading to the Constitution Act, 1982, were wide ranging, and among the topics proposed for reform was the Senate. It is significant that in the most ambitious constitutional undertaking since Confederation, the Senate – the institution whose reform had been discussed as much as or more than any other – did not appear except in Section 47(1). And the reason for this was the intransigence of the government of Saskatchewan, led by Allan Blakeney, who strongly opposed giving the Senate a veto over its own continued existence under the terms of the amending formula. As Romanow, Whyte, and Leeson recount in *Canada ... Notwithstanding*, the suspensive veto was the compromise reached after prolonged and fraught negotiation.

The intricacies of constitutional negotiation are peripheral to the focus of this discussion, which is on the intersection of federalism and the constitution. Nonetheless, the suspensive veto has assumed *ex post facto* a rationale that touches both of these topics though it was not heard at the time of its adoption. In this context, it needs to be remembered that at the same time the Senate's role was reduced to a delay of 180 days, provincial legislatures were incorporated into the assent process for amendments secured under Sections 38, 41, and 42 of the constitution:

> The logic of this constitutional structure was impeccable. The House of Commons speaks for the Canadian people. The Senate speaks for the regions. But the provinces are the regions. In these circumstances, the Senate should not be able to veto an amendment that has been agreed to by the House of Commons and the affected provinces.

By contrast, if a constitutional amendment does not involve the provinces, but is solely a federal matter to be made by Act of Parliament, it is the Senate that speaks for the regions. And it retains its veto to do so.[56]

It is a delicate matter to determine the effect of this change in amending procedure on the conduct of federalism. Rejection of the Meech Lake Accord as a result of the failure of some provincial legislatures to pass the necessary authorizing resolution would seem to point to a gain for the provinces. Failure of the Charlottetown Accord to win popular support in a majority of provinces in a referendum for which there was no constitutional requirement in the first place casts doubt on almost any conclusion drawn, since on the basis of these precedents each situation is so fact-specific. As for the federal government, is it weakened or strengthened by the disappearance of an absolute Senate veto? Comparisons are meaningless since the Senates of Australia and the United States, for example, are not limited to a suspensive veto when the matter before them is a constitutional amendment. The need to ask the question is a reminder, once again, of the long and unintended reach of Senate reform in Canada.

Whatever the intention of the Founding Fathers, the operation of the American federal system has been centralizing in its effect. The history of the Electoral College and of the U.S. Senate itself bears out that thesis. More than fifty years ago, William Riker noted that 'state officials had to use the political party, not state governments, to make their influence felt in Washington.'[57] By contrast, disputatious premiers reinforce a peripheralized federalism in Canada. One reason that may be suggested for the difference is the absence of provincial politicians with federal ambitions. Few attempt to move from one to the other 'sphere'; none succeed when they do. One who tried but failed was Duff Roblin, premier of Manitoba and unsuccessful contender in 1967 for the leadership of the federal Progressive Conservative Party. Three years earlier, André Laurendeau, co-chairman of the B-and-B Commission, had assessed Roblin's handicap as follows: 'There are some things it would be difficult for him to do on the provincial level – for example, in the area of French-language teaching and schools – that he would have to have done to be credible federally. So he's in a state of perpetual contradiction.'[58] The contrast here with politics in the United States is great, indeed. A more familiar explanation says that a weak Senate, as far as its being an effective federal institution, is to blame. Again, in this matter Canada and the United States appear as mirror images. If it is

the case, as Alan Tarr has argued, that 'limited judicial review of federalism disputes [in the United States] res[t]s in part on the purported
adequacy of the Senate as a political guarantor of state interests,' then
in Canada, the reverse seems true – courts play this role because the
upper chamber does not.[59]

Yet the courts have moved from being, predominantly, arbiters of
federalism to becoming guarantors of Charter rights. That at least is
one school of thought, and it is reinforced by another, which says that
the Supreme Court 'equates efficiency with centralism, and thus ...
favour[s] the national polity over regional ones.'[60] At one level this is
the argument Harold Laski advanced in 1939 in an article titled 'The
Obsolescence of Federalism' in *The New Republic*. There the danger to
federalism lay in capitalism and its requirement for administrative
uniformity. Now it lies in enforcing values associated with protecting
health or the environment. Standards, in short, are antithetical to federalism. One is reminded of Margaret Atwood's aphorism that 'straight
line wins over curve,' but also of her assessment, which echoes Harold
Innis's, that this occurs at a cost of vital energy.[61] It is Leclair's view
that this energy radiates from collective or communitarian identities,
whose distinguishing qualities are jeopardized by pan-Canadian values that transcend the particularities of federalism. These concerns
go beyond the frame of this chapter, except that they emphasize the
shifting theoretical base to federalism. It was William Livingston, for
instance, who argued forcefully for the proposition that values and attitudes 'produc[e] a demand for some kind of federal recognition of the
diversities.'[62] But it would appear that new values and new attitudes
may also challenge federalism. When that happens, who is to be the
judge?

# 7 The Habit of Federalism

**Mr McConkey** moved the second reading of the Bill: 'An Act to declare the first day of July, or Dominion Day, a legal holiday.'
**Mr. Ferguson** thought ... it would be unpleasant for some parties who were not much in love with Confederation to be called upon to celebrate the anniversary of its coming into force.

Commons *Debates*, 3 May 1869, 163

Here, so early, and at the heart of government, was an inauspicious sign for the future of the new federation. As with cancellation in 2009 of a plan to re-enact the battle of the Plains of Abraham, silence rather than celebration in 1869 seemed the better response to mark another momentous event in Canadian history.[1] Dominion (later Canada) Day did evolve into a holiday to mark the achievement of Confederation, though not until Canada's centennial could it be said that July 1 had superseded May 24 (Queen Victoria's birthday) as the undisputed date of national celebration. The eclipse of Empire, but more particularly agreement on a substitute form of symbolic representation, was a long time coming.

The undefined 'parties ... not much in love with Confederation' was a masterful statement of ambiguity, allowing wide latitude for inclusion of disaffected citizens, but also provinces. In the 1860s the outlier in this second category was Nova Scotia, whose support for Confederation was eventually and grudgingly acquired through the offer of a seat in cabinet for Joseph Howe and 'better (financial) terms.' In the 1880s discontent in Nova Scotia went so far as to spawn a secessionist movement, but the idea of secession is not regionally specific. There are periods in the country's history when Canadians in the east, the west, and the centre have flirted with or, more seriously, contemplated this prospect. The idea that the terms of union may be redefined or that they are renegotiable reveals an attitude toward federalism that is unrepublican in the American sense of the term, but is embedded in the layered allegiance that is a feature of monarchy.[2]

This historical vignette, with its reference to the exchange of loyalty for money or political influence, is of a piece with another perspective, one that describes federalism as a '*burden* of integration and accommodation in our divided and multinational society.'[3] As important as these mechanistic or instrumental conceptions may be in describing the political architecture of a federation, they are bloodless when it comes to communicating life in a federal system. Speaking of Australia, but it could equally well be said of Canada, Campbell Sharman complains that 'federalism is often seen as a narrow set of rules externally imposed on the political process instead of a formal expression of the diversity of social and political relationships that characterise … society. Because this diversity is lived through rather than thought about, the importance of the states [and provinces] in the political process is consistently underrated.'[4]

There can be no more familiar graphic depiction of Canadian federalism than the obligatory official photograph of first ministers arranged, by date of their province's entry into Confederation, as a stiff frieze on either side of Canada's prime minister. (When they meet, date of entry determines the order of speaking too, a convention that obtains even when the federal government is absent, as at the Confederation for Tomorrow Conference, chaired by Ontario premier John Robarts in 1967.) The same might be said of any arrangement of flags or floral emblems. In the Garden of the Provinces and Territories in Ottawa there is a minor variation on this ordering: the Canadian flag (on a taller flagpole than the rest) is surrounded by the flags of the four original provinces at one corner of the garden, while the six remaining provincial flags are grouped in another corner. The three territorial flags stand to one side. Along a wall on one other side, the floral emblems are displayed in the accepted order.

Perhaps too much may be made of symbolic representation of the units of the federation. Yet flags stir emotion in Canada: the great Maple Leaf flag debate of the 1960s; the question of whether to retain and, if so, when to display the Union Jack; the gigantic Maple Leaf flag displayed by the 'no' supporters in Dominion Square in Montreal on the eve of the 1995 Quebec referendum on sovereignty; or the flag of Louis Riel's provisional government flown at Fort Garry in 1869. The list of possible illustrations is longer than this. James Tully concurs in the importance of symbols: 'It is as if a person thought that "My Canada *includes* Quebec" and "Aboriginal government *within* Canada" were perspectiveless phrases that did not dispose us to one view rather than another – when in fact the subordination has already been accomplished ... The seating at First Ministers' Conferences seems to confirm this.'[5]

In the separate and coordinate worlds of Whearean federalism, why does the federal government command centre stage? Is there not, despite what the theorists say, an assumption that the constitution of political knowledge in a federation, reflected in the ordering of people and symbols, is hierarchical? Or, to put it in Tully's words: 'Canada appears to be a thing over and above the members that fit into it.' To the obdurate provinces, Pierre Trudeau used to ask: 'Who speaks for Canada?' Yet today, this question has an antiquated ring, for despite what the politicians might think, federalism is about more than governments and their relations. And this is true not only – and perhaps, not even mainly – because of the influence of the Charter with its emphasis on rights and freedoms.

It would be unwise in this study to embark on a postmodernist discussion of the decline of the grand narrative and the rise of the autonomous self. Still, somebody should make the attempt, for Canada's great national projects are confined to the past: the end of Empire, the end of western settlement, the end of wartime mobilization, and the end of postwar economic and social innovation, along with lowered expectations for unity through bilingualism, free trade and Mulroney, the Charter and Trudeau, national medical care and Pearson, 'unhyphenated Canadianism' and Diefenbaker, nation building (for example, the admission of Newfoundland as a province) and St Laurent – such ambitious goals and policies have disappeared, in part for reasons unique to Canada but also, in part, for reasons common to countries throughout the western world.

One way of explaining what has happened is to say that there has been a cultural revolution, in two senses of the term: an overturning of traditional values but also a displacement of other values by the cultural. Marriage, divorce, abortion, pornography, and more are no longer the preserve of state, church, or family to prescribe or proscribe. What was once public and proclaimed from outside is now private and determined by the individual. Conversely, what is the effect on government? When the public becomes private, what is a public duty? This shift in attitude and behaviour has major implications for the place of government in the lives of its citizens. Moreover, in a federation such as Canada's, where there is a single criminal code (as opposed to the United States, where there are fifty-one), the revolution in values alters the relationship between orders of government. This is for two reasons: first, Parliament has less control than it once did of these matters (and less ability to control, as witness its failure to agree on a Criminal Code amendment to regulate the provision of abortion in place of the section struck down by the Supreme Court in 1988); and second, the personal and the cultural are, under the Canadian Constitution, largely the domain of the provinces. The question of jurisdiction is highly relevant here, but so too is something else – churches, trade unions, voluntary associations, educational organizations, and many other groups are provincially based. The churches and equality groups campaigned for – or against – changes in the legal definition of marriage. The same organizations, along with others, have taken a leading role in advocating on behalf of the homeless and the hungry.

The list is long but the point is simple: the provinces (and the municipalities, which in Canada are creatures of the provinces) are the site of increasing activity in the quest for policies and laws that take the individual as their object of concern. Some of this activity is generated by innovations in provincial policy. An example would be human rights commissions and tribunals, which after 1945 became the accustomed method across Canada for dealing with human rights grievances. Claims of discrimination for reasons of race, religion, and sexual orientation, among others, promoted publicity, controversy, and associational activity – all within the province. The tribunal, rather than the court, as the choice of instrument led, in the words of an Ontario report, to 'human rights legislation [being] concerned less with punishment than with attempting to win the offender to the community consensus.'[6] Effecting a settlement rather than settling a score was the objective. Since so much of politics toward the end of the twentieth century turned on matters of rights and entitlements, the influence of this mode of resolution cannot be ignored.

Nor *should* it be ignored, for another reason. In a paper titled 'Parliament, Meetings, and Civil Society,' Australian scholar Judith Brett has noted that

neither in top level negotiations between companies, nor in settling community disputes do most people abide by formal rules based on parliamentary procedure. Changes in both the form of meetings, from formal and adversarial to informal and consensual ... have weakened the threads which once tied the general community to its parliament ... From the perspective of those experienced with the modern, informal meeting and its consensual means of reaching a decision, parliamentary procedure is no longer seen as enabling but as precluding cooperative action.[7]

Associational activity takes place within the unit (province, state, or canton) of a federation. When the subject of concern to an association is clearly federal, such as a matter that falls under the Criminal Code in Canada, the distance between citizen and government – already wide – requires substantial information, money, and energy to bridge. Brett's thesis – that '"the parliamentarisation" of associational life ... is now on the wane' – further separates the citizen from government by adding a psychological dimension to the institutional one. *Robert's Rules of Order*, or some similar guide (Brett cites several procedural manuals) made the club the essential unit of society and politics in the English-speaking world – even children formed them, in order 'to rehearse the skills and forms of adult life.' Such a desire to imitate has declined.

What is the implication of the individualization of politics for federalism and the constitution in Canada? One answer is that it 'flattens' federalism, because it contradicts the implicit assumption of a federal–provincial hierarchy. Yet in this effect, new circumstances abet the existing order. Associational life in the provinces has always been more complex and of greater moment for the practice of federalism than often acknowledged. For example, and in the words of Peter W. Hogg: 'Regulation of professions and trades typically takes the form of restrictions on entry, coupled with rules of conduct, which often include fee-setting, and administration by a governing body. Such regulation ... comes within property and civil rights in the province.'[8] This is true whether the subject is, for instance, realtors, electricians, engineers, pharmacists, lawyers, or doctors; and has been true since the beginning of the federation, though probably more visible in the prairie provinces, which began life *de novo* after their territorial era, than in those provinces, like Nova Scotia, whose constitutional base predated Confederation. W.F.A. Turgeon, Saskatchewan's second attorney general, illustrated the point in a speech outlining 'the problem confronting the first government of the newly created province. The government must not only administer the affairs of the province, but it must create the machinery with which

to administer ... He recited a number of governmental measures show-
ing the effort being made to establish the communal life of the people
on a sound basis.'[9] Here was the foundation being laid for Lipset's later
theory of Saskatchewan's distinctive community organization.

Self-regulation of professions is a long-standing practice in the
Anglo-American world. In Canada, as Hogg notes, but in the United
States and Australia too, the legal framework for professions is set by
the unit governments. The growth of the professions and of professionalism, as well as the related expansion of demand for education, is an
important dimension of Canadian federalism today. Two examples –
law and medicine – substantiate this assertion.

Law is provincial in multiple ways: law schools are established in and
by a province; students who attend these schools come overwhelmingly from within that province; articles are normally taken at firms within
the province; in turn, lawyers practise within the province; and it is
from their ranks that judges for the courts of the province are chosen.
Provincial jurisdiction and provincial jurisprudence ensure that provincial law societies, if not hermetic, are administratively worlds apart
from one another. Yet in practice, how separate are they? In what way
are they twined by the presence of a single Criminal Code and, now, by
the Canadian Charter of Rights and Freedoms? In sum, to what extent
does the legal system in Canada promote or suppress provincialism?

While there *may* be more interprovincial mobility among those seeking a career in medicine than in law, the provincial base of medicine
replicates that of law. Instead of law societies there are provincial colleges of physicians and surgeons, which have, among other powers, the
discretion to limit or deny hospital privileges to doctors. The doctors'
strike in Saskatchewan in 1962 and the importation of British doctors to
fill the void provided an opportunity for that province's College of Physicians and Surgeons to exercise its professional regulatory powers for
a time in some communities in just such a way. Since the introduction of
a national medical care program in the 1960s, which, in the words of a
former Saskatchewan minister of health (Allan Blakeney), 'has become
a badge of our common citizenship,' the tension between the national
program on the one hand and its provincial administration on the other
has grown.[10] Few subjects in Canada have been as thoroughly studied
as health care, while at the same time remaining as consistently controversial. Often the source of that controversy is a demand from the provinces for more money to support the medical services the provinces

provide. The financial dimension of medicare is enormous, expanding and a continual cause of federal–provincial strife.[11]

But there are other reasons why health care is so contentious: excessive waiting times for services covered by the public health system; prohibitions on the purchase of private health insurance for these same services; resistance to establishing private health providers in the provinces; unequal access to legalized abortions in a hospital after approval of a therapeutic abortion committee; street clinics for the treatment of heroin addiction; and much more. What is clear from this list, and from other items that might be added to it, is the intimate and personal nature of the matters it includes. Here, more than any other topic one might suggest, is a matter that interweaves federalism and the constitution – and the individual Canadian. The cliché that all politics is personal is usually repeated in the context of how politicians behave; it applies at least as well to how individuals behave. The personal and the provincial intersect because the constitution foresaw that they should; when necessary, that juncture may be the first step toward engaging the federal dimension as well. The story of how Canada became one of the first countries to legalize same-sex marriage illuminates this path. At the same time, that subject offers support for the claim made by Lisa Miller that 'remnants of activity remain on the levels at which they originated even as issues have migrated across levels.'[12] Evidence of the validity of that observation can be found in the decision of the government of Saskatchewan in 2009 to ask its Court of Appeal 'to give its opinion on two legislative options that would exempt at least some marriage commissioners from "marrying" a same sex couple if such a marriage is against their religious beliefs.'[13] In brief, there is a legislative echo in federal systems of government.

A familiar theme in the literature of federalism posits the units of the federation as laboratories for policy experimentation. 'No fault' insurance would be one example, though other examples are so plentiful as to throw doubt on the utility of the proposition itself. In fact, imitation has not been limited to provinces. Manitoba, for instance, copied the Australian practice of using independent electoral boundaries commissions to draw the boundaries of its provincial constituencies. Later, Parliament and the other provinces followed suit. The laboratory analogy is not wrong, but it offers little in the way of explanation. More fruitful is to think of experimentation and innovation as demonstrations of the habit of federalism, that is, of the creative potential of the provinces.

The provinces or, more accurately, people in the provinces have been unusually productive in promoting movements on behalf of social reform: temperance, prohibition, and the female franchise early in the last century; resistance to discrimination based on sex, race, and religion in this century. The churches, particularly Protestant denominations committed to promoting the social gospel, were especially active in the twentieth-century campaigns. The Roman Catholic Church and adherents of evangelical faiths have adopted strong positions against alteration to the definition of marriage in this century. From the perspective of this study, the important point to note is that the churches themselves were provincially based, though the mainline denominations were often organized into a federated structure. A case in point is the United Church of Canada: founded in 1925 as a result of union of the Methodist, Congregational, and a large portion of the Presbyterian churches, it is divided into thirteen 'conferences'; some, such as the Saskatchewan conference, comprise only a single province. Coterminous or near-coterminous boundaries in this matter – but also in quite different ones, such as business organizations, service clubs, and sports leagues – reinforce the provincial base and outlook of what might be called the federalism of small things to an extent seldom analysed in the literature on federalism.

This same line of argument – the development of parallel provincial organizations – was used by J.A. Corry to advance the proposition that there was in Canada in the 1950s a 'nationalizing of sentiment.'[14] In the United States, where the same thesis received publicity, two contributing factors usually offered for its occurrence were expansion of the mass media and arrival of an affluent consumer society. However, according to historian Margaret Prang, Corry 'identified welfare, trade union, business, agricultural, and educational elites, whose influence he believed was proving to be decisive in tipping Canadian opinion in favour of strong leadership from Ottawa.'[15] No evidence was offered to support the claim that the direction of influence was from province to nation – a surprising assertion in any case since jurisdiction in the five listed areas is so strongly provincial. Within less than a decade, a new interpretation of Canadian federalism disputed Corry's attribution of federal predominance, a reversal of fortune in which Prang herself appeared to concur: 'The increased power of provincial governments has fostered the growth of provincial branches of national organizations and has heightened the influence of regional and provincial networks.'[16]

What this chapter calls the habit of federalism clearly predates the period that Corry and Prang were speaking of. Arguably, absent that recognition and knowledge, it is not possible to explain some of the most extraordinary features of the Canadian political system. One obvious example is the rise and longevity of third parties in western Canada, such as the United Farmers of Alberta and Social Credit in Alberta, the Co-operative Commonwealth Federation in Saskatchewan, and the United Farmers of Manitoba. More apposite to the present discussion is the experience with third parties in three provinces that are often treated as part of a unity – the prairies. That common experience produced – and still does, if the recent history of the Reform Party is acknowledged – wildly different versions of politics, as practised within each province and in relationships with the federal government.

As noted in the previous chapter, the Social Credit series, published by the University of Toronto Press between 1950 and 1959, set out to explain the distinctiveness of Alberta politics, which was evident long before the Second World War. One of those volumes is W.E. Mann's *Sect, Cult, and Church in Alberta*.[17] The title indicates the importance of charismatic religion to the rise of Social Credit in Alberta – William Aberhart, Social Credit's first provincial leader, was the founder of the Calgary Prophetic Bible Institute – but Mann's choice of words also sets Alberta apart, religiously, from Saskatchewan, where the career of the leader of the CCF, T.C. Douglas, a Baptist minister, has been described by his biographers as *The Road to Jerusalem*,[18] and from Manitoba, where the biography of J.S. Woodsworth, a Methodist and then leader of the All People's Mission, is titled *A Prophet in Politics*.[19]

Comparative theology is not the issue here, but rather the location of the individual relative to the religious group and the group relative to the state or government. Nor is this a nonconformist concern only. The Roman Catholic principle of subsidiarity, a tenet of both Catholic philosophy and Quebec's view of federalism in the era before the Quiet Revolution, saw, in the words of the Tremblay Report, 'society as a complete organism into which Man is placed through the medium of institutions, groups and communities ... The role of the state [be it provincial or federal] is not to take the place of these natural groupings, but to help them achieve their purpose.'[20] More could be said of religion and Canadian federalism, beginning with constitutionally protected denominational schools, and moving on to the various means by which some current provincial governments provide support for faith-based education, or the intricate arrangements those same governments (or their predecessors) have employed to integrate religious colleges into public universities, or the role played by denominations in the education of Aboriginal children through residential schools, or the contribution since Confederation of Roman Catholic hospitals in the provision of health care across the country.

With the exception of residential schools, the sphere of jurisdiction involved in the foregoing activity is provincial, though that phrase needs to be used with caution. Jurisdiction is not the same as government, and by and large, voluntary organizations, whether their purpose is spiritual or sport, are private organizations. The residential schools exception may itself be a distinction without a difference. Section 91(24) of the Constitution Act, 1867, states that Parliament has legislative authority in the matter of 'Indians, and lands reserved for Indians.' Yet despite that apparent monopoly of authority, 'Canadian Indian policy' became, in the words of Alan Cairns, 'a classic case of state-sponsored fragmentation,'[21] evident, for instance, in the provincial base and focus of much of Aboriginal organization. The class action lawsuits launched on behalf of former residents, who claim to have suffered abuse while attending the schools, are provincial, since what is at issue is a tort. Because victims lived in several provinces, a unified settlement was deemed desirable; nonetheless, that settlement required the approval of each of the provinces.

Phrases excerpted from the titles of two publications, one in history and the other political science, on occasion have been used to describe provincial life. These are 'limited identities' and 'small worlds.'[22] While in their own context there may be justification for these attributions, as all-purpose descriptions they mislead. For those who live in Alberta, or Quebec, or Newfoundland and Labrador, or any other province, these are not small worlds, but *their* worlds. School, work, and recreation are provincially defined – usually by one province, for the large majority of Canadians who remain in the province of their birth (or settlement, if they are immigrants). Of course, there has been large out-migration from such provinces as Saskatchewan and Newfoundland and Labrador, and large in-migration to British Columbia, Alberta, and Ontario, but once the migration is complete, the influences on life in the receiving province are substantially unaltered, though the quality may be different.

For the individual citizen, federalism and the Constitution of Canada, to the extent these affect quality of life, have historically been provincial matters, augmented since the Second World War by equalization, medicare, and a host of other transfer payments from the federal government to the provinces directly or to their residents. The qualifier 'historically' is essential to that general statement, because in the last half-century the federal government has come to play a more direct role in matters considered to fall to the provinces.

An illustration is sport. As a glance at the sports section of any daily newspaper will reveal, there is still, among other activities, midget baseball and fastball, lacrosse, hockey, and basketball leagues, each with its own provincial and regional divisions. These are the kindergartens for the big leagues, which have flourished in the last five decades as a result of the introduction of televised coverage of sports, supplemented by specialty cable channels, and even nighttime major league baseball – the first game in a World Series under lights took place in 1971. Politics has always been involved in sport, as in awarding franchises and constructing arenas. However, federalism, in the sense of promoting Canada abroad or unity at home through sport, is a development that begins in 1961 with the proclamation of the Fitness and Amateur Sport Act. A minister of state and a branch (initially of Health and Welfare) with the same name distributed funds, which in the first twenty-five years increased from a quarter-million to fifty million dollars: 'The majority of it was used by eighty-five national organizations to pay the salaries of their administrative directors and national coaches, to assist athletes in training, and to fund participation in national and international competition. Grants were also given to the provinces to develop community activities.'[23] After 1960, two considerations drove the federal government's sports policy: 'concern about national unity' and 'losses suffered by the Canadian hockey team in international matches, as well as the poor performance of Canada's Olympic teams.'[24] Half a century later, in 2008, the two goals had been joined. In the words of the chief executive of the Canadian Olympic Committee: 'It's one of the few things that unifies [sic] the nation, when we have an athlete standing on the podium, representing our country.'[25]

The contribution of sport toward projecting Canada's international personality as bilingual and multicultural deserves study, as does the linkage between that objective and the organization and financing of sport nationally and within the provinces. Other parts of that study would include such subjects as women and sport, as well as lotteries, gaming, and sport. These are topics beyond the focus of this chapter, except in one important respect: policies that seek to promote the participation of women in sport, or that direct the proceeds of lotteries

toward expanding athletic activity across the country, are just that –
policies, and, more to the point, policies that emanate from the federal
government for a purpose other than, or in addition to, the promotion
of sport. That is the political dimension to sport that before 1960 was
largely absent. In the context of the current discussion, the habit of federalism in regard to sport has become two-dimensional: on the one hand,
the contribution of the voluntary sector to the development of amateur
sport, and on the other hand, the federal government's ambition to use
sport to promote Canada to Canadians as well as to non-Canadians.

In these two guises – provincial and federal – and in the sequence
in which they appear, sport is not exceptional. Consider, for example,
culture, another subject that goes unmentioned in the Constitution
Act, 1867. The National Gallery, the Canadian Broadcasting Corporation, and the National Film Board apart, there were no national cultural
institutions, and certainly no sense of a national cultural policy, before
the federal government's response to the recommendations of the Royal Commission on Arts, Letters, and Sciences (popularly known as the
Massey Commission after the name of its chairman, Vincent Massey).[26]
These responses included the introduction of federal university grants,
the creation of the Canada Council as a funding agency for the arts, and
the introduction of television through the means of a public agency. The
era of the commission and its report coincided with a period of federal
dominance, explained in part by a continuation of a presumption of
federal priority created during the Second World War. In 1949 the federal government had acted unilaterally to amend Section 91(1) to include
a domestic amending formula for the 'Constitution of Canada,' except
for subjects found in Section 92 and in a handful of other areas. The
principal motivation for the commission's recommendations, referred
to throughout the report, was concern about excessive American influence on Canadian life and institutions. As well, the report made clear its
conviction that because of Canada's large size and sparse population,
only the federal government was in a position to meet the cultural challenge presented by the United States.

Within a decade what might be called the 'survival' rationale for
federal paramountcy in the field of culture did not disappear so much
as find itself reinterpreted as a means of projecting Canada's linguistic
and cultural distinctiveness. The Massey Commission was not opposed
to bilingualism, though the term was not then in use, but there is nothing in its report to serve as an indication of the fundamental change that
resulted with the introduction of a regime of official languages. One

way of explaining these events is to say that a bilingual veneer, applied by (and to) the federal government, gave Canada a new look. As with sport, the object was to present Canada, abroad and at home, as a different place. That statement is unsatisfactory, however, for it does not convey the originality of what was being attempted. The image of Canada, whose loyalties had long been associated with its position as the senior member of the Empire/Commonwealth, was reinterpreted singularly in Canadian terms. Notwithstanding what the critics of bilingualism said, that reinterpretation was about more than language, and certainly about more than a language policy forced on Canadians by the federal government.

In 1972 the Association of Universities and Colleges of Canada appointed the Commission on Canadian Studies with T.H.B. Symons, founding president of Trent University, as its chairman. That commission, which was asked to inquire into the condition of studies relating to Canada in Canadian universities, issued a report in 1975 under the title *To Know Ourselves*.[27] The title is enigmatic. On the one hand, as its 'rationale' the report offers the following statement: 'The most valid and compelling argument for Canadian studies is the importance of self-knowledge ... who we are; where we are in time and space.' On the other hand, it also says that 'before the quest for such knowledge can begin, an individual or a collectivity must first be conscious of being Canadian.'[28] Arguably, the tensions between these two statements parallel tensions found in Canadian federalism – Canada the sum versus its provinces the parts. Perhaps that formula is to be expected, since the focus of the report is on universities – teaching, research, and learning – matters that under the constitution fall to the provinces. There is even a chapter titled 'The Canadian Component in Education for the Professions,' in which 'universities and professional associations [are encouraged to] accept joint responsibility for ensuring that appropriate continuing education courses are available to professionals.' Reinforcing the argument made earlier in this chapter about professional self-regulation, the report proposes that 'each profession possessing licensing authority over its members should consider requiring ... comprehensive examinations, as a condition for continued professional practice.'[29]

The report is more than an exposition in self-discovery. The commission had a research staff and a research agenda whose influence was evident, for instance, in the chapter on the university curriculum, which occupied almost half the report. A section of that chapter is titled 'Some

Other Areas of Opportunity and Need for Canadian Studies in Curriculum Development.' Here is found a discussion of 'ethnic studies and Canadian cultural pluralism'; it notes that 'the implications [of ethnic studies] pervade almost every aspect of the study of Canadian society.' It also records 'a major initiative ... following the Prime Minister's speech on the subject of multiculturalism to the House of Commons on 8 October 1971' in the form of 'scholarly studies of some twenty ethnic groups ... commissioned by the Department of the Secretary of State.'[30] Self-knowledge may be the report's goal, but its imperative is to recognize, through the study of Canada, the country's multiple – not limited – identities.

*To Know Ourselves* depicts Canada neither as a British country, though those roots were formative to its development, nor as a bilingual country, though its bicultural history coupled with the recognition of official bilingualism in 1969 signalled a conception of Canada very different from that of the past. Instead, and in alignment with the previous discussion about the influence of international competition on the reconceptualization of sport in Canada, the report adopts a Canada-in-the-world stance, albeit with far broader ramifications than in the matter of sport:

> We have failed to make the point to others (and perhaps also to ourselves) that Canada is worth studying for itself; that our geography, history, government, institutions and way of life are distinct and fascinating; that a knowledge of Canada and of its problems can also be helpful to an understanding of other cultures and of the problems of other societies ... In fact, the regional, bilingual, multi-cultural and federal character of Canada, and the geographic and economic diversity of the country, make Canada an ideal subject for the study of many themes which have world-wide relevance and which offer vigorous intellectual challenges.[31]

The Symons Report, more than any other initiative, may be credited with promoting Canadian studies abroad, which thirty years later is a large enterprise of visiting professorships, journals, and newsletters. In fact, the object of the report – 'to know ourselves,' not as inheritors of another culture but as creators of a new one – becomes realizable most fully when we see ourselves as we wish others to see us, as ethnically diverse and culturally inclusive.

In the preceding paragraphs two different kinds of federalism call for notice. Each is defined by the direction of movement required by the participant. Thus, what might be called outward federalism describes the activities of individuals in their provinces who organize to effect some behaviour or policy on the part of the federal government. Churches and changes to the laws on divorce, marriage, or abortion are an example. Here the habit of federalism is from neighbourhood to nation, from congregation and club to Commons. Conversely, there is, for want of a better term, inward federalism, where the principle of the federation – which is not necessarily the same thing as the federal principle, as Wheare or other theorists might define it – arises from outside through the agency of the federal government. As already suggested, this may result through the conduct of foreign policy and the presentation of Canada to non-Canadians in terms approved by the federal government. However, it may arise in a domestic context as well. Indeed, as Susan Phillips has noted in a paper on the voluntary sector: 'In some cases, strong relationships between NGOs [non-governmental organizations] and the national government have developed where certain groups were identified as central to the promotion of a national identity.' As examples, she cites women, and minority language and multicultural groups, 'even though the policies and programs that most directly affect them are the primary responsibility of provincial governments.'[32] Rather than the habit of federalism flowing up from community to country, here it flows down from governor to governed.

This reversal in the course of federalism lies, along with other factors, at the base of complaints about official bilingualism and about 'a "Citizens' constitution" derived from the Charter and the new constitutional status and identities that it gives to Canadians in general, and to racial minorities, the disabled, official-language minorities, and others in explicit terms.'[33] While not uniquely of prairie provenance, opposition to a perceived special status for the French language, and for designated categories of Canadians, found support in Canada's 'fourth realm,' heavily populated a century earlier by immigrants from central and eastern Europe.

One instrumental, but no less fundamental, means of bridging the regional and linguistic cleavages of the Canadian federation has been through the practice of elite accommodation. With cabinet's composition serving as the Platonic ideal, every federal government board and commission has been appointed, by Order in Council, to reflect the composition of federation: one member from each province – with Ontario and Quebec perhaps having two members each – and in recent years, separate members for each of the three territories. Significantly, for the subject of this chapter, that composition is not limited to government bodies. In a new study *Language Matters: How Canadian Voluntary Associations Manage French and English*, editors (and authors) David Cameron and Richard Simeon set out to answer this question: 'How well do associations in the Canadian voluntary sector reflect, represent, and accommodate linguistic dualism in their structures, in their practices, and in the work they do?'[34] An introductory list of acronyms includes more than one hundred organizations, from Amnesty International to the YWCA, but the seven case studies examine language usage by sector, as in farm, business, and health, among others.

The 'inspiration' for this work was the study completed for the Royal Commission on Bilingualism and Biculturalism by John Meisel and Vincent Lemieux, *Ethnic Relations in Canadian Voluntary Associations*.[35] The object of the more recent work was to determine whether the disparities in the use of English and French – English invariably being privileged forty years ago – had moderated. The thesis states that 'voluntary associations are central elements in the constitution of "civil society" [which] is essential to a healthy democratic politics.'[36] Cameron and Simeon conclude that the associations examined in the book 'have been more innovative and flexible in redefining relationships than have the governments of Canada in their successive efforts at constitutional renewal.'[37] For example, the case studies discuss accommodation through, among other means, construction of associational executives, with careful attention paid to linguistic competence and balance, as well as through 'weighted voting proportional to the financial contribution of each province.'[38]

If *Language Matters* owes a theoretical debt to a study done for the B-and-B Commission, then that earlier research is under its own obligation – this time to the theory of consociational democracy, identified most particularly with the work of Arend Lijphart. As discussed in chapter 2, the transformation of the study of Canadian federalism is associated with the onset of the Quiet Revolution in Quebec and with the introduction of new theories of the political system that arrive in Canada with the return of Canadian-born, American-trained political scientists. Among those theories is consociational democracy, which, according to the subtitle of the best-known Canadian book on the subject, is about 'political accommodation in segmented societies.'[39] (As an aside: consociationalism is associated with politics in the Low Countries, where society is divided into so-called 'pillars,' defined by religion and social values. Historically, politics there has been about accommodating difference through elite negotiation. With the decline in Christian identities in the last forty years and their replacement by a policy of multiculturalism, in response to massive immigration from Muslim countries, the pillars in the Netherlands became 'polders.' Yet in the words of Ian Buruma, 'the spirit of negotiation and watery compromise' remained – a recipe, it transpired, for acts of extremism.[40] In Belgium too, according to Tony Judt, 'the old "pillars" are in decline, and for similar reasons.'[41])

Consociationalism as a subject of academic study in Canada has disappeared, in large part because national political parties, the principal instruments for accommodating territorially based differences in the country – their so-called brokerage function – have themselves ceased to command national electoral support. The lasting effect of consociational democracy as a theory of Canadian politics rests in the conception that Canada is a 'segmented' society. From the time of Confederation, religious and linguistic differences had been recognized, along with growing regionalism in the wake of western settlement. Cabinet formation, as well as recruitment to the civil service, from Macdonald onward testified to this reality. But the national two-party system and, more crucially, the plurality electoral system rewarded pre- rather than post-election negotiation, thus discouraging the concept of segmentation. The provinces – those spheres of federalism – should take care of that, if acknowledgment were needed.

The Quiet Revolution in Quebec and the federal policy of two official languages across the country – especially in the federal bureaucracy – changed that perception. Paradoxically, bilingualism, which was intended to remove the barrier of language that French-speaking Canadians had long encountered outside Quebec, created a new cleavage. The 1996 Census revealed that 'less than 7 percent of Anglophones outside of Quebec were bilingual.'[42] How the large remaining, unilingual majority was to see itself in relation to national politics, where words had literally become instruments of government, remained unspecified but not, in truth, unprecedented. The whirligig of time that in the mid-nineteenth century had seen Canada West move, because of the large influx of immigrants, from being over- to under-represented in the legislature of the Parliament of United Canada (with its equal number of seats for each of the two sections), was now to be repeated in regard to language.

Prompted by questions about his experience in the federal bureaucracy, Escott Reid recalled, in 1970, its once exclusive character:

[Senior civil servants] were a pretty homogeneous group. They were all, I believe, WASPs or from WASP families even if, like Norman Robertson, they professed no religion. I think that ... almost all went to public schools, not private schools, and came from middle-class families. My guess is that of the dozen only two had any fluency in French, and that only two had lived in the Province of Quebec for more than a few months. There are, of course, no French Canadians in the group, no women, and, I think, no Roman Catholics. This was a group of people unrepresentative of Canada.

(It is interesting to speculate how much more limited would be the influence of a group of this kind in Ottawa today.)

But what is more significant ... is how far this homogeneity, this unrepresentativeness of Canada enabled these ... civil servants to accomplish what they did and disqualified them from accomplishing more.

Their task was facilitated by the special relations which they developed with the Liberal cabinet ministers in the unbroken period of Liberal rule from 1935 to 1957 and to the weakness of the House of Commons in this period and the weakness of the provinces, perhaps mainly because the depression and the war and the problems of the immediate post-war period concentrated power in Ottawa and in an inner group of cabinet ministers and senior civil servants in Ottawa.[43]

The world Reid describes is of a Canada before the Official Languages Act and before the Constitution Act, 1982, whose Section 16 entrenches English and French as the country's official languages. Section 133 of the Constitution Act, 1867, protected use of the two languages in legislatures and courts but said nothing of the bureaucracy, for the reason implicit in Reid's comment: government touched the lives of comparatively few citizens, at least until the expansion of social programs after 1945. Entrenching language rights reflected not only the practical need people now had to deal with government, but also the heightened awareness of fundamental rights, which in Canada extended to the languages of what the B-and-B Commission terms of reference called the two founding races.

As already noted in chapter 3, this reference to *two* founding races raised opposition to bilingualism on the prairies from immigrants (and their descendants) from central and eastern Europe who had arrived in Canada before the First World War. Also, it did not take account of the great waves of immigrants, mainly to central Canada, after the Second World War. According to the 2006 census, 47 per cent of the population of Metropolitan Toronto was born outside Canada. This makes Canada's most populous city as multicultural as the Netherlands, more multicultural than the United States, and less culturally fragile than either. Canadian cities – 40 per cent of Vancouver's population is foreign-born – demonstrate that 'a community and its core institutions can not only survive a massive and growing immigrant population but thrive with one.'[44] It is a matter that deserves serious study – elsewhere, however – whether the decline of Canada's once dominant Anglo-Protestant culture, the passage of the Official Languages Act followed by entrenchment of that principle in the Constitution, the adoption of a policy of multiculturalism, the failure to emulate in fact (as opposed to discuss in theory) consociational democratic practices found in segmented societies, the presence of a large Aboriginal population, and recognition of that presence in Canada today and in the past – whether these features account for Canada's success as a modern state.

A striking feature of Canada, when compared to the United States, is not only that the former is less homogeneous than the latter but also that throughout history homogeneity has been awarded less value in the former than in the latter – to talk of a Canadian way of life is invariably to court dissent from some region or group. 'First among our national goals, the prerequisite to all others ...,' said Lester Pearson in 1964, 'is national unity. That does not mean and cannot mean uniformity.'[45] Conversely, when Canada is compared to the Netherlands, the impressive point to note is how much more unified yet individualistic Canada – a behemoth of a country – is than the miniature segmented lowland state.

For a Canadian to describe his society as a success risks eliciting the charge of hubris. Still, Canada has experienced, in an amazingly short period of time, massive demographic and societal change with less overt tension as a result than many other countries. Of the foregoing reasons offered in explanation of this transformation, one not mentioned but relevant is the relationship between federalism and the constitution. Enough has been said in earlier chapters on the 'novel' constitution and 'parliamentary federalism' to suggest that the political condition of Canada is defined by its ambiguities, of which the following may be cited as illustrations: a federal union with 'a Constitution similar in Principle' to that of the world's most famous unitary state; a monarchy that is 'federalized'; a constitution that is a composite of common, civil, and codified criminal law; and the principle of legislative supremacy associated with an entrenched Charter of Rights and Freedoms. Literary theorist Harold Bloom once said that 'Shakespeare invented us'; borrowing that aphorism, it could be said that 'federalism makes us Canadians.'

Unlike some federal systems, Confederation was a Victorian creation for an imperial dependency, albeit one with substantial autonomy. Partly because of this colonial provenance, the act of union for the British North American colonies omitted a formula for its amendment other than by the Parliament at Westminster. Absent that formula but protected by the imperial Parliament, the procedures of the Canadian federation might have been rigorous, still they were never rigid. Political settlement became the basis for constitutional agreement, with the result that a change in government could have enormous secondary implications, such as a change in culture, attitude, and belief. A compelling case in support of this assertion was the second Trudeau government, elected in 1980. This was the government that patriated the constitution with a domestic amending formula and that introduced the Canadian Charter of Rights and Freedoms. The Constitution Act, 1982, should have been the act of constitutional completion. Yet as discussed in chapter 6, that did not happen, largely because of the rigid amending formula the Act established.

Instead, Section 43, which provides for a 'some but not all provinces' procedure, carries on the Canadian tradition of constitutional adaptability, a custom unaltered, it would appear, by recent events:

> It is remarkable that at the height of the tension over the Quebec Secession Reference case, the supposedly inflexible federal government and the supposedly intractable Parti Québécois government were able to come to a common view on the amendment of one of the two historic guarantees of the Constitution Act, 1867 directly applicable to Quebec, section 93 on education and denominational schools, and the amendment was made through the concurrence of the Senate and the House of Commons of Canada and the National Assembly of Quebec.[46]

Federalism as a matter of governments – federal and provincial; federalism as a matter of the two official languages; federalism as a matter of one government (the federal) promoting the identity and interests of selected (for instance, minority language) groups of Canadians for national purposes; or federalism as a matter of the provinces, together or singly, and their residents seeking better terms, new or improved or different policies from the federal government – all of these interchanges or exchanges provide context for the habit of federalism to evolve. Yet except for the relations between governments, the discussion of federalism that dominates the Anglo-American literature does little to illuminate the complexities of life in federal societies, nor does it take account of how varied that life is and how greatly and quickly it may change within one federal system.

Federalism is about more than theories, or governments and politics, or courts and jurisdictions. For every Canadian citizen who resides in a province, it is about myriad concerns: school curricula, licensing and insuring a motor vehicle, achieving some recognized level of certification for employment, enforcing maintenance orders, securing a provincial health card, and much, much more. Except on rare occasions, federal life is all interior. Yet at one level it is also solidly concrete. Most Canadian cities still have representative examples of the work of the Chief Architect's Branch of the Department of Public Works, whose greatest influence on the built environment occurred in the three decades before the First World War.[47] There are the former red-brick post offices, now devoted to some other use, immediately recognizable by their clock towers; there are armouries, drill halls, and customs buildings. All announced the federal presence in towns and cities from coast to coast, particularly in western Canada before 1914, where communities were simultaneously being created. Similarly, 'wartime housing,' the thirty thousand houses built during and after the Second World War, first under the Wartime Housing Corporation and later the Central (then Canadian) Mortgage and Housing Corporation, dot the urban landscape across the country. Again, most centres have a structure, such as an auditorium or hockey rink, that commemorates Canada's centennial in 1967.

Buildings have functions. The imposing red-brick, crenellated armoury in Regina is the home of the Royal Regina Rifles; its Hamilton counterpart is the home of the Royal Hamilton Light Infantry (Wentworth Regiment). The examples could easily be multiplied. The relationship between the military and federalism is not arcane, though it is rarely discussed in political science texts, unless in the context of the conscription crises of the two world wars. The military and defence are matters of federal jurisdiction (Section 91(7) of the Constitution Act, 1867). Yet men and women join the reserve or regular forces in their local communities, where those forces have deep historical roots. Proof to substantiate that statement lies in Remembrance Day ceremonies held at cenotaphs in the heart of towns and cities across the country. Re-enacted locally each year, before larger and larger audiences, and in company with the service from the National War Memorial in Ottawa, broadcast nationwide in French and English, the quintessentially federal matter of the military is recast in sentiments that are also personal, local, and provincial.

# 8 Conclusion

For an outsider, particularly a Canadian, the most striking feature of government in the United States is that its federal system reinforces its constitution, which is to say that the principle of each seeks to disperse power and institutions. The term 'checks and balances' is often employed to describe the countervailing influence of governmental institutions in the United States, though it appears nowhere in the United States Constitution. Nonetheless, the different terms of office for senators, congressmen, and the president and vice-president, the requirement for super-majorities (as in the case of treaty adoption), the presidential veto, and congressional override of that veto offer support for the proposition that – in the absence of strong party discipline – American politics is directed toward achieving a succession of agreements to secure passage of legislation. When to this arrangement is added the composition of the Electoral College and the assignment of equal state representation in the United States Senate, the incorporation of state voices in the institutions of the national government reinforces the metaphor of balance.

Once again, K.C. Wheare's dictum that 'the federal principle has come to mean what it does because the United States has come to be what it is' is singularly unilluminating when the subject at hand is the contribution of institutional balance to the well-being of the Canadian constitution. This is for the straightforward reason that there is no institutional balance in the Canadian constitution. One way of apotheosizing the difference between the two North American federations is to say that federalism in the United States lies in the legislative branch and in Canada in the executive branch. That terminology is preferable to saying that Canada has executive federalism, since that term has a specific, intergovernmental meaning. Instead, 'federalism in the executive branch' puts the emphasis where it is needed, on the prime minister and his monopoly of appointment power beginning (but not ending) with cabinet ministers drawn by convention from the different provinces of Canada.

It is the case, and needs to be acknowledged, that there is a literature that takes as its theme the desirability of political balance in Canada, but the subject is not institutional balance within the constitution – at least not until recently, when concern has been expressed about the decline in political accountability in a system of prime ministerial government. Instead, the idea of balance in Canadian politics has traditionally been reserved for reference to the relationship between the centrifugal and centripetal forces of federalism. More than half a century ago, W.P.M. Kennedy amplified the idea when he spoke of 'delicate balancings.'[1] But he and, more recently, R.C. Vipond are concerned about a balanced division of power between the central and provincial jurisdictions. The reason for the concern was, in the words of David Mills, 'to enable the different Governments to carry on their functions independentally [sic] and without interference.'[2] In short, the motivation was to give responsible government a chance, an opportunity denied it in the perpetual search for balance required to govern the province of United Canada. J.E. Hodgetts has written that 'from the administrative point of view [Union] was only skin deep.'[3] But from almost any other perspective the conclusion would be the same. For this historical reason the concept of balance in politics – as well as its cognate, coalition – had a bad reputation in post-Confederation Canada. In contrast, the dissolution of the Union dissolved French-English antipathy; or, stated positively, federalism rescued Canada's founding relationship.

There is another 'federal' dimension to the concept of balance, but it is one that is insufficiently explored in the study of Canadian politics. Christopher Dunkin's description of the 1867 federation as 'the three kingdoms' deserves further attention. It projects a sense of territorial harmony (and institutional, if the original composition of the Senate is recalled) that disappeared once the federation expanded westward. Indication of the first government's lack of clarity on the structure of the transcontinental state it was in the process of creating may be found in Macdonald's address to the House when introducing the Manitoba Act, 1870: 'It [is] not a matter of great importance whether the province shall be called a province or a territory. We have Provinces of all sizes, shapes and constitutions ... so that there [can]not be anything determined by the use of the word.'[4]

The area of Manitoba, as set down in the 1870 statute, was minute, compared to what the province was to become, or compared to most other jurisdictions then or later. That of course was of no consequence. The Manitoba Act was a political response to an immediate problem – the Riel uprising – with no thought given to the legislation's import for the federation, then or later. The four provinces that were to occupy the western territory did not possess the political, or economic, or cultural, or geographical unity that characterized in some respect each of Dunkin's kingdoms, and without that unity there could never be the harmony that Dunkin professed to see among the original members of Confederation. A quarter of a century ago, the cry was heard: 'The West Wants In.' But the strategy for inclusion, when it was revealed by the newly created Reform Party, championed provincial equality, a proposition the Fathers of Confederation rejected in the design they agreed upon for the new federal Canada.

Nor was the Macdonald government unique in introducing policies that appeared bereft of any theory of federalism. The Liberal government of Sir Wilfrid Laurier followed Macdonald's precedent in Manitoba in 1870 by withholding the transfer of natural resources to the new provinces of Alberta and Saskatchewan in 1905. Harold Innis was later to argue that this decision better deserved the label feudal than federal. In contrast to the principle of equal states set forth in the United States in the Northwest Ordinance of 1787 and hallowed in practice thereafter, Sir Robert Borden, in the absence of any theoretical justification, added vastly to the size of Ontario, Quebec, and Manitoba, when in 1912 his government transferred large portions of the North-West Territories to those provinces. According to Peter Onuf, from the founding of the Union the central measure of federalism in the United States was the equality principle, though he acknowledged that the meaning of that principle altered over time: at the beginning, states were 'measured directly against each other according to their relative size, population, or power.' After the Civil War, 'comparisons were ... made in a vertical framework: how did the states compare to each other in relation to federal authority?'[5] But in both instances the test was to promote republican government in company with the growth of the federation.

In the United States the constitution and the federation, treated as equals, were joined as one, a union the Civil War proved indissoluble.

At no time was this – that is, equivalency between the constitution and federation – the case in Canada. On the contrary, there was no theory of federalism in Canada to restrain the practice of using the constitution to alter the federation. Land, resources, and declaratory statements, among other means, have been employed by governments to promote some view of what this book refers to as either vertical or horizontal federalism. The motion passed by the House of Commons in November 2006 that 'recognizes that the Québécois form a nation within a united Canada' is one example. Two years later at celebrations to mark the four hundredth birthday of Quebec City, the prime minister, Stephen Harper, elaborated on his government's understanding of the significance of this motion: 'Passing the Quebec nation resolution was an act of recognition and reconciliation. Our government will take appropriate steps of recognition and accommodation where they're appropriate. For instance, we gave Quebec special representation at UNESCO, which is a world cultural organization. These are all the things we have done to strengthen Quebec's place in Canada.'[6]

International recognition of Quebec is a complicated story – with parallels to Canada's own search for acknowledgment as a political personality separate from the British Empire after 1918. In any event it is not directly relevant to the issue of reconfiguring the federation through resort to the constitution by means other than formal amendment. One that is, is the Constitutional Amendments Act, 1996 (S.C. 1996, c. 1), which at the initiative of the Chrétien Liberal government restored Quebec's constitutional veto, after the Supreme Court of Canada had found that no such veto existed. Whether Quebec should have a special role in amendments is not the issue here. Rather it is the government's unilateral decision, party discipline being the weapon it is in Canada's Parliament, to alter the arrangement of constitutional power as it affects the federation. To describe the 1996 Act as 'little short of a constitutional coup d'état by the Prime Minister' is perhaps extreme, or perhaps not.[7] The Clarity Act, 2000 (S.C. 2000, c. 26), which set conditions to assess a successful referendum's outcome on the question of secession of a province, is a third illustration. The parliamentary motion of 2006 and the statutes of 1996 and 2000 deal with Quebec and cultural federalism, but the Canadian disposition to bend the constitution to serve the needs of federalism in general is not restricted to a single province. The best-known demonstration to support that statement is the notwithstanding clause (Section 33) of the Canadian Charter of Rights and Freedoms, whereby an act or sections of an act of Parliament or the legislature of a province may be declared to operate notwith-standing certain sections of the Charter.

Federalism at the constitution's expense: John A. Macdonald would have something to say about that proposition, especially about the con-tribution made by the Judicial Committee of the Privy Council. Are there contrary examples, the constitution's benefiting at the expense of federalism? Yes, there are – and the courts again have been important determiners of that outcome. Consider, for instance, the SCC's opinion in *Reference re Ownership of Offshore Mineral Rights* (1968), in which it decided that 'the right to explore and exploit mineral resources in the seabed lying under the territorial waters and Continental Shelf adjacent to British Columbia was vested exclusively in Canada.'[8] Consider too the thesis, discussed in chapter 6, that the pan-Canadian rights guar-anteed in the Charter make small allowance for the diversities that federalism is intended to promote or protect. Or, a somewhat similar transfiguring argument that says: '"Canadian" values ... enabl[e] us to transcend the issues that constantly divide us (language, ethnic origin, etc.).'[9]

Federalism at the expense of the constitution, or the constitution at the expense of federalism: Which is it? The SCC has not answered this question, though its opinion, as stated in the *Secession Reference*, is that 'in interpreting our Constitution, the courts have always been concerned with the federalism principle, inherent in the structure of our constitutional arrangements, which has from the beginning been the lodestar by which the courts have been guided.'[10] More than that, as constitutional scholar John Whyte has noted, the Court has been con-sistent in its position:

> For the Supreme Court it [is] the principle of federalism – the division of governmental powers between the national government and the provinc-es – not the principle of bi-nationalism rooted in the two founding settler communities that [is] of primary constitutional significance. The Supreme Court ... made this choice in its 1981 decision in the *Patriation Reference* in setting out the constitutional convention of requiring some level of provin-cial consent in making requests to the United Kingdom for amendment. It reiterated that choice in the *Quebec Veto* case when it rejected Quebec's claim that its dissent should stop implementation. And, it made the same choice in the *Secession Reference*.[11]

For the theory of Canadian federalism, if not for the Court, the challenge lies in there being two federalisms. The Court has said that federalism is the lodestar of the constitution. If that were simply so, there would be no need for parliamentary resolutions and motions to assure Quebec of its historic place in the Canadian federation. The fact is that the Court has chosen, perhaps been forced to choose, one variation of Canadian federalism. Governments and Parliament have, equally necessarily, emphasized another variation. Parliamentary federalism has proved inadequate to the constitutional task at hand, and the 'novel' constitution Lord Monck invoked in the Throne Speech of 1868 has grown more singular in consequence of the Constitution Act, 1982.

To the divided jurisdiction that all federal governments display, and to the double federation – cultural and territorial – that is so much part of Canada's identity, must be added a political–judicial duality that influences the course of public policy. A long-standing criticism of executive federalism – that intergovernmental relations are in the hands of first ministers – is that it is unaccountable to legislatures and through legislatures to the people. The crux of the charge is that in a rivalry between executives and legislatures, legislatures lose. It is not difficult to appreciate the nature of the problem or why, in an attempt to address it, plebiscites, referendums, citizens' assemblies, and other mechanisms of consultation have gained popular acceptance as means of introducing legitimacy. There are other reasons for distrust of executive federalism, or elite accommodation for that matter: these procedures and practices no longer accord with the 'authorized vision' communities have of themselves, 'however variegated [their] constitutional elements.'[12]

While doubtless valid, the indictment of executive federalism is by now predictable, and diversionary. The division that seriously affects the course of federalism and its relationship to the constitution in Canada today is less the executive versus the legislature than it is the political – politicians federal *and* provincial, executive *and* legislative – versus the non-political – the courts, the media, and the people. No dichotomy is ever pure; still, it is the political class that promotes and protects cultural federalism. There are different views of binationalism in Canada, and some in this category may oppose the concept outright. Yet cultural federalism depends upon political agreements, whether in the form of intergovernmental accords, parliamentary resolutions, or statutes. Notwithstanding special terms of entry into Confederation, or side deals and accords later to recognize what are claimed to be unique circumstances, territorial federalism depends less on politicians (as it once did when political parties were truly national) and more on the judiciary and the public to sustain it. The difficult, indeed imponderable, challenge for Canadian federalism occurs when the two perspectives collide. Here, for example, is one source of the conundrum of Senate reform: essential to the federal agreement in 1867, the Senate of Canada is not essentially federalist in its composition.

Writing to the William Shawn, editor of *The New Yorker*, in 1964, Edmund Wilson, who the following year would publish his book *O Canada: An American's Notes on Canadian Culture*,[13] lamented that 'I found the subject of Canada extremely difficult to handle, because the country itself is so uncoordinated, and it is so hard to present the French and the English sides in any unified way.' True, indeed: what 'sides,' how 'unified'? If, as Eugene Forsey commented at almost the same time, 'the problems of Canadian federalism ... are not, for the most part, problems of federalism at all, but of Canadian dualism,' where then is the centre that coordinates?[14]

During the age of constitutional conferences this was the nub of Forsey's argument, when he tirelessly warned politicians and the public against innovations in the federation based on 'bad law, bad constitutionalism, and bad political science' that could lead to 'hemi-demi-semi-separatism.'[15] The letter and spirit of the constitution are the armature of federalism. Because in his mind the two were intimately connected, to experiment with federal structures and practices without paying close attention to the effects such experiments would have on constitutional processes was dangerous. In 1990, Forsey titled his memoirs *A Life on the Fringe*.[16] This was an accurate description of his position in the four-decades-long quest for a resolution to Canada's federal dilemma. From the sidelines he warned politicians of the undesirable and unintended consequences of their (and their advisers') schemes. His was not the only voice, though it was the most audible. It would be an exaggeration to say that his opposition thwarted these plans. What it did was keep central the proposition that federalism and the constitution must be connected if either is to prosper. The practices of American federalism and of the constitution of the United States had, in his mind, little applicability to Canada, except in this essential respect: the constitution and federalism were not severable in that country, or in any other.

Nor was this binary relationship the cause of a crisis. Canada continued united, and individual Canadians continued to prosper. While it is true that when using the democratic audit 'benchmarks' of participation, inclusiveness, and responsiveness, the Canadian federation (and all other federations, it may be presumed) earn low marks, there could be no other outcome since federations are non-majoritarian in structure, with divided powers and jurisdiction.[17] In any case, perhaps this is the wrong test. More than a century ago, Lord Haldane, whose reputation in Canada derived from his leading role as a member of the JCPC, burnished his legal reputation when acting as co-counsel for the Scottish Free Church before the House of Lords. Subsequent to that event, says David Schneiderman, Haldane was 'quoted famously for having stated the "test of personal identity of this Church lies not in its doctrine but in its life."'[18] Laski described the argument as a 'brilliant effort.' Brilliant or otherwise, with emendation the proposition may be applied to the subject of this book: that is to say, the test of Canadian federalism lies not in federal theory but in the life of Canadians. The Constitution Act, 1867, is no fount of structural federalism, as a theorist might conceive it. Still, the promise of federalism, the freedom and prosperity envisioned by the Fathers of Confederation, has been realized, if at a cost, unanticipated as recently as fifty years ago, of stronger regional sentiment in all parts of the country.

# Notes

## Abbreviations

| | |
|---|---|
| AC | Appeal Court (Judicial Committee of the Privy Council) |
| APSR | *American Political Science Review* |
| CBR | *Canadian Bar Review* |
| CHR | *Canadian Historical Review* |
| CJEPS | *Canadian Journal of Economics and Political Science* |
| CJPS | *Canadian Journal of Political Science* |
| CPA | *Canadian Public Administration* |
| CPR | *Canadian Parliamentary Review* |
| DLAUC | *Debates of the Legislative Assembly of United Canada* |
| DLR | *Dominion Law Reports* |
| DPC | Dominion-Provincial Conference |
| FC | Federal Court |
| FPC | Federal-Provincial Conference |
| HOC | House of Commons |
| IJCS | *International Journal of Canadian Studies* |
| IPSR | *International Political Science Review* |
| IRPP | Institute for Research on Public Policy |
| JCS | *Journal of Canadian Studies* |
| LAC | Library and Archives Canada |
| McGLJ | *McGill Law Journal* |
| PBA | *Proceedings of the British Academy* |
| QLJ | *Queen's Law Journal* |
| SAB | Saskatchewan Archives Board |
| SBR | *Saskatchewan Bar Review* |
| SCR | *Supreme Court Reports* |
| SCLR | *Supreme Court Law Review* |

TFCU    Task Force on Canadian Unity
TRSC    *Transactions of the Royal Society of Canada*
UBCLR   *University of British Columbia Law Review*
USA     University of Saskatchewan Archives
UTA     University of Toronto Archives
UTLJ    *University of Toronto Law Journal*
UWALR   *University of Western Australia Law Review*

**Preface**

1  Jean-Charles Falardeau, 'Roots and Values in Canadian Lives,' in Bernard
   Ostry and Janice Yalden, eds., *Visions of Canada: The Alan B. Plaunt Memorial
   Lectures, 1958–1992* (Montreal and Kingston: McGill-Queen's University
   Press, 2004), 75–98 at 76 and 77.
2  W.E. Gladstone, *Gleanings of Past Years*, I:225 (6 vols., 1879), in Sir Ivor
   Jennings, *Cabinet Government*. 3rd ed. (Cambridge: Cambridge University
   Press, 1959), 8.
3  J.R. Mallory, *The Structure of Canadian Government*, rev. ed. (Toronto: Gage,
   1984), 273.
4  'Some Notes on the Constitution and Government of Canada and on the
   Canadian Federal System' (reference paper prepared for the information of
   a delegation from the National Convention of Newfoundland), LAC, MG
   26L, vol. 36, Newfoundland National Convention and Canada, Government Meetings 1947, Part 1.

**Chapter 1**

1  Philip Ziegler, *Osbert Sitwell* (New York: Knopf, 2000), 265.
2  See John Kendle, *Ireland and the Federal Solution: The Debate over the United
   Kingdom Constitution* (Montreal and Kingston: McGill-Queen's University Press, 1989); and Nicholas Mansergh, *Survey of British Commonwealth
   Affairs: Problems of External Policy, 1931–1939* (London: Oxford University
   Press, 1952), 347–53.
3  From Plant. 33, Laski Archives, London School of Economics ('Lecture
   Notes'), in David Schneiderman, 'Harold Laski, Viscount Haldane, and the
   Law of the Canadian Constitution in the Early Twentieth Century,' *UTLJ* 48
   (1998): 521–60 at 534.
4  K.C. Wheare, *Federal Government* (London: Oxford University Press, 1946).
5  Geoffrey Marshall, 'Kenneth Clinton Wheare,' *PBA* 67 (1981): 491–507 at
   497.

6  William S. Livingston, *Federalism and Constitutional Change* (Oxford: Clarendon, 1956).
7  Kenneth C. Wheare, 'Federalism and the Making of Nations,' in Arthur W.
   Macmahon, ed., *Federalism Mature and Emergent* (Garden City: Doubleday,
   1962), 30.
8  See, however, M.P. Singh and Chandra Mohan, eds., *Regionalism and
   National Identity: Canada, India – Interdisciplinary Perspectives* (Delhi: Pragati,
   1994).
9  Malcolm M. Feeley and Edward Rubin, *Federalism: Political Identity and
   Tragic Compromise* (Ann Arbor: University of Michigan Press, 2008), ch. 1,
   'What Is Federalism?'
10  William H. Stewart, 'Metaphors, Models, and the Development of Federal
    Theory,' *Publius* 12 (Spring 1982): 5–24.
11  Deil S. Wright, *Understanding Intergovernmental Relations: Public Policy and
    Participants' Perspectives in Local, State, and National Governments* (North
    Scituate: Duxbury, 1978), 19, quoted in Stewart, 'Metaphors, Models, and
    the Development of Federal Theory,' 6.
12  Alan C. Cairns, 'The Governments and Societies of Canadian Federalism,'
    *CJPS* 10, no. 4 (December 1977): 695–725; Richard Simeon, *Federal-
    Provincial Diplomacy: The Making of Recent Policy in Canada* (Toronto: Uni-
    versity of Toronto Press, 1972).
13  *Parliamentary Debates on the subject of Confederation of the British North
    American Provinces* (Quebec: Hunter, Rose and Co., 1865, reprinted Ottawa:
    King's Printer, 1951), 146.
14  Daniel J. Elazar, 'Our Thoroughly Federal Constitution,' in Robert A.
    Goldwin and William A. Schambra, eds., *How Federal Is Our Constitution?*
    (Washington: American Enterprise Institute for Public Policy Research,
    1987), 43; and Peter S. Onuf, *The Origins of the Federal Republic: Jurisdictional
    Controversies in the United States, 1775–1787* (Philadelphia: University of
    Pennsylvania Press, 1983), xviii.
15  Canada. Department of External Affairs, *Documents on Relations between
    Canada and Newfoundland: vol. 2, 1940–1949, Confederation, Part 1,* Paul
    Bridle, ed. (Ottawa: Supply and Services, 1984); Norman Robertson
    (Under-Secretary of State for External Affairs) to the Prime Minister (Louis
    St Laurent), 18 August 1943, 78, and high commissioner (C.J. Burchell) to
    Robertson, 16 November 1943, 87.
16  Lorne Sossin, 'The Ambivalence of Executive Power in Canada,' in Paul
    Craig and Adam Tomkins, eds., *The Executive and Public Law: Power and
    Accountability in Comparative Perspective* (New York: Oxford University
    Press, 2006), 52–88 at 53.

17 Kirk Cameron and Graham White, *Northern Governments in Transition: Political and Constitutional Development in the Yukon, Nunavut, and the Western Northwest Territories* (Montreal: Institute for Research on Public Policy, 1995), 130 and 131.
18 Harold A. Innis, *Political Economy in the Modern State* (Toronto: Ryerson, 1946), xi–xii.
19 Peter H. Russell, *Constitutional Odyssey: Can Canadians Ever Become a Sovereign People?* 3rd ed. (Toronto: University of Toronto Press, 2004).
20 See selection of articles on 'The Gomery Effect,' *Policy Options* (June 2005); Canada, Commission of Inquiry into the Sponsorship Program and Advertising Activities, *Who Is Responsible? Summary* (Ottawa: Ministry of Public Works, 2005).
21 Allan Blakeney, *An Honourable Calling: Political Memoirs* (Toronto: University of Toronto Press, 2008), 45.
22 Wheare, *Federal Government*, 12.
23 Patricia Cline Cohen, *A Calculating People: The Spread of Numeracy in Early America* (Chicago: University of Chicago Press, 1982).
24 Lord Elgin to Lord Grey, 23 March 1850, in Sir A. G. Doughty, ed., *The Elgin-Grey Papers, 1846–1852.* 4 vols. (Ottawa: King's Printer, 1937), II:609.
25 David E. Smith, *The Republican Option in Canada, Past and Present* (Toronto: University of Toronto Press, 1999), 104.
26 Geoffrey Marshall, 'Canada's New Constitution (1982): Some Lessons in Constitutional Engineering,' in Vernon Bogdanor, ed., *Constitutions in Democratic Politics* (Brookfield: Gower, 1981), 158.
27 Laurence H. Tribe, *The Invisible Constitution* (New York: Oxford University Press, 2008), Part III, 'Explorations beyond the Text.'
28 Elazar, 'Our Thoroughly Federal Constitution,' 51.
29 See, for instance, Seymour Martin Lipset, *Continental Divide: The Values and Institutions of the United States and Canada* (New York: Routledge, 1990); Michael Adams, *Fire and Ice: The United States, Canada, and the Myth of Converging Values* (Toronto: Penguin Canada, 2003); Andrew Cohen, *The Unfinished Canadian: The People We Are* (Toronto: McClelland and Stewart, 2007).
30 Nova Scotia, *Royal Commission on Donald Marshall, Jr., Prosecution* (Halifax: Queen's Printer, 1989); *Report of the Commission of Inquiry into the Wrongful Conviction of David Milgaard* (Regina: Queen's Printer, 2008); *Report of the Commission of Inquiry Re: Neil Stonechild* (Regina: Queen's Printer, 2004); *Report of the Kaufman Commission on Proceedings Involving Guy Paul Morin* (Toronto: Queen's Printer, 1998).
31 David E. Smith, 'Politics and Police,' in R.C. Macleod and David Schnei-

derman, eds., *Police Powers in Canada: The Evolution and Practice of Authority* (Toronto: University of Toronto Press, 1994), 184–208.

32  For a statement of this position, see Donald V. Smiley and Ronald L. Watts, *Intrastate Federalism in Canada* (Toronto: University of Toronto Press in cooperation with the Royal Commission on the Economic Union and Development Prospects for Canada, 1985).

33  David R. Cameron and Jacqueline D. Krikorian, 'The Study of Federalism, 1960–1999: A Content Review of Several Leading Canadian Academic Journals,' *CPA* 45, no. 3 (Fall 2002): 329–63 at 352.

34  http://www.forumfed.org/en/about/index.php (accessed 26 February 2009).

35  'Minister Dion Affirms That a Better Knowledge of Other Federations Strengthens Canadian Unity,' *CanadaNewsWire*, 19 March 1999, quoted in Cameron and Krikorian, 'The Study of Federalism, 1960–1999,' 329.

36  George Anderson, *Federalism: An Introduction* (Toronto: Oxford University Press, 2008).

37  See *Federations* 7, no. 3 (July 2008).

38  Elazar, 'Our Thoroughly Federal Constitution,' 56.

39  Richard Simeon, *Political Science and Federalism: Seven Decades of Scholarly Engagement*. 2000 Kenneth R. MacGregor Lecturer, Institute of Intergovernmental Relations, School of Policy Studies, Queen's University, 2002, 1.

40  For example: Richard Simeon, ed., *Must Canada Fail?* (Montreal and Kingston: McGill-Queen's University Press, 1977); R. Kent Weaver, ed., *The Collapse of Canada?* (Washington: Brookings Institution, 1992); Thomas O. Hueglin, *Federalism and Fragmentation: A Comparative View of Political Accommodation in Canada* (Kingston: Institute of Intergovernmental Relations, 1984).

**Chapter 2**

1  K.C. Wheare, *Federal Government* (Toronto: Oxford University Press, 1946); William S. Livingston, *Federalism and Constitutional Change* (Oxford: Clarendon, 1956); Arthur W. Macmahon, *Federalism, Mature and Emergent* (Garden City: Doubleday, 1962).

2  Typed sheet headed 'Saskatchewan Brief,' n.d. [1945] in LAC, MG30 A 25, Papers of Eugene Alfred Forsey (file 57/58 disallowance of provincial acts (2), 1945, 1948).

3  Ronald L. Watts, 'Canada's Constitutional Options: An Outline,' in Ronald L. Watts and Douglas M. Brown, eds., *Options for A New Canada* (Toronto: University of Toronto Press, 1991), 15–30 at 25.

4 S. Rufus Davis, *The Federal Principle: A Journey through Time in Quest of a Meaning* (Berkeley: University of California Press, 1978), 38.

5 A.V. Dicey, *Introduction to the Study of the Law of the Constitution.* 10th ed. (London: Macmillan, 1962), 155.

6 HOC, *Debates*, 8 March 1870, 283.

7 Nathan Keyfitz, 'Robert Hamilton Coats, 1874–1960,' *Proceedings of the Royal Society of Canada* (1960), 99–104 at 99.

8 Government of Saskatchewan, News Release, 4 October 2007, 'Province Launches Constitutional Challenge.' http://www.gov.sk.ca/news?newsId=4b4264al-c946-4eaa-8c5d-75160118af47, accessed 19 March 2009.

9 'Prior to 1870, "North-Western Territory" referred to the area outside Rupert's Land but still administered by the Hudson's Bay Company, mostly consisting of the lands that drained into the Arctic Ocean rather than Hudson Bay. After the 1870 transfer of both regions to Canada, they became (minus the new province of Manitoba) "the North-West Territory," a name that has since evolved into "Northwest Territories."' Garrett Wilson, *Farewell Frontier: The 1870s and the End of the Old West* (Regina: Canadian Plains Research Center, 2007), xviii.

10 Canada. Energy, Mines and Resources. Surveys and Mapping Branch, *Territorial Evolution of Canada* (Ottawa 1969).

11 Norman L. Nicholson, *The Boundaries of Canada, Its Provinces and Territories* (Ottawa: Department of Mines and Technical Surveys, Geographical Branch, 1964), 82.

12 Ibid., 86 and 88.

13 Memorandum on Representation of the Maritime Provinces, *Canadian Sessional Papers* (1914), no. 118a, pp. 1–3, reprinted in R. MacGregor Dawson, ed., *Constitutional Issues in Canada, 1900–1931* (Oxford: Oxford University Press, 1933), 173–5.

14 Canada. Royal Commission on Dominion-Provincial Relations, *Report of Proceedings*, 2 May 1938, 7434.

15 Vincent Ostram, 'State Administration of Natural Resources in the West,' *APSR* 47, no. 2 (June 1953): 478–93.

16 HOC, *Debates*, 21 February 1905, cols. 1426-7.

17 See, for example, Michael Burgess, 'Competing National Visions: Canada-Quebec Relations in a Comparative Perspective,' in Alain-G. Gagnon and James Tully, eds., *Multinational Democracies* (Cambridge: Cambridge University Press, 2001), 257–74 at 269–71; and David Milne, 'Asymmetry in Canada, Past and Present,' Asymmetry Series 2005(1), Institute of Intergovernmental Relations, School of Policy Studies, Queen's Univer-

sity. http://www.queensu.ca/iigr/working/asymmetricfederalism/
Milne2005.pdf

18  Mikhail Filippov, Peter C. Ordeshook, and Olga Shvetsova, *Designing Federalism: A Theory of Self-Sustainable Federal Institutions* (New York: Cambridge University Press, 2004), 67.

19  This report appears as a research note, in Patrick Fafard and François Rocher, 'The Evolution of Federalism Studies in Canada: From Centre to Periphery,' *CPA* 52, no. 2 (June 2009): 290–311.

20  David W. Fransen, 'Unscrewing the Unscrutable: The Rowell-Sirois Commission, the Ottawa Bureaucracy, and Public Finance Reform, 1935–1941,' (PhD diss., University of Toronto, 1982), 23; also see Robert B. Bryce, *Maturing in Hard Times: Canada's Department of Finance through the Great Depression* (Montreal and Kingston: McGill-Queen's University Press, 1986), 188. For personal recollections of the commission by its press secretary, as well as impressions of the premiers who appeared before it, see Wilfrid Eggleston, *While I Still Remember* (Toronto: Ryerson, 1968), ch. 14, 'A Royal Commission.'

21  MacKay to Premier A.A. Dysart, 6 November 1937, in LAC, MG30 E 159, Papers of Robert A. MacKay (file Rowell-Sirois 'D' Correspondence 1937–1941).

22  T.C. Davis to Gardiner, 13 September 1937, SAB, R1022, Papers of James G. Gardiner, 41329–31. For more on the social sciences in Saskatchewan, see Robin Neill, 'Economic Historiography in the 1950s: The Saskatchewan School,' *JCS* 34, no. 3 (Autumn 1999): 243–60; and Shirley Spafford, *No Ordinary Academics: Economics and Political Science at the University of Saskatchewan, 1910–1960* (Toronto: University of Toronto Press, 2000). Spafford notes that one (former) member of the Saskatchewan department, Pete McQueen, was on the research staff of the Royal Commission, while another, W.A. Carrothers, who had subsequently joined the Department of Economics at the University of British Columbia, prepared the province of British Columbia's brief to the commission.

23  J.A. Corry, *Democratic Government and Politics* (Toronto: University of Toronto Press, 1946).

24  Ibid., 355–6.

25  R. MacGregor Dawson, *The Government of Canada*. 5th ed., rev. by Norman Ward (Toronto: University of Toronto Press, 1970).

26  J.R. Mallory, *The Structure of Canadian Government*. Rev. ed. (Toronto: Gage, 1984).

27  A.R.M. Lower, F.R. Scott, et al., *Evolving Canadian Federalism* (Durham: Duke University Press, 1958).

28 *ASPR* 53, no. 3 (1959): 803; *CHR* 40, no. 2 (1959): 162–3.
29 Gia Metherell, 'Clark's History Itself Is Now Historical,' *Canberra Times*, 9 May 2004, 4.
30 Raphael Samuel, *Theatres of Memory, Vol. 1: Past and Present in Contemporary Culture* (London: Verso, 1994), 15.
31 Alan Cairns, 'The Constitutional World We Have Lost,' in C.E.S. Franks, J.E. Hodgetts, O.P. Dwivedi, Doug Williams, and V. Seymour Williams, eds., *Canada's Century: Governance in a Maturing Society* (Montreal and Kingston: McGill-Queen's University Press, 1995), 43–67.
32 Reginald Whitaker, 'Confused Alarms of Struggle and Flight: English-Canadian Political Science in the 1970s,' *CHR* 60, no. 1 (1979): 1–18 at 14. A critical view of the same development but from another discipline's perspective is found in John English, 'The Second Time Around: Political Scientists Writing History,' *CHR* 67, no. 1 (1986): 1–16.
33 David Easton, *The Political System: An Inquiry into the State of Political Science* (New York: Knopf, 1953).
34 For a critical 'in-house' Canadian assessment of this academic transformation of the social sciences, see S.D. Clark, 'Canadian Studies and the Social Sciences' [1981], a hand-written nine-page essay on University of Tsukuba (Japan) letterhead, in UTA, B1990–0029, Papers of S.D. Clark (file 002 Correspondence Tsukuba, 1981–82).
35 W.P.M. Kennedy, *Statutes, Treaties, and Documents of the Canadian Constitution, 1713–1929* (Toronto: Oxford University Press, 1930).
36 Kennedy to Dafoe, 5 November 1928, 'Private and Confidential,' in LAC, MG30 D 45, Papers of John W. Dafoe (file M 75).
37 Edwin R. Black and Alan C. Cairns, 'A Different Perspective on Canadian Federalism,' *CPA* 9, no. 1 (March 1966): 27–45.
38 David R. Cameron and Jacqueline D. Krikorian, 'The Study of Federalism, 1960–99: A Content Review of Several Leading Canadian Academic Journals,' *CPA* 45, no. 3 (Fall 2002): 328–63.
39 Canada. Royal Commission on Bilingualism and Biculturalism, *A Preliminary Report* (Ottawa: Queen's Printer, 1965), 13.
40 Laurence H. Tribe, *The Invisible Constitution* (New York: Oxford University Press, 2008), 68–9 (emphasis in original).
41 R. Young, P. Faucher, and A. Blais, 'The Concept of Province-Building: A Critique,' *CJPS* 17, no. 4 (December 1984): 783–818.
42 Ontario. Confederation for Tomorrow Conference, *Proceedings*, Toronto, 27–30 November 1967, 11 and 4.
43 David R. Cameron, 'Not Spicer and Not the B and B: Reflections of an Insider on the Workings of the Pepin-Robarts Task Force on Canadian Unity,' *IJCS* 7–8 (Spring–Fall 1993): 333–45.

44  *Reference re Secession of Quebec*, [1998] 2 *SCR* 217 (para. 96).

**Chapter 3**

1  HOC, *Debates*, 1867–68, 5–6.
2  *Reference re Secession of Quebec*, [1998] 2 *SCR* 217 (paras. 49–82).
3  J.R. Mallory, 'The Continuing Evolution of Canadian Constitutionalism,' in Alan Cairns and Cynthia Williams, research coordinators, *Constitutionalism, Citizenship, and Society in Canada* (Toronto: University of Toronto Press in cooperation with the Royal Commission on the Economic Union and Development Prospects for Canada, 1985), 55.
4  Warren J. Newman, '"Grand Entrance Hall," Back Door or Foundation Stone? The Role of Constitutional Principles in Construing and Applying the Constitution of Canada' (2001), 14 *SCLR* (2d) 197, see n77, and 199.
5  K.C. Wheare, *Federal Government*. 3rd ed. (Toronto: Oxford University Press, 1953), 12.
6  Australia, *Official Report of the National Australasian Convention Debates*. Adelaide Session (1897) (Sydney: Legal Books Pty., 1986), 175.
7  John Gooch, *Manual or explanatory development of the Act for the union of Canada, Nova Scotia, and New Brunswick in one dominion under the name of Canada synthetical and analytical with the text of the Act etc., and the index to the Act and the treaties* ([Ottawa: s.n.], 1867).
8  Richard Simeon, 'Making Federalism Work,' in *Open Federalism: Interpretations, Significance* (Kingston: Institute of Intergovernmental Relations, 2006), 1.
9  William S. Livingston, *Federalism and Constitutional Change* (Oxford: Clarendon, 1956), 10.
10  Frank Underhill, 'The Cabinet and Leadership,' *Canadian Forum*, January 1930: 116–17, in R. MacGregor Dawson, ed., *Constitutional Issues in Canada, 1900–1931* (London: Oxford University Press, 1933), 135.
11  J. Noel Lyon, 'The Central Fallacy of Canadian Constitutional Law,' *McGLJ* 22 (1976): 45 and 42–3.
12  HOC, *Debates*, 3 April 1868, 450.
13  David E. Smith, 'The Politics of the Federal Cabinet,' in Glen Williams and Michael Whittington, eds., *Canadian Politics in the Eighties*, 2nd ed. (Toronto: Methuen, 1984), 351–70. See also Frederick W. Gibson, *Cabinet Formation and Bicultural Relations: Seven Case Studies* (No. 6, Studies of the Royal Commission on Bilingualism and Biculturalism) (Ottawa: Information Canada, 1970).
14  *Parliamentary Debates on the Subject of the Confederation of the British North*

*American Provinces* (Quebec: Hunter, Rose & Co., Parliamentary Printers, 1865 [Ottawa: King's Printer, 1951]), 29.

15  M.J.C. Vile, *Constitutionalism and the Separation of Powers* (Oxford: Clarendon, 1967).

16  *Parliamentary Debates on the Subject of the Confederation*, 32 and 33.

17  John Taylor, *An Inquiry into the Principles and Policy of the United States* (New Haven: Yale University Press, 1950, first published 1814), quoted in Gordon S. Wood, *Revolutionary Characters: What Made the Founders Different* (New York: Penguin, 2006), 201.

18  Wood, *Revolutionary Characters*, 201 (emphasis added).

19  Arthur Sheps, 'The American Revolution and the Transformation of English Republicanism,' *Historical Reflections* 2, no. 1 (Summer 1975): 20 (emphasis in original).

20  David E. Smith, *The People's House of Commons: Theories of Democracy in Contention* (Toronto: University of Toronto Press, 2007).

21  Roy Jenkins, *Churchill* (London: Macmillan, 2001), 67.

22  Peter C. Oliver, *The Constitution of Independence: The Development of Constitutional Theory in Australia, Canada, and New Zealand* (Oxford: Oxford University Press, 2005), 112.

23  *Parliamentary Debates on the Subject of the Confederation*, 30 and 31 (emphasis added).

24  See Andrew Smith, *British Businessmen and Canadian Confederation: Constitution-Making in an Era of Anglo-Globalization* (Montreal and Kingston: McGill-Queen's University Press, 2008), 116 and 210n30.

25  Ibid., 126.

26  HOC, *Debates*, 1867–68, 53–54 (E.M. McDonald).

27  *The Speeches and Public Letters of Joseph Howe*, II:490–1, quoted in Hon. Judge P.J.T. O'Hearn, 'Nova Scotia and Constitutional Amendment,' *McGLJ* 12, no. 4 (1966–7): 433–42 at 433.

28  HOC, *Debates*, 3 April 1868, 455.

29  'Memorandum on Representation of the Maritime Provinces,' Canadian Sessional Papers, 1914, no. 118a, pp. 1–3, reprinted in R. MacGregor Dawson, ed., *Constitutional Issues in Canada, 1900–1931* (Oxford: Oxford University Press, 1933), 173–5.

30  Duff Spafford, '"Effective Representation": Reference Re: Provincial Electoral Boundaries,' *SBR* 56 (1992): 197–208.

31  'Bystander' [Goldwin Smith], 'Colonel Gray on Confederation,' *Canadian Monthly* 2 (August 1872): 173–83 at 180–1.

32  Reginald Whitaker, *A Sovereign Idea: Essays on Canada as a Democratic Community* (Montreal and Kingston: McGill-Queen's University Press, 1992), 207.

33  Bora Laskin, *The British Tradition in Canadian Law* (London: Stevens and Sons, 1969), 121.

34  Mark Sproule-Jones, 'The Enduring Colony? Political Institutions and Political Science in Canada,' *Publius* 14, no. 1 (1984): 93–108.

35  H. McD. Clokie, 'Judicial Review, Federalism, and the Canadian Constitution,' *CJEPS* 8, no. 4 (November 1942): 537–56 at 541.

36  Oliver, *The Constitution of Independence*, 143.

37  Norman McL. Rogers, 'The Compact Theory of Confederation,' *Papers and Proceedings of the Annual Meeting of the Canadian Political Science Association* 3 (May 1931): 205–30.

38  Oliver, *The Constitution of Independence*, 144.

39  Clokie, 'Judicial Review, Federalism, and the Canadian Constitution,' 549.

40  *Parliamentary Debates on the Subject of Confederation*, 88.

41  HOC, *Debates*, 8 March 1870, 280.

42  David E. Smith, *The Regional Decline of a National Party: Liberals on the Prairies* (Toronto: University of Toronto Press, 1981).

43  David E. Smith, 'Party Government, Representation, and National Integration in Canada,' in Peter Aucoin, ed., *Party Government and Regional Representation in Canada* (Toronto: University of Toronto Press in cooperation with the Royal Commission on the Economic Union and Development Prospects for Canada, 1985), 1–68.

44  O'Hearn, 'Nova Scotia and Constitutional Amendment,' 433.

45  Ibid., 434.

46  Canada. Department of Justice, *A Consolidation of the Constitution Acts 1867 to 1982* (Ottawa: Public Works and Government Services, 2001).

47  An exception is J.E. Read, 'The Early Provincial Constitutions,' *CBR* 26, no. 4 (April 1948): 621–37.

48  Robert C. Vipond, *Liberty and Community: Canadian Federalism and the Failure of the Constitution* (Albany: SUNY Press, 1991).

49  Eggleston, *While I Still Remember*, 227.

50  HOC, *Debates*, 25 April 1870, 1181.

51  A useful chronicle of the Manitoba School Question ('Quebecers, the Roman Catholic Church and the Manitoba School Question: A Chronology') is found at http://faculty.marianopolis.edu/c.belanger/Quebec History/chronos/Manitoba.htm (accessed 15 December 2008).

52  *Attorney General of Manitoba v. Forest*, [1979] 2 SCR 1032.

53  Richard Goreham, *Language Rights and the Court Challenges Program: A Review of Its Accomplishments and Impact of Its Abolition*. Report submitted to the Commissioner of Official Languages (Ottawa: 1992), 3.

54  These events are chronicled in Frances Russell, *The Canadian Crucible:*

*Manitoba's Role in Canada's Great Divide* (Winnipeg: Heartland Associates, 2003), ch. 11.

55 Hon. Howard Pawley, 'The Lessons of a Very Political Life,' *CPR* 30, no. 2 (2007): 7–13 at 11.

56 See, for example, Eugene Forsey, 'Canada: Two Nations or One?' *CJEPS* 28 (November 1962): 485–501.

57 See speech on the Official Languages Bill from Senate *Debates*, 8 July 1969, reprinted in Senator Paul Yuzyk, *For a Better Canada: A Collection of Selected Speeches Delivered in the Senate of Canada and at Banquets and Conferences in Various Centres across Canada* (Toronto: Ukrainian National Association, [1973]), 123. A fictional portrayal of immigrant life in Winnipeg's North End that provides backdrop to the emotions expressed in this debate is found in John Marlyn, *Under the Ribs of Death* (London: Arthur Barker, [1957]).

58 Ramsay Cook, *Provincial Autonomy, Minority Rights, and the Compact Theory, 1867–1921*, Studies of the Royal Commission on Bilingualism and Biculturalism (Ottawa: Queen's Printer, 1969).

59 Daniel J. Elazar, 'Contrasting Unitary and Federal Systems,' *IPSR* 18, no. 3 (1997): 237–51 at 241.

60 Hugh MacLennan, *Two Solitudes* (Toronto: Macmillan, 1945).

## Chapter 4

1 Richard Gwyn, *John A.: The Man Who Made Us* (Toronto: Random House Canada, 2007), 427.

2 The authoritative study is by John T. Saywell, *The Office of Lieutenant-Governor* (Toronto: University of Toronto Press, 1957).

3 Michael Jackson, Rachele Dabraio, and Suzanne Moffett, 'Honours in a Federal State,' in Michael Jackson, ed., *Honouring Commonwealth Citizens: Proceedings of the First Conference on Commonwealth Honours and Awards* (Toronto: Honours and Awards Secretariat, Ontario Ministry of Citizenship and Immigration, 2007), 115–27.

4 New Brunswick, *Position Paper of the Government of New Brunswick: Bill S-4, An Act to Amend the Constitution Act, 1867 (Senate Tenure)*. Presented to the Standing Senate Committee on Legal and Constitutional Affairs, 20 April 2007. 12p.

5 *DLAUC*, 27 May 1850 (IX-I-1850), 259–60.

6 Eugene Forsey, 'Extension of the Life of Legislatures,' *CJEPS* 26 (November 1960): 604–16, reprinted in *Freedom and Order: Collected Essays* (Toronto: McClelland and Stewart, 1974), 205–22.

7  FP (file 57/17 Corrections to 'Canadians and Their Government: Towards a New Canada,' CBA report, n.d. [1979]).

8  David R. Cameron, 'Not Spicer and Not the B and B: Reflections of an Insider on the Workings of the Pepin-Robarts Task Force on Canadian Unity,' *IJCS* 7–8 (Spring–Fall 1993): 333–45.

9  Robert Décary, 'Politics and the Constitution,' 28 July 1978 (first draft), in LAC, RG33/118, Task Force on Canadian Unity (hereafter TFCU), (Section 1V, no. 362).

10  TFCU, *A Future Together*, 102.

11  *Maritime Bank* v. *Receiver General of New Brunswick* (1892) A.C. 437 at 441–2.

12  Saywell, *The Office of the Lieutenant-Governor*, 219.

13  *Initiative and Referendum Act* (1919) A.C. 935.

14  David E. Smith, *The Invisible Crown: The First Principle of Canadian Government* (Toronto: University of Toronto Press, 1995), ch. 3, 'Canadianizing the Crown.'

15  Angela Hall, 'Liberal Leader Makes Appeal to the West,' *Leader-Post*, 17 February 2009, A1 and A2. The events of December 2008 and January 2009 are discussed in Peter H. Russell and Lorne Sossin, eds., *Parliamentary Democracy in Crisis* (Toronto: University of Toronto Press, 2009).

16  Tom Flanagan, 'Only Voters Have the Right to Decide on the Coalition,' *Globe and Mail*, 9 January 2009, A13. For another view, see W.T. Stanbury, 'Write It Down: Codify the Unwritten Conventions for Canada's Sake,' *Hill Times*, 15 December 2008, 13 and 22.

17  Ralph Heintzman, 'The Formal Executive,' 9 July 1978 (first draft), TFCU (Section 1V, Doc. no. 322).

18  Saywell, *The Office of Lieutenant-Governor*, 220 (quotation from *Re the Power of the Governor General in Council to Disallow Provincial Legislation and the Power of Reservation of a Lieutenant Governor*, [1938] *SCR*, 71; see too K.C. Wheare, *The Statute of Westminster and Dominion Status*, 4th ed. (London: Oxford University Press, 1949).

19  [Enoch Powell], 'Eyrie in the Hills,' *The Listener*, 15 March 1979, 372.

20  'The Question of a Reconstituted Senate,' 1 December 1977, TFCU (Section 1V, no. 364); and Ghislain Fortin, 'The House of the Federation Proposal Revisited,' 24 August 1978 (first draft), TFCU (Section 1V, no. 413).

21  Dr Ronald L. Watts, 'Politics and the Constitution: Senate,' 7 September 1978, TFCU (Section 1V, no. 423-A).

22  Donald V. Smiley and Ronald L. Watts, *Intrastate Federalism in Canada* (Toronto: University of Toronto Press in cooperation with the Royal Commission on the Economic Union and Development Prospects for Canada, 1985), 144.

23  Canada, *Responsive Institutions for a Modern Canada* (Ottawa: Minister of Supply and Services, 1991), 11.
24  Tom Kent, 'An Elected Senate: Key to Redressing the Democratic Deficit, Revitalizing Federalism,' *Policy Options* (April 2004): 49–53.
25  For a detailed analysis of the Senate Appointments Consultations Act, see Bruce M. Hicks and André Blais, 'Restructuring the Canadian Senate through Elections,' *IRPP Choices* 14, no. 15 (November 2008). Concern as to the constitutionality of Bill C-20 led the Canadian Bar Association to recommend that the Government of Canada refer the bill to the Supreme Court of Canada 'to ensure that its provisions are constitutionally valid.' Canadian Bar Association, 'Bill C-20 Senate Appointment Consultations Act' (National Constitutional and Human Rights Section, April 2008), 11p.
26  An exception is Jennifer Smith, ed., *The Democratic Dilemma: Reforming the Canadian Senate* (Institute of Intergovernmental Relations, School of Public Policy, Queen's University, and Montreal and Kingston: McGill-Queen's University Press, 2009).
27  http://www12.statcan.ca/census-recensement/2006/as-sa/97-550/index-eng.cfm?CFID=362, 18 May 2010.
28  Parliament, Senate, Special Senate Committee on Senate Reform, *Report on the Motion to Amend the Constitution of Canada (western regional representation in the Senate)*, October 2006. Report and proceedings available online at http://www.parloge.ca/39/1/parlbus/commbus/senate/Com-e/refo-e/rep-e/rep02oct06-e.htm (19 May 2010).
29  Seymour Martin Lipset, *Agrarian Socialism: The Cooperative Commonwealth Federation in Saskatchewan: A Study in Political Sociology* (Berkeley: University of California Press, 1950). Of the ten volumes in the Social Credit series, the most applicable to this discussion are C.B. Macpherson, *The Theory and Practice of a Quasi-Party System* (Toronto: University of Toronto Press, 1953); John Richards and Larry Pratt, *Prairie Capitalism: Power and Influence in the New West* (Toronto: McClelland and Stewart, 1979).
30  Nelson Wiseman, *In Search of Canadian Political Culture* (Vancouver: UBC Press, 2007); see ch. 5, 'Regions and Political Culture.'
31  HOC, *Debates*, 20 January 1908, col. 1557 (Geo. Smith).
32  Ronald L. Watts, *Comparing Federal Systems in the 1990s* (Kingston: Institute of Intergovernmental Relations, 1996), 87 and 89.
33  *British Columbia in the Canadian Confederation* (A Submission presented to the Royal Commission on Dominion-Provincial Relations by the Government of the Province of British Columbia, Victoria: King's Printer, 1938), 17.
34  Louis Massicotte, 'Possible Repercussions of an Elected Senate on Official

Language Minorities in Canada,' Report for the Office of the Commissioner of Official Languages, March 2007), 16. Massicotte finds support
for his opinion from Alain Noël: 'The real threat associated with regional
majorities does not derive from decentralization, but rather from intrastate
federalism.' Alain Noël, 'Is Decentralization Conservative? Federalism
and the Contemporary Debate on the Canadian Welfare State,' in Robert
Young, ed., *Stretching the Federation: The Art of the State in Canada* (Kingston: Institute of Intergovernmental Relations, Queen's University, 1999),
195–218 at 204.

35  Massicotte, 'Possible Repercussions,' 21.
36  Canada, Office of the Commissioner of Official Languages, *Annual Report
    2007–2008*, http://www.ocol-clo.gc.ca/html/ar_ra_2007_08_chap2_1_e
    .php (accessed 27 November 2008).
37  Reference re: Legislative Authority of Parliament in relation to the Upper
    House (1980), 1 *SCR* 54 (quotations in this paragraph are from pages 77
    and 56).
38  John D. Whyte, 'What Does the Constitution Say?' in Jennifer Smith, ed.,
    *The Democratic Dilemma: Reforming the Canadian Senate* (Montreal and
    Kingston: McGill-Queen's University Press, 2009), 91–109 at 103.
39  John C. Courtney, *Commissioned Ridings: Designing Canada's Electoral Dis-
    tricts* (Montreal and Kingston: McGill-Queen's University Press, 2001), 26.
40  Canada, 'Federal Government Restores Principle of Representation by
    Population in the House of Commons,' 14 November 2007. http://news
    .gc.ca/web/view/en/index.jsp?articleid=361279& (22 November 2007).
    Bill C-12, introduced on 1 April 2010, provided for an additional thirty
    seats in the Commons: eighteen to Ontario, seven to British Columbia,
    and five to Alberta. John Ibbitson, 'House Reform Boosts Fastest-Growing
    Provinces,' *Globe and Mail*, 2 April 2010, A1, A6.
41  Canadian Press, 'Ontario to Get 21 More Seats in Commons: McGinty,' 17
    December 2008. http://www.cbc.ca/canada/toronto/story/2008/12/17/
    ont-parliament.html (accessed 12 February 2009).
42  David C. Docherty, *Legislatures* (Vancouver: UBC Press, 2005), 109.
43  W.P.M. Kennedy, 'Law and Custom in the Canadian Constitution,' in *The
    Round Table* (December 1929), reprinted in Robert MacGregor Dawson,
    *Constitutional Issues in Canada, 1900–1931* (London: Oxford University
    Press, 1933), 50–62 at 51.
44  Kennedy, 'The Law and Custom,' 61.
45  HOC, *Debates*, 3 April 1868, 450 and 453.
46  Donald J. Savoie, *Governing from the Centre: The Concentration of Power in
    Canadian Politics* (Toronto: University of Toronto Press, 1999), 339.

47 'The Long Labors of Willard Wirtz,' National Public Radio (Weekend Edition), 20 December 2008, http://www.npr.org/templates/story/story .php?storyId=98558213 (accessed 18 February 2009).

48 Canada, *Report of the Royal Commission on the Economic Union and Development Prospects for Canada* (Macdonald Commission), 1985, vol. 3, 83.

49 Canada, *Responsive Institutions for a Modern Canada*, 7.

50 See, for example, Donald Desserud, 'The Confidence Convention under the Canadian Parliamentary System,' *Parliamentary Perspectives* no. 7 (Ottawa: Canadian Study of Parliament Group, October 2006).

51 Norman Ward, *The Canadian House of Commons: Representation*. 2nd ed. (Toronto: University of Toronto Press, 1963), 65.

52 Robert MacGregor Dawson, *Constitutional Issues in Canada, 1900–1931* (London: Oxford University Press, 1933), ch. 8: 'Political Parties,' Section 3: 'Revolts against the Old Parties.'

53 John English, *The Decline of Politics: The Conservatives and the Party System, 1901–1920* (Toronto: University of Toronto Press, 1977).

54 *Wells* v. *Newfoundland*, [1999] 3 *SCR* 199, para. 54. Cited in Lorne Sossin, 'The Ambivalence of Executive Power in Canada,' in Paul Craig and Adam Tomkins, eds., *The Executive and Public Law: Power and Accountability in Comparative Perspective* (New York: Oxford University Press, 2006), 52–88 at 58.

55 Bruce Hicks, 'Bilingualism and the House of Commons 40 Years after B and B,' *Parliamentary Perspectives* no. 8 (Ottawa: Canadian Study of Parliament Group, June 2008).

56 HOC, *Debates*, 20 January 1908, col. 1571.

## Chapter 5

1 Donald V. Smiley and Ronald L. Watts, *Intrastate Federalism in Canada* (Toronto: University of Toronto Press in cooperation with the Royal Commission on the Economic Union and Development Prospects for Canada, 1985), xv.

2 Guy Laforest, 'Quebec beyond the Federal Regime of 1867–1982: From Distinct Society to National Community,' in Ronald L. Watts and Douglas M. Brown, eds., *Options for a New Canada* (Toronto: University of Toronto Press, 1991), 103–22 at 103.

3 David Cameron and Richard Simeon, 'Intergovernmental Relations in Canada: The Emergence of Collaborative Federalism,' *Publius* 32, no. 2 (Spring 2002): 49–71 at 49.

4 Richard Johnston, André Blais, Elisabeth Gidengil, and Neil Nevitte, 'The

People and the Charlottetown Accord,' in Ronald L. Watts and Douglas M. Brown, eds., *Canada: The State of the Federation, 1993* (Kingston: Institute of Intergovernmental Relations, 1993), 19–43 at 39.

5 Hamish Telford, 'The Federal Spending Power in Canada: Nation-Building or Nation-Destroying?' *Publius* 33, no. 1 (2003): 23–44. For a thorough examination of the subject of the spending power and the Constitution, see *QLJ* 34, no. 1 (Fall 2008). The title of the issue is 'Open Federalism and the Spending Power.'

6 Richard Simeon, *Federal-Provincial Diplomacy: The Making of Recent Policy in Canada* (Toronto: University of Toronto Press, 1972).

7 Royal Commission on the Economic Union and Development Prospects for Canada, *Report.* 3 vols. (Ottawa: Minister of Supply and Services Canada, 1985); Royal Commission on Electoral Reform and Party Financing, *Report* (Ottawa: Minister of Supply and Services Canada, 1991).

8 Harold D. Lasswell, *Politics: Who Gets What, When, How* (New York: World, 1958).

9 'Official Synopsis of the Report of the Royal Commission on Agricultural Credit,' 1913, abridged and reprinted in David E. Smith, *Building a Province: A History of Saskatchewan in Documents* (Saskatoon: Fifth House, 1992), Document 60, 211–28.

10 E.P. Neufeld, *The Financial System of Canada: Its Growth and Development* (Toronto: Macmillan of Canada, 1972), 295 and 384–5.

11 Duff Spafford, 'Notes on Re-reading Lipset's *Agrarian Socialism*,' in David E. Smith, ed., *Lipset's 'Agrarian Socialism': A Re-examination* (Regina: Canadian Plains Research Center and Saskatchewan Institute of Public Policy, 2007), 23–33 at 30.

12 Janice MacKinnon, *Minding the Public Purse: The Fiscal Crisis, Political Trade-Offs, and Canada's Future* (Montreal and Kingston: McGill-Queen's University Press, 2003).

13 Ernest R. Forbes, *The Maritime Rights Movement, 1919–1927: A Study in Canadian Regionalism* (Montreal and Kingston: McGill-Queen's University Press, 1979).

14 *Toronto Electric Commissioners v. Snider* [1925] A.C. 396. See W.H. McConnell, *Commentary on the British North America Act* (Toronto: Macmillan of Canada, 1977), 148–9.

15 For a political science discussion of Saskatchewan's innovative labour legislation, see David E. Smith, ed., *Building a Province*, Documents 86 and 87 and pages 36–7.

16 See, for instance, 'The Agreement on Internal Trade (AIT): Implications for Canadian-Certified Teachers Wanting to Work in BC,' http://www

.bcct.ca/documents/FormsandPublications/BecomeTeacher/MiscForms/
AIT_implications.pdf (accessed 11 September 2009).

17 Richard Simeon, *Political Science and Federalism: Seven Decades of Scholarly Engagement* (Kingston: Institute of Intergovernmental Relations, 2002), 13. The ten volumes, with publication dates in parentheses, were published by the University of Toronto Press: W.L. Morton, *The Progressive Party in Canada* (1950); D.C. Masters, *The Winnipeg General Strike* (1950); Jean Burnet, *Next-Year Country* (1951); C.B. Macpherson, *Democracy in Alberta* (1953); J.R. Mallory, *Social Credit and the Federal Power in Canada* (1954); W.E. Mann, *Sect, Cult, and Church in Alberta* (1955); V.C. Fowke, *The National Policy and the Wheat Economy* (1957); Lewis G. Thomas, *The Liberal Party in Alberta* (1959); S.D. Clark, *Movements of Social Protest in Canada, 1640–1840* (1959); and J.A. Irving, *The Social Credit Movement* (1959).

Two volumes planned but never proceeded to completion were 'Economic Development of the Pacific Coast Region' (W.T. Easterbrook) and 'The Economic Background of Social Credit and the Monetary Experiment' (W.J. Waines and J.L. Graham).

18 Fowke to Del Clark, 11 October 1949, in USA, 95/5, Papers of Vernon C. Fowke, (XIX Manuscripts (K) *National Policy and the Wheat Economy*). Clark had originally assumed that the emphasis would be upon 'the efforts of the farmers to protect their interests.' Clark to Fowke, 3 August 1944, ibid.

19 J.R. Mallory, *Social Credit and the Federal Power in Canada* (Toronto: University of Toronto Press, 1954), 189.

20 Clark to Lynd, 15 February 1947, and Clark to Brebner, 11 April 1947, in UTA, S.D. Clark Papers, B 1990-0029 (file 014, University of Toronto Correspondence, personal and general 1946–50).

21 See S.D. Clark, 'The Attack on the Authority Structure of Canadian Society,' *TRSC* 14 (1976): 5–15.

22 MacKay to Dr Joseph Sirois, 16 July 1938, and Skelton to MacKay, 22 July 1938, in LAC, Papers of Robert A. MacKay, MG 30 E159, vol. 8 (files Rowell-Sirois Correspondence, 1938–1940, 'Sirois' and Rowell-Sirois Correspondence, 1937–1941 'S'). The O'Connor Report is titled Senate of Canada, Session 1939, *Report, pursuant to resolution of the Senate to the Honourable The Speaker, by the Parliamentary Counsel, Relating to The Enactment of the British North America Act, 1867, any lack of congruence between its terms and judicial construction of them and cognate matters* (Ottawa: Queen's Printer, 1961). (Hereafter *Report to the Senate of Canada on the B.N.A. Act.*)

23 O'Connor to Cronkite, 29 April 1940, in USA, F.C. Cronkite Papers, MG

33 (file B. Publications (3) 1934–1949). See too, W.F. O'Connor, *Report to the Senate of Canada on the B.N.A. Act*, 11-3.

24 Mackay to H.F. Angus, 18 July 1938, in LAC, MacKay Papers (file Rowell-Sirois Correspondence, 1938–1941A). O'Connor corroborated MacDonald's influence in a letter (29 April 1940) to Cronkite in USA, Cronkite Papers (file B. Publications (3)).

25 DPC (1941), 14 January 1941, 9 (King) and DPC (1945), Memorandum submitted by ... Province of Quebec, 25 April 1946 (English translation), 354 (Duplessis). (Unless otherwise noted, all references to DPC and FPC are to *Proceedings* of intergovernmental meetings.)

26 DPC (1941), 14 January 1941, 25 and 23.

27 Mackay to R.M. Fowler, Legal Secretary to the Chairman, 28 May 1938, in LAC, Mackay Papers (file 'Rowell-Sirois Correspondence, 1937–1939, 'F').

28 Kirk Makin, 'High Stakes Battle Looms over Oil-Sands Pollution,' *Globe and Mail*, 15 August 2007, A1 and A4.

29 For a succinct history and analysis of recent changes to the equalization program, see Michael Holden, 'Equalization: Implications of Recent Changes' (Ottawa: Library of Parliament, 2006), http://www.parl.gc.ca/information/library/PRBpubs/prb0591-e.htm (accessed 1 January 2009).

30 H. Blair Neatby, *William Lyon Mackenzie King, 1924–1932: The Lonely Heights*, vol. 2 (Toronto: University of Toronto Press, 1963), 221.

31 Christopher Dunn, 'Canadian Federalism and the Newfoundland and Labrador Royal Commission,' in *Constructing Tomorrow's Federalism / Bâtir Le Fédéralisme de Demain* (Regina: Saskatchewan Institute of Public Policy, 2004), 15–16.

32 FPC (1950), 5 December 1950, 58.

33 FPC (1955), 3 October 1955, 49.

34 Canada, Royal Commission on Government Organization, *Report*, 5 vols. (Ottawa: Queen's Printer, 1962). See also Luc Juillet and Ken Rasmussen, *Defending a Contested Ideal: Merit and the PSC of Canada, 1908–2008* (Ottawa: University of Ottawa Press, 2008).

35 Robert MacGregor Dawson, *The Principle of Official Independence: With Particular Reference to the Political History of Canada* (London: P.S. King and Son, 1922), ch. 3.

36 For a history of the GSC, see Morris Zaslow, *Reading the Rocks: The Story of the Geological Survey of Canada, 1842–1972* (Toronto and Ottawa: Macmillan of Canada in association with the Department of Energy, Mines and Resources and Information Canada, 1975).

37 DPC (1945), 9 January 1946, 261 ('Saskatchewan Replies to Dominion Gov-

ernment Proposals Delivered to the Dominion-Provincial Conference on Reconstruction').

38 Communication, 'Politics and National Symbols,' by Don Phillipson on the H-Canada discussion list, 6 November 2007, http:www.h-net.msu.edu.

39 DPC (1927), 10 November 1927, 31 (Precis of Discussion).

40 Phillipson, 'Reply: Politics and National Symbols.'

41 H.G. Thorburn, 'Federalism, Pluralism, and the Canadian Community,' in David P. Shugarman and Reginald Whitaker, eds., *Federalism and Political Community: Essays in Honour of Donald Smiley* (Peterborough: Broadview, 1989), 173–85 at 180.

42 FPC (1966), 25 October 1966, 19.

43 C.P. Snow, *The Two Cultures and the Scientific Revolution* (intro. by Stephan Collini) (New York: Cambridge University Press, 1998).

44 Will Kymlicka, 'The Paradox of Liberal Nationalism,' *Literary Review of Canada* 4, no. 10 (November 1995): 13.

45 Peter Graefe and Andrew Bourns, 'The Gradual Defederalization of Canadian Health Policy,' *Publius* 39, no. 1 (2009): 187–209 at 203. The Romanow Commission citation is Canada, Commission on the Future of Health Care in Canada, *Building on Values: The Future of Health Care in Canada* (Ottawa: Commission on the Future of Health Care in Canada, 2003).

46 Donald V. Smiley, *Canada in Question: Federalism in the Seventies* (Toronto: McGraw-Hill Ryerson, 1972), 98.

47 DPC (1935), 13 December 1935, 46.

48 DPC (1927), 3 November 1927, 9 (Precis of Discussion); and DPC (1935), 28 and 46.

49 Hon. E. Peter Lougheed, John Stack Memorial Lecture, Saskatoon, 9 February 2009 (question-and-answer session).

50 Philip Resnick, *The Politics of Resentment: British Columbia Regionalism and Canadian Unity* (Vancouver: UBC Press, 2000).

51 J. Peter Meekison, 'The Western Premiers' Conference: Intergovernmental Co-operation at the Regional Level,' in J. Peter Meekison, Hamish Telford, and Harvey Lazar, eds., *Reconsidering the Institutions of Canadian Federalism: Canada: The State of the Federation, 2002* (Montreal and Kingston: McGill-Queen's University Press, 2004), 183–209 at 191.

52 Janice MacKinnon, *Minding the Public Purse*, 159.

53 David McKay, 'William Riker on Federalism: Sometimes Wrong but More Right Than Anyone Else' (paper presented at the Conference on Constitutions, Voting, and Democracy, Center for New Institutional Social Sciences, Washington University, St Louis, 7–8 December, 2001), 3–4, quoted in Malcolm M. Feeley and Edward Rubin, *Federalism: Political Identity and Tragic*

*Compromise* (Ann Arbor: University of Michigan Press, 2008), 2 (emphasis in original).

54 Feeley and Rubin, *Federalism*, 89.

55 See for example, Richard Simeon, 'Federalism and Decentralization in Canada' (paper presented at the 2nd International Conference on Decentralization), http://www.forumfed.org/libdocs/IntConfDecent02/20031213-ca-RichardSimeon.pdf (accessed March 2009); Robin Boadway, 'The Folly of Decentralizing the Canadian Federation,' *Dalhousie Review* 75, no. 3 (Winter 1996): 313–49; and Harvey Lazar, 'Managing Interdependencies in the Canadian Federation: Lessons from the Social Union Framework Agreement' (Constructive and Co-operative Federalism? A Series of Commentaries on the Council of the Federation, Institute of Intergovernmental Relations / Institute for Research on Public Policy, 2003).

56 Peter H. Russell, *Constitutional Odyssey: Can Canadians Become a Sovereign People?* 3rd ed. (Toronto: University of Toronto Press, 2004).

## Chapter 6

1 K.C. Wheare, *Federal Government*. 3rd ed. (London: Oxford University Press, 1953), 65–6.

2 John T. Saywell, *The Lawmakers: Judicial Power and the Shaping of Canadian Federalism*. Osgoode Society for Canadian Legal History (Toronto: University of Toronto Press, 2002), 269. The Duplessis-Lévesque quotation is cited in Alan C. Cairns, 'Who Should the Judges Be? Canadian Debates about the Composition of a Final Court of Appeal,' in Harry N. Scheiber, ed., *North American and Comparative Federalism: Essays for the 1990s* (Berkeley: University of California, Institute of Governmental Studies Press, 1992), 82n5.

3 Jean Leclair, 'The Supreme Court of Canada's Understanding of Federalism: Efficiency at the Expense of Diversity,' *QLJ* 28 (2002–3): 411–53 at 437.

4 Geoffrey Marshall, *Constitutional Theory* (Oxford: Clarendon, 1971), 6.

5 See, for instance, *Attorney-General for Canada* v. *Attorney-General for Ontario and Others* (1937) A.C. 355 (Re Employment and Social Insurance Act).

6 *Attorney-General for Canada* v. *Attorney-General for Ontario and Others* (1937) A.C. 326 (Re Weekly Hours, Minimum Wages and Hours of Labour Acts).

7 Bora Laskin, '"Peace, Order, and Good Government" Re-Examined,' in W.R. Lederman, ed., *The Courts and the Canadian Constitution* (Toronto: McClelland and Stewart, 1964), 92, cited in David Schneiderman, 'Harold

Laski, Viscount Haldane, and the Law of the Canadian Constitution in the Early Twentieth Century,' *UTLJ* 48 (1998): 521–60 at 525.

8  Frank R. Scott, 'The Privy Council and Mr. Bennett's "New Deal" Legislation,' in *Essays on the Constitution: Aspects of Canadian Law and Politics* (Toronto: University of Toronto Press, 1977), ch. 7. The piece first appeared in the *CJEPS* 3 (1937): 234–40. Further comments were added to it from 'The Consequences of the Privy Council Decisions,' *CBR* 15 (1937): 485–92.

9  Paul Romney, *Getting It Wrong: How Canadians Forgot Their Past and Imperilled Confederation* (Toronto: University of Toronto Press, 1999), 173–4.

10  USA, MG 33, Cronkite Papers (C.3, Speeches and Articles), Faculty Club (University of Saskatchewan), [1938].

11  A.R.M. Lower, 'Theories of Canadian Federalism – Yesterday and Today,' in A.R.M. Lower, F.R. Scott, et al., *Evolving Canadian Federalism* (Durham: Duke University Press, 1958), 1–53 at 19.

12  Quebec, *Report of the Royal Commission of Inquiry on Constitutional Problems*, 4 vols. in 5. (Quebec: Province of Quebec, 1956), vol. 2, 165 and 171 (hereafter Tremblay Report), quoted in Bruce Ryder, 'The Demise and Rise of Classical Federalism: Promoting Autonomy for the Provinces and First Nations,' *McGLJ* 36 (1990–91): 308–81 at 340.

13  Tremblay Report, vol. 2, 151.

14  *Great West Saddlery Co.* v. *The King* (1921) 2 A.C. 91.

15  Jean-Charles Falardeau, 'Roots and Values in Canadian Lives,' in Bernard Ostry and Janice Yalden, eds., *Visions of Canada: The Alan B. Plaunt Memorial Lectures, 1958–1992* (Montreal and Kingston: McGill-Queen's University Press, 2004), 75–98 at 76.

16  Brooke Claxton, *Memoirs*, vol. 2, 287 (no additional bibliographic information provided) and Graham Spry, 'Broadcasting in Canada: Comment,' *CHR* 46 no. 2 (1965): 137–8, both quoted in Ron Faris, *The Passionate Educators: Voluntary Organizations and the Struggle for Control of Adult Educational Broadcasting in Canada, 1919–1952* (Toronto: Peter Martin Associates, 1975), 15 and 16.

17  Faris, *The Passionate Educators*, 16 (quoting Spry).

18  LAC, MG 31, E 46, Papers of Escott M. Reid, vol. 24 (file 1: The Effect of the Depression on Canadian Politics), for typed transcripts of interviews.

19  Rogers to Reid, 17 April 1933, ibid., vol. 35 (file 69: Rogers, Norman (1)).

20  E. Barker, *Political Thought in England 1848 to 1914* (London: Oxford University Press, 1963), 158, quoted in David Schneiderman, 'Harold Laski and the Law of the Canadian Constitution,' 529.

21  Schneiderman, 'Harold Laski,' 530.

22  H.J. Laski, *The Foundations of Sovereignty and Other Essays* (New York: Harcourt, Brace and Company, 1921), 55, quoted in Scheiderman, 'Harold Laski,' 535.

23  Geoffrey Sawer, 'Implication and the Constitution: Part 1,' *Res Judicatae* 4 (1948–50) at 19.

24  FPC (1950), 10–12 January 1950, 35.

25  Anne Twomey, *The Constitution of New South Wales* (Sydney: Federation Press, 2004).

26  David E. Smith, *The Republican Option in Canada, Past and Present* (Toronto: University of Toronto Press, 1999), 145.

27  Richard C. Risk, 'The Puzzle of Jurisdiction,' 46 *SCLR* (1994–5): 703–18 at 718.

28  K.C. Wheare, *Federal Government*. 3rd ed. (London: Oxford University Press, 1953), 63.

29  K.M. Lysyk, 'Reshaping Canadian Federalism,' *UBCLR*, 13 (1978): 1 at 16, cited in Saywell, *The Lawgivers*, 270.

30  Éric Montpetit, *Le Fédéralisme d'ouverture: La Recherche d'une légitimité Canadienne au Québéc* (Quebec: Septentrion, 2007), 66–7.

31  Allan Blakeney to Rt. Hon. Pierre Elliott Trudeau, 10 October 1978, in Department of Intergovernmental Affairs, *Resources: The Saskatchewan Position*, First Ministers Conference on the Constitution, Ottawa, 1980, Appendix in *'Confederation and Saskatchewan': Selected Saskatchewan Documents*, December 1976 to September 1980 (Regina, n.d.), quoted in David E. Smith, ed., *Building a Province: A History of Saskatchewan in Documents* (Saskatoon: Fifth House, 1992), Document 132, 436–8.

32  Canada. *Task Force on Canadian Unity: A Future Together* (Ottawa: Supply and Services Canada, January 1979), 130.

33  *Reference re: Objection to a Resolution to Amend the Constitution*, [1982] 2 *SCR* 793, paras. 22 and 86 (hereinafter Quebec Veto Reference).

34  Cris de Clercy, '"Holding Hands with the Public:" Trudeau and the Task Force on Canadian Unity, 1977–1979,' unpublished MA thesis, University of Saskatchewan, 1992.

35  Mollie Dunsmuir and Brian O'Neal, 'Quebec's Constitutional Veto: The Legal and Historical Context' (Ottawa: Political and Social Affairs Division, Library of Parliament, May 1992), 5, http://dsp-psd.pwgsc.gc.ca/Collection-R/LoPBdP/BP/bp295-e.htm (accessed 20 September 2007). See, too, Peter C. Oliver, 'Quebec and the Amending Formula: Protection, Promotion, and Federalism,' in Stephen Tierney, ed., *Accommodating Cultural Diversity* (Aldershot: Ashgate, 2007), 167–97.

36  For a history of this development, see Quebec, *Quebec's Positions on Con-*

*stitutional and Intergovernmental Issues from 1936 to March 2001* (Quebec: Publications du Québec, 2001).

37 *Reference re Resolution to Amend the Constitution*, [1981] 2 *SCR* 753 at 905 (hereinafter Patriation Reference).

38 Gilles Bourque and Jules Duchastel, *L'Identité fragmente: Nation et citoyenneté dans les débats constitutionnels Canadiens, 1941–1992* (Montreal: Editions Fides, 1996), 120.

39 Graeme Mitchell, Ian Peach, David E. Smith, and John Donaldson Whyte, eds., *A Living Tree: The Legacy of 1982 in Canada's Political Evolution* (Markham: LexisNexis, 2007).

40 Conference organizing memorandum, John Whyte, 23 April 2006 (in author's possession).

41 Marc-Antoine Adam, 'The Constitution Act, 1982, and the Dilemma of Canadian Duality Since 1760,' in Mitchell et al., *The Living Tree*, 625–48 at 627; and Garth Stevenson, 'Twenty-Five Years of Constitutional Frustration: The Amending Formula and the Continuing Legacy of 1982,' in Mitchell et al., *The Living* Tree, 681–705 at 681.

42 Roy Romanow, John Whyte, and Howard Leeson, *Canada ... Notwithstanding: The Making of the Constitution, 1976–1982* (Toronto: Carswell/Methuen, 1984), 24.

43 Ibid., 274–5.

44 Stevenson, 'Twenty-Five Years,' 683.

45 Romanow, Whyte, and Leeson, *Canada ... Notwithstanding*, 102.

46 Warren Newman, 'Living with the Amending Procedures: Prospects for Future Constitutional Reform in Canada,' in Mitchell et al., *The Living Tree*, 747–80 at 749–50.

47 James Ross Hurley, *Amending Canada's Constitution: History, Processes, Problems and Prospects* (Ottawa: Supply and Services Canada, 1996), 93.

48 Donald Dennison, 'Two Steps Forward, One Step Sideways,' in Mitchell et al., *The Living Tree*, 85–99 at 93.

49 Janet L. Hiebert, 'The Canadian Charter of Rights and Freedoms,' in John C. Courtney and David E. Smith, eds., *The Oxford Handbook of Canadian Politics* (New York: Oxford University Press, 2010), ch. 4. Internal quotation is from Heather MacIvor, *Canadian Politics and Government in the Charter Era* (Toronto: Thomson-Nelson, 2006), 221–2.

50 Montpetit, *Le Fédéralisme d'ouverture*, 24.

51 Carolyn J. Tuohy, *Policy and Politics in Canada: Institutionalized Ambivalence* (Philadelphia: Temple University Press, 1992), 5.

52 Hiebert, in *The Oxford Handbook of Canadian Politics*.

53 Montpetit, *Le Fédéralisme d'ouverture*, 66.

54  Kirk Makin, 'Judges Garner Greater Trust Than Politicians, Survey finds,' *Globe and Mail*, 9 April 2007, A5.
55  Allan Blakeney, *An Honourable Calling: Political Memoirs* (Toronto: University of Toronto Press, 2008), 189–90.
56  Mark Audcent, *The Senate Veto: Opinion of the Law Clerk and Parliamentary Counsel* (Ottawa: Senate of Canada, 1999), 23.
57  William H. Riker, *The Development of American Federalism* (Boston: Kluwer, 1987), 138.
58  *The Diary of André Laurendeau: Written during the Royal Commission on Bilingualism and Biculturalism, 1964–1967* (selected and with an intro. by Patricia Smart, trans. Patricia Smart and Dorothy Howard) (Toronto: Lorimer, 1991), 33.
59  G. Alan Tarr, 'Symmetry and Asymmetry in American Federalism,' paper presented at The Federal Idea: Conference in Honour of Ronald L. Watts, Institute of Intergovernmental Relations, Queen's University, Kingston, October 2007, 28, http://www.queensu.ca/iigr/conf/Watts/papers.html (accessed 26 April 2009).
60  Leclair, 'The Supreme Court of Canada's Understanding of Federalism,' 413.
61  Margaret Atwood, *Survival: A Thematic Guide to Canadian Literature* (Toronto: Anansi, 1972), 123.
62  William S. Livingston, *Federalism and Constitutional Change* (Oxford: Clarendon, 1956), 6.

**Chapter 7**

1  Canadian Press, 'Plains of Abraham Re-Enactment Cancelled,' 17 February 2009, http://www.thestar.com/news/canada/article/588670 (accessed 5 May 2009).
2  David E. Smith, *The Republican Option in Canada, Past and Present* (Toronto: University of Toronto Press, 1999), 172 and n91, 286.
3  Richard Simeon, 'Building Legislative Federalism,' *Constructing Tomorrow's Federalism* (Regina: Saskatchewan Institute of Public Policy, 2004), 53 (emphasis added).
4  Campbell Sharman, 'Underestimating Federalism' (University of Tasmania School of Government public lecture series, University of Tasmania, Hobart, 11 October 2001), 12 (paper in author's possession).
5  James Tully, 'Diversity's Gambit Declined,' in Curtis Cook, ed., *Constitutional Predicament: Canada after the Referendum of 1992* (Montreal and Kingston: McGill-Queen's University Press, 1994), 149–98 at 159 (emphasis in original).

6  Ontario Human Rights Commission, *Life Together: A Report on Human Rights in Ontario* (Toronto: Queen's Printer for Ontario, 1977), 18.

7  Judith Brett, 'Parliament, Meetings and Civil Society' (paper presented as a lecture in the Department of the Senate Occasional Lecture Series at Parliament House, Canberra, Australia, 27 July 2001), http://www.aph.gov.au/SENATE/pubs/pops/pop38/c08.pdf (accessed 7 May 2009).

8  Peter W. Hogg, *Constitutional Law in Canada*. 3rd ed. (Toronto: Carswell, 1992), 546.

9  *Estevan Mercury*, 13 April 1911.

10  Allan Blakeney, *An Honourable Calling: Political Memoirs* (Toronto: University of Toronto Press, 2008), 62–6.

11  Commission on the Future of Health Care in Canada, *Building on Values: The Future of Health Care in Canada – Final Report* (Saskatoon: Commission on the Future of Health Care in Canada, 2002).

12  Lisa L. Miller, 'The Representational Bias of Federalism: Scope and Bias in the Political Process, Revisited,' *Perspectives in Politics* 5, no. 2 (June 2007): 305–21 at 307.

13  'Saskatchewan Seeks Ruling on Marriage Commissioner Bill,' 28 July 2009, http://www.todaysfamilynews.ca/sexuality/saskatchewan-seeks-ruling-on-marriage-commissioner-bill.html (accessed 30 July 2009).

14  J.A. Corry, 'Constitutional Trends and Federalism,' in A.R.M. Lower, F.R. Scott, et al., *Evolving Canadian Federalism* (Durham: Duke University Press, 1958), 97 and 109–10.

15  Margaret Prang, 'Networks and Associations and the Nationalizing of Sentiment in English Canada,' in R. Kenneth Carty and W. Peter Ward, eds., *National Politics and Community in Canada* (Vancouver: UBC Press, 1986), 48–62 at 48.

16  Prang, 'Networks and Associations,' 60.

17  W.E. Mann, *Sect, Cult, and Church in Alberta* (Toronto: University of Toronto Press, 1955). The other volumes in the series are listed in ch. 5n17.

18  Thomas H. McLeod and Ian McLeod, *Tommy Douglas: The Road to Jerusalem* (Edmonton: Hurtig, 1987).

19  K.W. McNaught, *A Prophet in Politics: A Biography of J.S. Woodsworth* (Toronto: University of Toronto Press, 1959).

20  David Kwavnick, ed., *The Tremblay Report: Report of the Royal Commission of Inquiry on Constitutional Problems*. Carleton Library (Toronto: McClelland and Stewart, 1973), 69.

21  Alan C. Cairns, 'Author's Introduction,' in Douglas E. Williams, ed., *Constitutional Government and Society in Canada: Selected Essays by Alan C. Cairns* (Toronto: McClelland and Stewart, 1988), 14.

22 J.M.S. Careless, '"Limited Identities" in Canada,' *CHR* 50, no. 1 (1969): 1–10; David J. Elkins and Richard Simeon, *Small Worlds: Provinces and Parties in Canadian Political Life* (Toronto: Methuen, 1980).

23 Jean Harvey and Roger Proulx, 'Sport and the State in Canada,' in Jean Harvey and Hart Cantelon, eds., *Not Just a Game: Essays in Canadian Sport Sociology* (Ottawa: University of Ottawa Press, 1988), 93–120 at 102.

24 Ibid., 103 and 97.

25 Andrew Mayeda, 'Harper Government Plans to Study Athletics Funding,' *Leader-Post*, 27 November 2008, A15.

26 Maria Tippet, *Making Culture: English-Canadian Institutions and the Arts before the Massey Commission* (Toronto: University of Toronto Press, 1990).

27 T.H.B. Symons, *To Know Ourselves: The Report of the Commission on Canadian Studies.* 2 vols. (Ottawa: Association of Universities and Colleges of Canada, 1975).

28 Ibid., I:12.

29 Ibid., I:181.

30 Ibid., I:81 and 82.

31 Ibid., II:3.

32 Susan D. Phillips, 'Voluntary Sector: State Relationships in Federal Systems' (Forum of Federations: International Conference on Federalism, 1999), 3.

33 Alan C. Cairns, 'Ritual, Taboo, and Bias in Constitutional Controversies in Canada, or Constitutional Talk in Canadian Style,' in Alan C. Cairns, *Disruptions: Constitutional Struggles, from the Charter to Meech Lake,* ed. Douglas E. Williams (Toronto: McClelland and Stewart, 1991), 199–222 at 205.

34 David Cameron and Richard Simeon, eds., *Language Matters: How Canadian Voluntary Associations Manage French and English* (Vancouver: UBC Press, 2009).

35 John Meisel and Vincent Lemieux, *Ethnic Relations in Canadian Voluntary Associations.* Studies of the Royal Commission on Bilingualism and Biculturalism, Document 13 (Ottawa: Queen's Printer, 1972).

36 Cameron and Simeon, *Language Matters,* 4 and 5.

37 Ibid., 181.

38 Ibid., 113.

39 Kenneth D. McRae, ed., *Consociational Democracy: Political Accommodation in Segmented Societies.* Carleton Library (Toronto: McClelland and Stewart, 1974). Lijphart's seminal article, 'Consociational Democracy,' *World Politics* 21, no. 2 (1969): 207–25, appears in the McRae volume of essays.

40 Ian Buruma, *Murder in Amsterdam: Liberal Europe, Islam, and the Limits of Tolerance* (New York: Penguin, 2007), 46–53.

41  Tony Judt, *Reappraisals: Reflections on the Forgotten Twentieth Century* (New York: Penguin, 2008), 246, ch. 14, 'The Stateless State: Why Belgium Matters.'

42  Louise Marmen and Jean-Pierre Corbeil, *New Canadian Perspectives: Languages in Canada: 1996 Census* (Ottawa: Minister of Public Works and Government Services Canada, 1999), 45, quoted in Cameron and Simeon, *Language Matters*, 15.

43  Reid to Iain McKellar (Humanities and Social Sciences Division, Canada Council), 15 December 1970, LAC, MacKay Papers (vol. 36, file: Smith, Ruth C. (2) 1970–2).

44  Will Wilkinson, 'The Immigration Fallacy,' Cato Institute: Commentary, 27 April 2009, (accessed 9 June 2009). For a concerned view of the effects of immigration on Anglo-Protestant culture in the United States, see Samuel P. Huntington, *Who Are We? The Challenges to America's Identity* (New York: Simon and Schuster, 2004).

45  FPC, 1 September 1968, cited in Gary R. Miedema, *For Canada's Sake: Public Religion, Centennial Celebrations, and the Remaking of Canada in the 1960s* (Montreal and Kingston: McGill-Queen's University Press, 2005), 45.

46  Warren Newman, 'Living with the Amending Procedures: Prospects for Future Constitutional Reform in Canada,' in Mitchell et al., *A Living Tree*, 747–80 at 772.

47  Margaret Archibald, *By Federal Design: The Chief Architect's Branch of the Department of Public Works, 1881–1914* (Ottawa: Parks Canada, 1983).

## Chapter 8

1  R.C.B. Risk, 'The Many Minds of W.P.M. Kennedy,' in R.C.B. Risk, *A History of Canadian Legal Thought: Collected Essays*, ed. and intro. by G. Blaine Baker and Jim Phillips (Toronto: Osgoode Society for Canadian Legal History by University of Toronto Press, 2006), 300–40 at 321.

2  HOC, *Debates*, 28 November 1867, 154, cited in Robert C. Vipond, *Liberty and Community: Canadian Federalism and the Failure of the Constitution* (Albany: SUNY Press, 1991), 40–1.

3  J.E. Hodgetts, *Pioneer Public Service: An Administrative History of the United Canadas, 1841–1867* (Toronto: University of Toronto Press, 1955), 56.

4  HOC, *Debates*, 2 May 1870, 1287.

5  Peter Onuf, 'New State Equality: The Ambiguous History of a Constitutional Principle,' *Publius* 18 (1988): 68.

6  Marianne White, 'Happy 400th Birthday Quebec City,' *Leader-Post*, 4 July 2008, B12.

7 Miro Cernetig, 'Chrétien's Distinct Society Backfires in West,' *Globe and Mail*, 29 November 1995, quoted in Peter H. Russell, *Constitutional Odyssey: Can Canadians Become a Sovereign People?* 3rd ed. (Toronto: University of Toronto Press, 2004), 238.

8 Cited in W.H. McConnell, *Commentary on the British North America Act* (Toronto: Macmillan of Canada, 1977), 407. Case citation: *Reference re Ownership of Offshore Mineral Rights* [1968], 65 *D.L.R.* [2d] 353.

9 Jean Leclair, 'The Supreme Court of Canada's Understanding of Federalism: Efficiency at the Expense of Diversity,' *QLJ* 28 (2002–03): 411–53 at 439.

10 *Reference re Secession of Quebec*, [1998] 2 *SCR* 217 (para. 56).

11 John D. Whyte, 'Constitutional Meaning: Text and Experience' (lecture delivered to the first-year class at the College of Law, University of Saskatchewan, Saskatoon, 6 November 2006).

12 Peter Walker Johnston and Stanley D. Hotop, 'Patches on an Old Garment or New Wineskins for New Wine? Constitutional Reform in Western Australia – Evolution or Revolution?' *UWALR* 20 (1990): 428–44 at 430.

13 Edmund Wilson, *Letters on Literature and Politics, 1912–1972*, ed. Elena Wilson (New York: Farrar, Straus and Giroux, 1977), 636. *O Canada* was published by Farrar, Straus and Giroux in 1965.

14 Eugene Forsey, 'Concepts of Federalism: Some Canadian Aspects,' in J. Peter Meekison, ed., *Canadian Federalism; Myth or Reality?* (Toronto: Methuen, 1968), 348–54 at 348.

15 Eugene Forsey, 'Our Present Discontents,' in *Freedom and Order: Collected Essays*. Carleton Library no. 73 (Toronto: McClelland and Stewart, 1974), 306–32. This piece earlier appeared in Ontario Advisory Committee on Confederation, *Background Papers and Reports*, vol. 2, (1970), 60–84.

16 Eugene A. Forsey, *A Life on the Fringe: The Memoirs of Eugene Forsey* (Toronto: Oxford University Press, 1990).

17 Jennifer Smith, *Federalism* (Vancouver: UBC Press, 2004). See ch. 1, 'Auditing Federalism in Canada.'

18 Quoted in David Schneiderman, 'Harold Laski, Viscount Haldane, and the Law of the Canadian Constitution in the Early Twentieth Century,' *UTLJ* 48 (1998): 521–60 at 532.

# Bibliography

**Primary Sources**

*Manuscript: Personal*

Library and Archives Canada
John W. Dafoe MG30D45
Eugene Alfred Forsey MG30A25
Robert A. MacKay MG30E159
Escott M. Reid MG31E46
Saskatchewan Archives Board
James G. Gardiner R1022
University of Saskatchewan Archives
Frederick C. Cronkite MG33
Vernon C. Fowke MG95
University of Toronto Archives
Samuel Delbert Clark B1990-0029

*Government Records*

AUSTRALIA
Official Report of the National Australasian Convention Debates, Sydney, 1891. Sydney: Legal Books Pty. Ltd., 1986.
Official Report of the National Australasian Convention Debates, Adelaide Session, 1897. Sydney: Legal Books Pty. Ltd., 1986.
Official Report of the Debates of the Australasian Federal Convention, Sydney, 1897. Sydney: Legal Books Pty. Ltd., 1986.
Official Record of the Debates of the Australasian Federal Convention, Melbourne, 1898. Sydney: Legal Books Pty. Ltd., 1986.

CANADA

Canadian Sessional Papers, 1914, no. 118a, 'Memorandum on Representation
of the Maritime Provinces.' Reprinted in R. MacGregor Dawson, ed., *Consti-
tutional Issues in Canada, 1900–1931*. London: Oxford University Press, 1933.
Dominion-Provincial Conferences. *Proceedings*.
Energy, Mines and Resources. Surveys and Mapping Branch. *Territorial Evolu-
tion of Canada* (Map). Ottawa, 1969.
Federal-Provincial Conferences. *Proceedings*.
Legislative Assembly of United Canada. *Debates*.
– Parliamentary Debates on the Subject of the Confederation of the British
North American Provinces. Quebec, 1865. Ottawa: King's Printer, 1951.
Parliament. House of Commons. *Debates*.
– Senate. Special Senate Committee on Senate Reform. *Report on the Motion to
Amend the Constitution of Canada (western regional representation in the Senate)*,
October 2006. http://www.senate-senat.ca/senref.asp.

NEW BRUNSWICK

New Brunswick. *Position Paper of the Government of New Brunswick: Bill S-4, An
Act to Amend the Constitution Act, 1867 (Senate Tenure)*.

*Non-Governmental Records*

Audcent, Mark. *The Senate Veto: Opinion of the Law Clerk and Parliamentary
Counsel*. Ottawa: Senate of Canada, 1999.
Blakeney, Allan, to Rt. Hon. Pierre Elliott Trudeau, 10 October 1978, in Depart-
ment of Intergovernmental Affairs, *Resources: The Saskatchewan Position*,
First Ministers Conference on the Constitution, Ottawa, 1980, Appendix in
*'Confederation and Saskatchewan': Selected Saskatchewan Documents*, Decem-
ber 1976 to September 1980 (Regina, n.d.), quoted in David E. Smith, ed.,
*Building a Province: A History of Saskatchewan in Documents*. Saskatoon: Fifth
House, 1992.
British Columbia. *British Columbia in the Canadian Confederation*. A Submis-
sion presented to the Royal Commission on Dominion-Provincial Relations
by the Government of the Province of British Columbia, Victoria: King's
Printer, 1938.
Canada. 'Federal Government Restores Principle of Representation by Popula-
tion in the House of Commons.' 14 December 2007. http://news.gc.ca/
web/view/en/index.jsp?articleid=361279&.
Canadian Bar Association. 'Bill C-20 Senate Appointment Consultations Act.'
Ottawa: National Constitutional and Human Rights Section, April 2008.

Commission of Inquiry into the Sponsorship Program and Advertising Activities. *Who Is Responsible? Summary.* Ottawa: Ministry of Public Works, 2005.

Commission on the Future of Health Care in Canada. *Building on Values: The
Future of Health Care in Canada – Final Report.* Saskatoon: Commission on the
Future of Health Care in Canada, 2002.

Department of External Affairs. *Documents on Relations between Canada and
Newfoundland: Vol. 2, 1940–1949, Confederation, Part 1.* Paul Bridle, ed.
Ottawa: Supply and Services, 1984.

Doughty, Sir A.G., ed. *The Elgin-Grey Papers, 1846–1852.* 4 vols. Ottawa: King's
Printer, 1937.

Dunsmuir, Mollie, and Brian O'Neal. 'Quebec's Constitutional Veto: The
Legal and Historical Context.' Ottawa: Political and Social Affairs Division,
Library of Parliament, May 1992. http://dsp-psd.pwgsc.gc.ca/Collection-
R/LoPBdP/BP/bp295-e.htm.

Gooch, John. *Manual or explanatory development of the Act for the union of Canada, Nova Scotia, and New Brunswick in one dominion under the name of Canada
synthetical and analytical with the text of the Act etc., and the index to the Act and
the treaties.* [Ottawa: s.n.], 1867.

Goreham, Richard. *Language Rights and the Court Challenges Program: A Review
of Its Accomplishments and Impact of Its Abolition.* Ottawa: Commissioner of
Official Languages, 1992.

Marmen, Louise, and Jean-Pierre Corbeil. *New Canadian Perspectives: Languages
in Canada: 1996 Census.* Ottawa: Minister of Public Works and Government
Services, 1999.

Massicotte, Louis. 'Possible Repercussions of an Elected Senate on Official
Language Minorities in Canada.' Report for the Office of the Commissioner
of Official Languages, March 2007.

Newfoundland and Labrador. Royal Commission on Renewing and Strengthening Our Place in Canada, *Final Report.* St John's: Queen's Printer, 2003.
http://www.exec.gov.nl.ca/royalcomm/finalreport/default.html.

Nova Scotia. *Royal Commission on Donald Marshall, Jr., Prosecution.* Halifax:
Queen's Printer, 1989.

Office of the Commissioner of Official Languages, *Annual Report 2007–2008.*
http://www.ocol-clo.gc.ca/html/ar_ra_2007_08_chap2_1_e.php.

Ontario. Confederation for Tomorrow Conference, *Proceedings.* Toronto:
Queen's Printer, 1967.

Ontario. *Report of the Kaufman Commission on Proceedings Involving Guy Paul
Morin.* Toronto: Queen's Printer, 1998.

Ontario Human Rights Commission. *Life Together: A Report on Human Rights in
Ontario.* Toronto: Queen's Printer for Ontario, 1977.

Quebec. *Report of the Royal Commission of Inquiry on Constitutional Problems*. 4 vols. in 5. Quebec: Province of Quebec, 1956.

– *Quebec's Positions on Constitutional and Intergovernmental Issues from 1936 to March 2001*. Quebec: Publications du Québec, 2001.

*Responsive Institutions for a Modern Canada*. Ottawa: Minister of Supply and Services, 1991.

Royal Commission on Bilingualism and Biculturalism. *A Preliminary Report*. Ottawa: Queen's Printer, 1965.

Royal Commission on Dominion-Provincial Relations. *Report*. Reprinted in one volume. Ottawa: Queen's Printer, 1954.

Royal Commission on Dominion-Provincial Relations. *Report of Proceedings*, 2 May 1938.

Royal Commission on the Economic Union and Development Prospects for Canada. *Report*. 3 vols. Ottawa: Minister of Supply and Services Canada, 1985.

Royal Commission on Electoral Reform and Party Financing. *Report*. Ottawa: Minister of Supply and Services Canada, 1991.

Royal Commission on Government Organization. *Report*. 5 vols. Ottawa: Queen's Printer, 1962.

Royal Commission on Energy. *Second Report*. Ottawa: [Queen's Printer], 1959.

Saskatchewan. *Report of the Commission of Inquiry into the Wrongful Conviction of David Milgaard*. Regina: Queen's Printer, 2008.

– *Report of the Commission of Inquiry Re: Neil Stonechild*. Regina: Queen's Printer, 2004.

Senate of Canada, Session 1939. *Report, pursuant to resolution of the Senate to the Honourable The Speaker, by the Parliamentary Counsel, Relating to The Enactment of the British North America Act, 1867, any lack of congruence between its terms and judicial construction of them and cognate matters*. Ottawa: Queen's Printer, 1961.

'Some Notes on the Constitution and Government of Canada and on the Canadian Federal System' (A Reference Paper Prepared for the Information of a Delegation from the National Convention of Newfoundland). Newfoundland National Convention and Canada, Government Meetings 1947, Part 1.

Symons, T.H.B. *To Know Ourselves: The Report of the Commission on Canadian Studies*. 2 vols. Ottawa: Association of Universities and Colleges of Canada, 1975.

Task Force on Canadian Unity. *A Future Together: Observations and Recommendations*. Ottawa: Supply and Services, 1979.

Task Force on Canadian Unity. Unpublished Studies and Documents. Robert Décary, 'Politics and the Constitution'; Ghislain Fortin, 'The House of the

Federation Proposal Revisited'; Ralph Heintzman, 'The Formal Executive';
n/a, 'The Question of a Reconstituted Senate'; and Ronald L. Watts, 'Politics
and the Constitution: Senate.'

## Secondary Sources

*Books*

Adams, Michael. *Fire and Ice: The United States, Canada, and the Myth of Converging Values*. Toronto: Penguin Canada, 2003.

Anderson, George. *Federalism: An Introduction*. Toronto: Oxford University Press, 2008.

Archibald, Margaret. *By Federal Design: The Chief Architect's Branch of the Department of Public Works, 1881–1914*. Ottawa: Parks Canada, 1983.

Atwood, Margaret. *Survival: A Thematic Guide to Canadian Literature*. Toronto: Anansi, 1972.

Barker, E. *Political Thought in England 1848 to 1914*. London: Oxford University Press, 1963.

Blakeney, Allan. *An Honourable Calling: Political Memoirs*. Toronto: University of Toronto Press, 2008.

Bourque, Gilles, and Jules Duchastel. *L'Identité fragmentée: Nation et citoyenneté dans les débats constitutionnels Canadiens, 1941–1992*. Montreal: Editions Fides, 1996.

Bryce, Robert B. *Maturing in Hard Times: Canada's Department of Finance through the Great Depression*. Montreal and Kingston: McGill-Queen's University Press, 1986.

Burnet, Jean. *Next-Year Country*. Toronto: University of Toronto Press, 1951.

Buruma, Ian. *Murder in Amsterdam: Liberal Europe, Islam, and the Limits of Tolerance*. New York: Penguin, 2007.

Cameron, David, and Richard Simeon, eds. *Language Matters: How Canadian Voluntary Associations Manage French and English*. Vancouver: UBC Press, 2009.

Cameron, Kirk, and Graham White. *Northern Governments in Transition: Political and Constitutional Development in the Yukon, Nunavut, and the Western Northwest Territories*. Montreal: Institute for Research on Public Policy, 1995.

Clark, S.D. *Movements of Social Protest in Canada, 1640–1840*. Toronto: University of Toronto Press, 1959.

Cohen, Andrew. *The Unfinished Canadian: The People We Are*. Toronto: McClelland and Stewart, 2007.

Cohen, Patricia Cline. *A Calculating People: The Spread of Numeracy in Early America*. Chicago: University of Chicago Press, 1982.

Cook, Ramsay. *Provincial Autonomy, Minority Rights, and the Compact Theory, 1867–1921*. Studies of the Royal Commission on Bilingualism and Biculturalism. Ottawa: Queen's Printer, 1969.

Corry, J.A. *Democratic Government and Politics*. Toronto: University of Toronto Press, 1946.

Courtney, John C. *Commissioned Ridings: Designing Canada's Electoral Districts*. Montreal and Kingston: McGill-Queen's University Press, 2001.

Davis, S. Rufus. *The Federal Principle: A Journey through Time in Quest of Meaning*. Berkeley: University of California Press, 1978.

Dawson, R. MacGregor, ed. *Constitutional Issues in Canada, 1900–1931*. London: Oxford University Press, 1933.

– *The Government of Canada*. 5th ed. Revised by Norman Ward. Toronto: University of Toronto Press, 1970.

– *The Principle of Official Independence: With Particular Reference to the Political History of Canada*. London: P.S. King and Son, 1922.

Dicey, A.V. *Introduction to the Study of the Law of the Constitution*. 10th ed. London: Macmillan, 1962.

Docherty, David C. *Legislatures*. Vancouver: UBC Press, 2005.

Easton, David. *The Political System: An Inquiry into the State of Political Science*. New York: Knopf, 1953.

Eggleston, Wilfrid. *While I Still Remember*. Toronto: Ryerson, 1968.

Elkins, David J., and Richard Simeon. *Small Worlds: Provinces and Parties in Canadian Political Life*. Toronto: Methuen, 1980.

English, John. *The Decline of Politics: The Conservatives and the Party System, 1901–1920*. Toronto: University of Toronto Press, 1977.

Faris, Ron. *The Passionate Educators: Voluntary Organizations and the Struggle for Control of Adult Educational Broadcasting in Canada, 1919–1952*. Toronto: Peter Martin Associates, 1975.

Feeley, Malcolm M., and Edward Rubin. *Federalism: Political Identity and Tragic Compromise*. Ann Arbor: University of Michigan Press, 2008.

Filippov, Mikhail, Peter C. Ordeshook, and Olga Shvetsova. *Designing Federalism: A Theory of Self-Sustainable Federal Institutions*. New York: Cambridge University Press, 2004.

Forbes, Ernest R. *The Maritime Rights Movement, 1919–1927: A Study in Canadian Regionalism*. Montreal and Kingston: McGill-Queen's University Press, 1979.

Forsey, Eugene A. *A Life on the Fringe: The Memoirs of Eugene Forsey*. Toronto: Oxford University Press, 1990.

Fowke, V.C. *The National Policy and the Wheat Economy*. Toronto: University of Toronto Press, 1957.

Gwyn, Richard. *John A.: The Man Who Made Us*. Toronto: Random House Canada, 2007.

Gibson, Frederick W. *Cabinet Formation and Bicultural Relations: Seven Case Studies*. Studies of the Royal Commission on Bilingualism and Biculturalism. Ottawa: Information Canada, 1970.

Harvey, Jean, and Hart Cantelon, eds. *Not Just a Game: Essays in Canadian Sport Sociology*. Ottawa: University of Ottawa Press, 1988.

Hodgetts, J.E. *Pioneer Public Service: An Administrative History of the United Canadas, 1841–1867*. Toronto: University of Toronto Press, 1955.

Hogg, Peter W. *Constitutional Law in Canada*. 3rd ed. Toronto: Carswell, 1992.

Hueglin, Thomas O. *Federalism and Fragmentation: A Comparative View of Political Accommodation in Canada*. Kingston: Institute of Intergovernmental Relations, 1984.

Huntington, Samuel P. *Who Are We? The Challenges of American Identity*. New York: Simon and Schuster, 2004.

Hurley, James Ross. *Amending Canada's Constitution: History, Processes, Problems, and Prospects*. Ottawa: Supply and Services Canada, 1996.

Innis, Harold A. *Political Economy in the Modern State*. Toronto: Ryerson, 1946.

Irving, J.A. *The Social Credit Movement*. Toronto: University of Toronto Press, 1959.

Jenkins, Roy. *Churchill*. London: Macmillan, 2001.

Jennings, Sir Ivor. *Cabinet Government*. 3rd ed. Cambridge: Cambridge University Press, 1959.

Judt, Tony. *Reappraisals: Reflections on the Forgotten Twentieth Century*. New York: Penguin, 2008.

Juillet, Luc, and Ken Rasmussen. *Defending a Contested Ideal: Merit and the PSC of Canada, 1908–2008*. Ottawa: University of Ottawa Press, 2008.

Kendle, John. *Ireland and the Federal Solution: The Debate over the United Kingdom Constitution*. Montreal and Kingston: McGill-Queen's University Press, 1989.

Kennedy, W.P.M. *Statutes, Treaties, and Documents of the Canadian Constitution, 1713–1929*. Toronto: Oxford University Press, 1930.

Kwavnick, David, ed. *The Tremblay Report: Report of the Royal Commission of Inquiry on Constitutional Problems*. Carleton Library. Toronto: McClelland and Stewart, 1973.

Laskin, Bora. *The British Tradition in Canadian Law*. London: Stevens and Sons, 1969.

Lasswell, Harold D. *Politics: Who Gets What, When, How*. New York: World, 1958.

Laurendeau, André. *The Diary of André Laurendeau: Written during the Royal*

*Commission on Bilingualism and Biculturalism, 1964–1967.* Selected and with an introduction by Patricia Smart. Toronto: Lorimer, 1991.

Lipset, Seymour Martin. *Continental Divide: The Values and Institutions of the United States and Canada.* New York: Routledge, 1990.

– *Agrarian Socialism: The Cooperative Commonwealth Federation in Saskatchewan: A Study in Political Sociology.* Berkeley: University of California Press, 1950.

Livingston, William S. *Federalism and Constitutional Change.* Oxford: Clarendon, 1956.

Lower, A.R.M., F.R. Scott, et al. *Evolving Canadian Federalism.* Durham: Duke University Press, 1958.

MacIvor, Heather. *Canadian Politics and Government in the Charter Era.* Toronto: Thomson-Nelson, 2006.

MacKinnon, Janice. *Minding the Public Purse: The Fiscal Crisis, Political Trade-Offs, and Canada's Future.* Montreal and Kingston: McGill-Queen's University Press, 2003.

MacLennan, Hugh. *Two Solitudes.* Toronto: Macmillan, 1945.

Macmahon, Arthur W. *Federalism, Mature and Emergent.* Garden City: Doubleday, 1962.

Macpherson, C.B. *Democracy in Alberta: The Theory and Practice of a Quasi-Party System.* Toronto: University of Toronto Press, 1953.

Mallory, J.R. *The Structure of Canadian Government.* Revised edition. Toronto: Gage, 1984.

Mallory, J.R. *Social Credit and the Federal Power in Canada.* Toronto: University of Toronto Press, 1954.

Mann, W.E. *Sect, Cult, and Church in Alberta.* Toronto: University of Toronto Press, 1955.

Mansergh, Nicholas. *Survey of British Commonwealth Affairs: Problems of External Policy, 1931–1939.* London: Oxford University Press, 1952.

Marlyn, John. *Under the Ribs of Death.* London: Arthur Barker [1957].

Marshall, Geoffrey. *Constitutional Theory.* Oxford: Clarendon, 1971.

Masters, D.C. *The Winnipeg General Strike.* Toronto: University of Toronto Press, 1950.

McConnell, W.H. *Commentary on the British North America Act.* Toronto: Macmillan of Canada, 1977.

McLeod, Thomas H., and Ian McLeod. *Tommy Douglas: The Road to Jerusalem.* Edmonton: Hurtig, 1987.

McNaught, K.W. *A Prophet in Politics: A Biography of J.S. Woodsworth.* Toronto: University of Toronto Press, 1959.

McRae, Kenneth D., ed. *Consociational Democracy: Political Accommodation in Segmented Societies.* Carleton Library. Toronto: McClelland and Stewart, 1974.

Meisel, John, and Vincent Lemieux. *Ethnic Relations in Canadian Voluntary Associations*. Studies of the Royal Commission on Bilingualism and Biculturalism, Document 13. Ottawa: Queen's Printer, 1972.

Miedema, Gary R. *For Canada's Sake: Public Religion, Centennial Celebrations, and the Remaking of Canada in the 1960s*. Montreal and Kingston: McGill-Queen's University Press, 2005.

Mitchell, Graeme, Ian Peach, David E. Smith, and John Donaldson Whyte, eds. *A Living Tree: The Legacy of 1982 in Canada's Political Evolution*. Markham: LexisNexis, 2007.

Montpetit, Éric. *Le Fédéralisme d'ouverture: La Recherche d'une légitimité Canadienne au Québec*. Québec: Septentrion, 2007.

Morton, W.L. *The Progressive Party in Canada*. Toronto: University of Toronto Press, 1950.

Neatby, H. Blair. *William Lyon Mackenzie King, 1924–1932: The Lonely Heights*, vol. 2. Toronto: University of Toronto Press, 1963.

Neufeld, E.P. *The Financial System of Canada: Its Growth and Development*. Toronto: Macmillan of Canada, 1972.

Nicholson, Norman L. *The Boundaries of Canada, Its Provinces and Territories*. Ottawa: Department of Mines and Technical Surveys, Geographical Branch, 1964.

Oliver, Peter C. *The Constitution of Independence: The Development of Constitutional Theory in Australia, Canada, and New Zealand*. Oxford: Oxford University Press, 2005.

Onuf, Peter S. *The Origins of the Federal Republic: Jurisdictional Controversies in the United States, 1775–1787*. Philadelphia: University of Pennsylvania Press, 1983.

Richards, John, and Larry Pratt. *Prairie Capitalism: Power and Influence in the New West*. Toronto: McClelland and Stewart, 1979.

Riker, William H. *The Development of American Federalism*. Boston: Kluwer, 1987.

Romanow, Roy, John Whyte, and Howard Leeson. *Canada … Notwithstanding: The Making of the Constitution, 1976–1982*. Toronto: Carswell/Methuen, 1984.

Romney, Paul. *Getting It Wrong: How Canadians Forgot Their Past and Imperilled Confederation*. Toronto: University of Toronto Press, 1999.

Resnick, Philip. *The Politics of Resentment: British Columbia Regionalism and Canadian Unity*. Vancouver: UBC Press, 2000.

Russell, Frances. *The Canadian Crucible: Manitoba's Role in Canada's Great Divide*. Winnipeg: Heartland Associates, 2003.

Russell, Peter H. *Constitutional Odyssey: Can Canadians Ever Become a Sovereign People?* 3rd ed. Toronto: University of Toronto Press, 2004.

Russell, Peter H., and Lorne Sossin, eds. *Parliamentary Democracy in Crisis.* Toronto: University of Toronto Press, 2009.

Samuel, Raphael. *Theatres of Memory, Vol. 1: Past and Present in Contemporary Culture.* London: Verso, 1994.

Savoie, Donald J. *Governing from the Centre: The Concentration of Power in Canadian Politics.* Toronto: University of Toronto Press, 1999.

Saywell, John T. *The Office of Lieutenant-Governor.* Toronto: University of Toronto Press, 1957.

– *The Lawmakers: Judicial Power and the Shaping of Canadian Federalism.* Osgoode Society for Canadian Legal History. Toronto: University of Toronto Press, 2002.

Simeon, Richard. *Federal–Provincial Diplomacy: The Making of Recent Policy in Canada.* Toronto: University of Toronto Press, 1972.

– *Political Science and Federalism: Seven Decades of Scholarly Engagement.* 2000 Kenneth R. MacGregor Lecturer, Institute of Intergovernmental Relations, School of Policy Studies, Queen's University, 2002.

– ed. *Must Canada Fail?* Montreal and Kingston: McGill-Queen's University Press, 1977.

Singh, M.P., and Chandra Mohan, eds. *Regionalism and National Identity: Canada, India – Interdisciplinary Perspectives.* Delhi: Pragati, 1994.

Smiley, Donald V. *Canada in Question: Federalism in the Seventies.* Toronto: McGraw-Hill Ryerson, 1972.

Smiley, Donald V., and Ronald L. Watts. *Intrastate Federalism in Canada.* Toronto: University of Toronto Press in cooperation with the Royal Commission on the Economic Union and Development Prospects for Canada, 1985.

Smith, Andrew. *British Businessmen and Canadian Confederation: Constitution-Making in an Era of Anglo-Globalization.* Montreal and Kingston: McGill-Queen's University Press, 2008.

Smith, David E., ed. *Building a Province: A History of Saskatchewan in Documents.* Saskatoon: Fifth House, 1992.

– *The Invisible Crown: The First Principle of Canadian Government.* Toronto: University of Toronto Press, 1995.

– *The People's House of Commons: Theories of Democracy in Contention.* Toronto: University of Toronto Press, 2007.

– *The Regional Decline of a National Party: Liberals on the Prairies.* Toronto: University of Toronto Press, 1981.

– *The Republican Option in Canada, Past and Present.* Toronto: University of Toronto Press, 1999.

Smith, Jennifer. *Federalism.* Vancouver: UBC Press, 2004.

– ed. *The Democratic Dilemma: Reforming the Canadian Senate*. Institute of Intergovernmental Relations, School of Public Policy, Queen's University, and Montreal and Kingston: McGill-Queen's University Press, 2009.

Snow, C.P. *The Two Cultures and the Scientific Revolution*. Introduction by Stephan Collini. New York: Cambridge University Press, 1998.

Spafford, Shirley. *No Ordinary Academics: Economics and Political Science at the University of Saskatchewan, 1910–1960*. Toronto: University of Toronto Press, 2000.

Taylor, John. *An Inquiry into the Principles and Policy of the United States*. New Haven: Yale University Press, 1950, first published 1814.

Thomas, Lewis G. *The Liberal Party in Alberta*. Toronto: University of Toronto Press, 1959.

Tippet, Maria. *Making Culture: English-Canadian Institutions and the Arts before the Massey Commission*. Toronto: University of Toronto Press, 1990.

Tribe, Laurence H. *The Invisible Constitution*. New York: Oxford University Press, 2008.

Tuohy, Carolyn J. *Policy and Politics in Canada: Institutionalized Ambivalence*. Philadelphia: Temple University Press, 1992.

Twomey, Anne. *The Constitution of New South Wales*. Sydney: Federation Press, 2004.

Vile, M.J.C. *Constitutionalism and the Separation of Powers*. Oxford: Clarendon, 1967.

Vipond, Robert C. *Liberty and Community: Canadian Federalism and the Failure of the Constitution*. Albany: SUNY Press, 1991.

Ward, Norman. *The Canadian House of Commons: Representation*. 2nd ed. Toronto: University of Toronto Press, 1963.

Watts, Ronald L. *Comparing Federal Systems in the 1990s*. Kingston: Institute of Intergovernmental Relations, 1996.

Weaver, R. Kent, ed. *The Collapse of Canada?* Washington: Brookings Institution, 1992.

Wheare, K.C. *Federal Government*. London: Oxford University Press, 1946.

– *The Statute of Westminster and Dominion Status*. 4th ed. London: Oxford University Press, 1949.

Whitaker, Reginald. *A Sovereign Idea: Essays on Canada as a Democratic Community*. Montreal and Kingston: McGill-Queen's University Press, 1992.

Wilson, Edmund. *Letters on Literature and Politics, 1912–1972*. Elena Wilson, ed. New York: Farrar, Straus and Giroux, 1977.

Wilson, Garrett. *Farewell Frontier: The 1870s and the End of the Old West*. Regina: Canadian Plains Research Center, 2007.

Wiseman, Nelson. *In Search of Canadian Political Culture*. Vancouver: UBC Press, 2007.

Wood, Gordon S. *Revolutionary Characters: What Made the Founders Different*. New York: Penguin, 2006.

Wright, Deil S. *Understanding Intergovernmental Relations: Public Policy and Participants' Perspectives in Local, State, and National Governments*. North Scituate: Duxbury, 1978.

Yuzyk, Senator Paul. *For a Better Canada: A Collection of Selected Speeches Delivered in the Senate of Canada and at Banquets and Conferences in Various Centres across Canada*. Toronto: Ukrainian National Association [1973].

Zaslow, Morris. *Reading the Rocks: The Story of the Geological Survey of Canada, 1842–1972*. Toronto/ Ottawa: Macmillan of Canada in association with the Department of Energy, Mines and Resources, and Information Canada, 1975.

Ziegler, Philip. *Osbert Sitwell*. New York: Knopf, 2000.

*Chapters in Books*

Adam, Marc-Antoine. 'The Constitution Act, 1982, and the Dilemma of Canadian Duality Since 1760.' In Graeme Mitchell, Ian Peach, David E. Smith, and John Donaldson Whyte, eds., *The Living Tree: The Legacy of 1982 in Canada's Constitutional Evolution*. 625–48. Markham: LexisNexis, 2007.

Burgess, Michael. 'Competing National Visions: Canada-Quebec Relations in a Comparative Perspective.' In Alain-G. Gagnon and James Tully, eds., *Multinational Democracies*. 257–74. Cambridge: Cambridge University Press, 2001.

Cairns, Alan C. 'Author's Introduction.' In Douglas E. Williams, ed., *Constitutional Government and Society in Canada: Selected Essays by Alan C. Cairns*. 11–24. Toronto: McClelland and Stewart, 1988.

– 'The Constitutional World We Have Lost.' In C.E.S. Frank, J.E. Hodgetts, O.P. Dwivedi, Doug Williams, and V. Seymour Williams, eds., *Canada's Century: Governing a Maturing Society*. 43–67. Montreal and Kingston: McGill-Queen's University Press.

– 'Ritual, Taboo, and Bias in Constitutional Controversies in Canada, or Constitutional Talk Canadian Style.' In Douglas E. Williams, ed., *Disruptions: Constitutional Struggles, from the Charter to Meech Lake*. 199–222. Toronto: McClelland and Stewart, 1991.

– 'Who Should the Judges Be? Canadian Debates about the Composition of a Final Court of Appeal.' In Harry N. Scheiber, ed., *North American and Comparative Federalism: Essays for the 1990s*. 57–88. Berkeley: University of California Press, 1992.

Corry, J.A. 'Constitutional Trends and Federalism.' In A.R.M. Lower, F.R. Scott, et al., *Evolving Canadian Federalism*. 91–125. Durham: Duke University Press, 1958.

Dennison, Donald. 'Two Steps Forward, One Step Sideways.' In Graeme Mitchell, Ian Peach, David E. Smith, and John Donaldson Whyte, eds., *The Living Tree: The Legacy of 1982 in Canada's Constitutional Evolution*. 85–99. Markham: LexisNexis, 2007.

Elazar, Daniel J. 'Our Thoroughly Federal Constitution.' In Robert A. Goldwin and William A. Schambra, eds., *How Federal Is Our Constitution?* 38–66. Washington: American Enterprise Institute for Public Policy Research, 1987.

Falardeau, Jean-Charles. 'Roots and Values in Canadian Lives.' In Bernard Ostry and Janice Yalden, eds., *Visions of Canada: The Alan B. Plaunt Memorial Lectures, 1958–1992*. 75–98. Montreal and Kingston: McGill-Queen's University Press, 2004.

Forsey, Eugene. 'Concepts of Federalism: Some Canadian Aspects.' In J. Peter Meekison, ed., *Canadian Federalism: Myth or Reality?* 348–54. Toronto: Methuen, 1968.

– 'Our Present Discontents.' In *Freedom and Order: Collected Essays*. 306–32. Carleton Library No. 73, Toronto: McClelland and Stewart, 1974.

Harvey, Jean, and Roger Proulx. 'Sport and the State in Canada.' In Jean Harvey and Hart Cantelon, eds., *Not Just a Game: Essays in Canadian Sport Sociology*. 93–120. Ottawa: University of Ottawa Press, 1988.

Hiebert, Janet L. 'The Canadian Charter of Rights and Freedoms.' In John C. Courtney and David E. Smith, eds., *The Oxford Handbook of Canadian Politics*. 54–71. New York: Oxford University Press, 2010.

Jackson, Michael, Rachele Dabraio, and Suzanne Moffett. 'Honours in a Federal State.' In Michael Jackson, ed., *Honouring Commonwealth Citizens: Proceedings of the First Conference on Commonwealth Honours and Awards*. 115–27. Toronto: Honours and Awards Secretariat, Ontario Ministry of Citizenship and Immigration, 2007.

Johnston, Richard, André Blais, Elisabeth Gidengil, and Neil Nevitte. 'The People and the Charlottetown Accord.' In Ronald L. Watts and Douglas M. Brown, eds., *Canada: The State of the Federation, 1993*. 19–43. Kingston: Institute of Intergovernmental Relations, 1993.

Kennedy, W.P.M. 'Law and Custom in the Canadian Constitution.' In Robert MacGregor Dawson, ed., *Constitutional Issues in Canada, 1900–1931*. 50–62. London: Oxford University Press, 1933.

Laforest, Guy. 'Quebec beyond the Federal Regime of 1867–1982: From Distinct Society to National Community.' In Ronald L. Watts and Douglas

M. Brown, eds., *Options for a New Canada*. 103–22. Toronto: University of Toronto Press, 1991.

Laskin, Bora. '"Peace, Order, and Good Government" Re-Examined.' In W.R. Lederman, ed., *The Courts and the Canadian Constitution*. 66–104. Toronto: McClelland and Stewart, 1964.

Lower, A.R.M. 'Theories of Canadian Federalism: Yesterday and Today.' In A.R.M. Lower, F.R. Scott, et al., *Evolving Canadian Federalism*. 1–53. Durham: Duke University Press, 1958.

Mallory, J.R. 'The Continuing Evolution of Canadian Constitutionalism.' In Alan Cairns and Cynthia Williams, eds., *Constitutionalism, Citizenship, and Society in Canada*. 51–97. Toronto: University of Toronto Press, in cooperation with the Royal Commission on the Economic Union and Development Prospects for Canada, 1985.

Marshall, Geoffrey. 'Canada's New Constitution (1982): Some Lessons in Constitutional Engineering.' In Vernon Bogdanor, ed., *Constitutions in Democratic Politics*. 56–70. Brookfield: Gower, 1988.

Meekison, J. Peter. 'The Western Premiers' Conference: Intergovernmental Co-operation at the Regional Level.' In J. Peter Meekison, Hamish Telford, and Harvey Lazar, eds., *Reconsidering the Institutions of Canadian Federalism: Canada: The State of the Federation, 2002*. 183–209. Montreal and Kingston: McGill-Queen's University Press, 2004.

Newman, Warren. 'Living with the Amending Procedures: Prospects for Future Constitutional Reform in Canada.' In Graeme Mitchell, Ian Peach, David E. Smith, and John Donaldson Whyte, eds., *The Living Tree: The Legacy of 1982 in Canada's Constitutional Evolution*. 747–80. Markham: LexisNexis, 2007.

Noël, Alain. 'Is Decentralization Conservative? Federalism and the Contemporary Debate on the Canadian Welfare State.' In Robert Young, ed., *Stretching the Federation: The Art of the State in Canada*. 195–218. Kingston: Institute of Intergovernmental Relations, Queen's University, 1999.

Oliver, Peter C. 'Quebec and the Amending Formula: Protection, Promotion, and Federalism.' In Stephen Tierney, ed., *Accommodating Cultural Diversity*. 167–97. Aldershot: Ashgate, 2007.

Prang, Margaret. 'Networks and Associations and the Nationalizing of Sentiment in English Canada.' In R. Kenneth Carty and W. Peter Ward, eds., *National Politics and Community in Canada*. 48–62. Vancouver: UBC Press, 1986.

Risk, R.C.B. 'The Many Minds of W.P.M. Kennedy.' In R.C.B. Risk, *A History of Canadian Legal Thought: Collected Essays*. 300–40. Ed. and intro. by G. Blaine Baker and Jim Phillips. Toronto: Osgoode Society for Canadian Legal History by University of Toronto Press, 2006

Saskatchewan. *Official Synopsis of the Report of the Royal Commission on Agri-*

*cultural Credit* (1913). In David E. Smith, *Building a Province: A History of Saskatchewan in Documents*. 211–28. Saskatoon: Fifth House, 1992.

Scott, Frank R. 'The Privy Council and Mr. Bennett's "New Deal" Legislation.' In *Essays on the Constitution: Aspects of Canadian Law and Politics*. 90–101. Toronto: University of Toronto Press, 1977.

Simeon, Richard. 'Making Federalism Work.' In Keith G. Banting et al., *Open Federalism: Interpretations, Significance*. 1–5. Kingston: Institute of Intergovernmental Relations, 2006.

Smith, David E. 'The Politics of the Federal Cabinet.' In Glen Williams and Michael Whittington, eds., *Canadian Politics in the Eighties*. 351–70. 2nd ed. Toronto: Methuen, 1984.

– 'Party Government, Representation, and National Integration in Canada.' In Peter Aucoin, ed., *Party Government and Regional Representation in Canada*. 1–68. Toronto: University of Toronto Press, in cooperation with the Royal Commission on the Economic Union and Development Prospects for Canada, 1985.

– 'Politics and Police.' In R.C. Macleod and David Schneiderman, eds., *Police Powers in Canada: The Evolution and Practice of Authority*. 184–208. Toronto: University of Toronto Press, 1994.

Sossin, Lorne. 'The Ambivalence of Executive Power in Canada.' In Paul Craig and Adam Tomkins, eds., *The Executive and Public Law: Power and Accountability in Comparative Perspective*. 52–88. New York: Oxford University Press, 2006.

Spafford, Duff. 'Notes on Re-reading Lipset's *Agrarian Socialism*.' In David E. Smith, ed., *Lipset's 'Agrarian Socialism': A Re-examination*. 23–33. Regina: Canadian Plains Research Center and Saskatchewan Institute of Public Policy, 2007.

Stevenson, Garth. 'Twenty-Five Years of Constitutional Frustration: The Amending Formula and the Continuing Legacy of 1982.' In Graeme Mitchell, Ian Peach, David E. Smith, and John Donaldson Whyte, eds., *The Living Tree: The Legacy of 1982 in Canada's Constitutional Evolution*. 681–705. Markham: LexisNexis, 2007.

Thorburn, H.G. 'Federalism, Pluralism, and the Canadian Community.' In David P. Shugarman and Reginald Whitaker, eds., *Federalism and Political Community: Essays in Honour of Donald Smiley*. 173–85. Peterborough: Broadview, 1989.

Tully, James. 'Diversity's Gambit Declined.' In Curtis Cook, ed., *Constitutional Predicament: Canada after the Referendum of 1992*. 149–98. Montreal and Kingston: McGill-Queen's University Press, 1994.

Watts, Ronald L. 'Canada's Constitutional Options: An Outline.' In Ronald L. Watts and Douglas M. Brown, eds., *Options for A New Canada*. 15–30. Toronto: University of Toronto Press, 1991.

Wheare, Kenneth C. 'Federalism and the Making of Nations.' In Arthur
W. Macmahon, ed., *Federalism Mature and Emergent.* 28–43. Garden City:
Doubleday, 1962.

Whyte, John D. 'What Does the Constitution Say?' In Jennifer Smith, ed., *The
Democratic Dilemma: Reforming the Canadian Senate.* 91–109. Montreal and
Kingston: McGill-Queen's University Press, 2009.

*Articles in Journals*

Black, Edwin R., and Alan C. Cairns. 'A Different Perspective on Canadian
Federalism.' *CPA* 9, no. 1 (March 1966): 27–45.

Boadway, Robin. 'The Folly of Decentralizing the Canadian Federation.' *Dalhousie Review* 75, no. 3 (Winter 1996): 313–49.

'Bystander.' 'Colonel Gray on Confederation.' *Canadian Monthly* 2 (August
1872): 173–83.

Cairns, Alan C. 'The Governments and Societies of Canadian Federalism.'
*CJPS* 10, no. 4 (December 1977): 695–725.

Cameron, David R. 'Not Spicer and Not the B and B: Reflections of an Insider
on the Workings of the Pepin-Robarts Task Force on Canadian Unity.' *IJCS*
7–8 (Spring–Fall 1993): 333–45.

Cameron, David R., and Jacqueline D. Krikorian. 'The Study of Federalism,
1960–99: A Content Review of Several Leading Canadian Academic Journals.' *CPA* 45, no. 3 (Fall 2002): 329–63.

Cameron, David, and Richard Simeon. 'Intergovernmental Relations in Canada: The Emergence of Collaborative Federalism.' *Publius* 32, no. 2 (Spring
2002): 49–71.

Careless, J.M.S. '"Limited Identities" in Canada.' *CHR* 50, no. 1 (1969): 1–10.

Clark, S.D. 'The Attack on the Authority Structure of Canadian Society.' *TRSC*
14 (1976): 5–15.

Clokie, H. McD. 'Judicial Review, Federalism, and the Canadian Constitution.'
*CJEPS* 8, no. 4 (November 1942): 537–56.

Desserud, Donald. 'The Confidence Convention under the Canadian Parliamentary System.' *Parliamentary Perspectives* 7 (Ottawa: Canadian Study of
Parliament Group, October 2006).

Elazar, Daniel J. 'Contrasting Unitary and Federal Systems.' *IPSR* 18, no. 3
(1997): 237–51.

English, John. 'The Second Time Around: Political Scientists Writing History.'
*CHR* 67, no. 1 (1986): 1–16.

Fafard, Patrick, and François Rocher. 'The Evolution of Federalism Studies in
Canada: From Centre to Periphery.' *CPA* 52 no. 2 (June 2009): 291–311.

Forsey, Eugene. 'Canada: Two Nations or One?' *CJEPS* 28 (November 1962): 485–501.

– 'Extension of the Life of Legislatures.' *CJEPS* 26 (November 1960): 604–16.

Graefe, Peter, and Andrew Bourns. 'The Gradual Defederalization of Canadian Health Policy.' *Publius* 39 no. 1 (Winter 2009): 187–209.

Hicks, Brian. 'Bilingualism and the Canadian House of Commons 40 Years after B and B.' *Parliamentary Perspectives*, no. 8 (Ottawa: Canadian Study of Parliament Group, June 2008).

Hicks, Bruce M., and André Blais. 'Restructuring the Canadian Senate through Elections.' *IRPP Choices* 14, no. 15 (November 2008).

Johnston, Peter Walker, and Stanley D. Hotop. 'Patches on an Old Garment or New Wineskins for New Wine? Constitutional Reform in Western Australia?' *UWALR* 20 (1990): 428–44.

Kent, Tom. 'An Elected Senate: Key to Redressing the Democratic Deficit, Revitalizing Federalism.' *Policy Options* (April 2004): 49–53.

Keyfitz, Nathan. 'Robert Hamilton Coats, 1874–1960.' *Proceedings of the Royal Society of Canada* (1960): 99–104.

Kymlicka, Will. 'The Paradox of Liberal Nationalism.' *Literary Review of Canada* 4, no. 10 (November 1995): 13–15.

Leclair, Jean. 'The Supreme Court of Canada's Understanding of Federalism: Efficiency at the Expense of Diversity.' *QLJ* 28 (2002–3): 411–53.

Lyon, J. Noel. 'The Central Fallacy of Canadian Constitutional Law.' *McGLJ* 22 (1976): 40–61.

Marshall, Geoffrey. 'Kenneth Clinton Wheare.' *PBA* 67 (1981): 491–507.

Miller, Lisa L. 'The Representational Bias of Federalism: Scope and Bias in the Political Process, Revisited.' *Perspectives on Politics* 5, no. 2 (June 2007): 305–21.

Neill, Robin. 'Economic Historiography in the 1950s: The Saskatchewan School.' *JCS* 34, no. 3 (Autumn 1999): 243–60.

Newman, Warren J. '"Grand Entrance Hall," Back Door or Foundation Stone? The Role of Constitutional Principles in Construing and Applying the Constitution of Canada.' *SCLR* 14 (2d) (2001): 197–242.

O'Hearn, Hon. Judge P.J.T. 'Nova Scotia and Constitutional Amendment.' *McGLJ* 12 (1966–7): 433–42.

Onuf, Peter. 'New State Equality: The Ambiguous History of a Constitutional Principle.' *Publius* 18, no. 4 (Summer 1988): 53–69.

Ostram, Vincent. 'State Administration of Natural Resources in the West.' *APSR* 47, no. 2 (June 1953): 478–93.

Pawley, Hon. Howard. 'The Lessons of a Very Political Life.' *CPR* 30, no. 2 (2007): 7–13.

Read, J.E. 'The Early Provincial Constitutions.' *CBR* 26, no. 4 (April 1998):
621–37.

Risk, Richard C. 'The Puzzle of Jurisdiction.' *SCLR* 46 (1994–5): 703–18.

Rogers, Norman McL. 'The Compact Theory of Confederation.' *Papers and
Proceedings of the Annual Meeting of the Canadian Political Science Association* 3
(May 1931): 205–30.

Ryder, Bruce. 'The Demise and Rise of Classical Federalism: Promoting
Autonomy for the Provinces and First Nations.' *McGLJ* 36 (1990–91): 308–
81.

Sawer, Geoffrey. 'Implication and the Constitution: Part 1.' *Res Judicatae* 4
(1948–50): 15–20.

Schneiderman, David. 'Harold Laski, Viscount Haldane, and the Law of the
Canadian Constitution in the Early Twentieth Century.' *UTLJ* 48 (1998):
521–60.

Scott, F.R. 'The Consequences of the Privy Council Decisions.' *CBR* 15 (1937):
485–92.

Sheps, Arthur. 'The American Revolution and the Transformation of English
Republicanism.' *Historical Reflections* 2, no. 1 (Summer 1975): 3–28.

Spafford, Duff. '"Effective Representation": Reference Re: Provincial Electoral
Boundaries.' *SBR* 56 (1992): 197–208.

Sproule-Jones, Mark. 'The Enduring Colony? Political Institutions and Political Science in Canada.' *Publius* 14, no. 1 (1984): 93–108.

Spry, Graham. 'Broadcasting in Canada: Comment.' *CHR* 46, no. 2 (1965): 137–8.

Stewart, William H. 'Metaphors, Models, and the Development of Federal
Theory.' *Publius* 12 (Spring 1982): 5–24.

Telford, Hamish. 'The Federal Spending Power in Canada: Nation-Building or
Nation-Destroying?' *Publius* 33, no. 1 (Winter 2003): 23–44.

Underhill, Frank. 'The Cabinet and Leadership.' *Canadian Forum,* January
1930, 116–17. Cited in R. MacGregor Dawson, ed., *Constitutional Issues in
Canada, 1900–1931* (London: Oxford University Press, 1933), 133–5.

Whitaker, Reginald. 'Confused Alarms of Struggle and Flight: English-
Canadian Political Science in the 1970s.' *CHR* 60, no. 1 (1979): 1–18.

Young, R., P. Faucher, and A. Blais. 'The Concept of Province-Building: A Critique.' *CJPS* 17, no. 4 (December 1984): 783–818.

*Theses*

De Clercy, Cris. '"Holding Hands with the Public:" Trudeau and the Task
Force on Canadian Unity, 1977–1979.' MA thesis, University of Saskatchewan, 1992.

Fransen, David W. 'Unscrewing the Unscrutable: The Rowell-Sirois Commission, the Ottawa Bureaucracy, and Public Finance Reform, 1935–1941.' PhD diss., University of Toronto, 1982.

*News Articles*

Canadian Press. 'Plains of Abraham Re-Enactment Cancelled.' 17 February 2009. http://www.thestar.com/news/canada/article/588670.
– 'Ontario to Get 21 More Seats in Commons: McGinty.' 17 December 2008. http://www.cbc.ca/canada/toronto/story/2008/12/17/ont-parliament. html.
Cernetig, Miro. 'Chrétien's Distinct Society Backfires in West.' *Globe and Mail*, 29 November 1995.
Flanagan, Tom. 'Only Voters Have the Right to Decide on the Coalition.' *Globe and Mail*, 9 January 2009, A13.
Government of Saskatchewan News Release. 'Province Launches Constitutional Challenge.' 4 October 2007. http://www.gov.sk.ca/news?newsId=4b4264al-c946-4eaa-8c5d-7516011af47.
Hall, Angela. 'Liberal Leader Makes Appeal to the West.' *Leader Post*, 17 February 2009, A1 and A2.
Ibbitson, John. 'House Reform Boosts Fastest-Growing Provinces.' *Globe and Mail*, 2 April 2010, A1, A6.
Makin, Kirk. 'High Stakes Battle Looms over Oil-Sands Pollution.' *Globe and Mail*, 15 August 2007, A1 and A4.
– 'Judges Garner Greater Trust Than Politicians, Survey Finds.' *Globe and Mail*, 9 April 2007, A5.
Mayeda, Andrew. 'Harper Government Plans to Study Athletics Funding.' *Leader-Post*, 27 November 2008, A15.
Metherell, Gia. 'Clark's History Itself Is Now Historical.' *Canberra Times*, 9 May 2004, 4.
'Minister Dion Affirms That a Better Knowledge of Other Federations Strengthens Canadian Unity.' CanadaNewsWire, 19 March 1999.
[Powell, Enoch]. 'Eyrie in the Hills.' *The Listener*, 15 March 1979, 372.
Stanbury, W.T. 'Write It Down: Codify the Unwritten Conventions for Canada's Sake.' *Hill Times*, 15 December 2008, 13 and 22.
'The Long Labors of Willard Wirtz.' National Public Radio (Weekend Edition), 20 December 2008. http://www.npr.org/templates/story/story.php?storyId=98558213
White, Marianne. 'Happy 400th Birthday Quebec City.' *Leader-Post*, 4 July 2008, B12.

*Court Cases*

*Attorney-General for Canada* v. *Attorney-General for Ontario and Others*, [1937] AC 355.
*Attorney-General for Canada* v. *Attorney-General for Ontario and Others*, [1937] AC 326.
*Attorney-General for Manitoba* v. *Forest*, [1979] 2 SCR 1032.
*Bilodeau* v. *Attorney-General for Manitoba*, [1986] 1 SCR 449.
*Great West Saddlery Co.* v. *The King*, [1921] 2 AC 91.
*Maritime Bank* v. *Receiver General of New Brunswick*, [1892] AC 437.
*Re Initiative and Referendum Act*, [1919] AC 944.
*Reference re Legislative Authority of Parliament in Relation to the Upper House*, [1980] 1 SCR 54.
*Reference re Objection to a Resolution to Amend the Constitution*, [1982] 2 SCR 793.
*Re Manitoba Language Rights*, [1985] 1 SCR 721.
*Re Manitoba Public Schools Act Reference*, [1993] 1 SCR 839.
*Reference re Provincial Electoral Boundaries*, [1991] 2 SCR 158.
*Reference re Secession of Quebec*, [1998] 2 SCR 217.
*Toronto Electric Commissioners* v. *Snider*, [1925] AC 396.


*Websites and Electronic Mail*

Forum of Federations. http://www.forumfed.org/en/about/index.php (26 February 2009).
Government of Saskatchewan, News Release, 4 October 2007. 'Province Launches Constitutional Challenge.' http://www.gov.sk.ca/news?newsId=464264al-c946-4eaa-8c5d-7516011af47 (19 March 2009).
Holden, Michael. 'Equalization: Implications of Recent Changes.' Ottawa: Library of Parliament, 2006. http://www.parl.gc.ca/information/library/PRBpubs/prb059-e.htm (1 January 2009).
'Quebecers, the Roman Catholic Church and the Manitoba School Question: A Chronology.' http://faculty.marianopolis.edu/c.belanger/QuebecHistory/chronos/Manitoba.htm (15 December 2008).
Phillipson, Don. Communication: 'Politics and National Symbols.' H-Canada discussion list (6 November 2007). http://www.h-net.msu.edu.
'Saskatchewan Seeks Ruling on Marriage Commissioner Bill.' 28 July 2009. http://www.todaysfamilynews.ca/Sexuality/saskatchewan-seeks-ruling-on-marriage-commissioner-bill.html (18 May 2010).
Wilkinson, Will. 'The Immigration Fallacy.' Cato Institute: Commentary, 27 April 2009. http://www.cato.org/pub_display.php?pub_id=10149 (9 June 2009).

*Unpublished Papers*

Brett, Judith. 'Parliament, Meetings and Civil Society' (paper presented as a
   lecture in the Department of the Senate Occasional Lecture Series at Parlia-
   ment House, Canberra, Australia, 27 July 2001). http://www.aph.gov.au/
   SENATE/pubs/pops/pop38/c08.pdf (7 May 2009).
Dunn, Christopher. 'Canadian Federalism and the Newfoundland and
   Labrador Royal Commission,' *Constructing Tomorrow's Federalism* (Regina:
   Saskatchewan Institute of Public Policy, 2004).
Lazar, Harvey. 'Managing Interdependencies in the Canadian Federation:
   Lessons from the Social Union Framework Agreement' (Constructive and
   Co-operative Federalism? A Series of Commentaries on the Council of the
   Federation, Institute of Intergovernmental Relations / Institute for Research
   on Public Policy, 2003).
Lougheed, Hon. E. Peter. John Stack Memorial Lecture (Saskatoon, 9 February
   2009).
McKay, David. 'William Riker on Federalism: Sometimes Wrong but More
   Right Than Anyone Else' (paper presented at the Conference on Constitu-
   tions, Voting, and Democracy, Center for New Institutional Social Sciences,
   Washington University, St Louis, 7–8 December 2001).
Phillips, Susan D. 'Voluntary Sector: State Relationships in Federal Systems'
   (Forum of Federations: International Conference on Federalism, 1999).
Sharman, Campbell. 'Underestimating Federalism' (University of Tasmania
   School of Government Public Lecture Series, University of Tasmania,
   Hobart, 11 October 2001).
Simeon, Richard. 'Building Legislative Federalism,' *Constructing Tomorrow's
   Federalism* (Regina: Saskatchewan Institute of Public Policy, 2004).
– 'Federalism and Decentralization in Canada' (paper presented at the 2nd
   International Conference on Decentralization). http://www.forumfed.org/
   libdocs/IntConfDecent02/20031213-ca-RichardSimeon.pdf.
Tarr, G. Alan. 'Symmetry and Asymmetry in American Federalism' (paper
   presented at The Federal Idea: Conference in Honour of Ronald L. Watts,
   Institute of Intergovernmental Relations, Queen's University, Kingston,
   October 2007). http://www.queensu.ca/iigr/conf/Watts/papers.html.
Whyte, John D. 'Constitutional Meaning: Text and Experience' (lecture deliv-
   ered to the first-year class at the College of Law, University of Saskatch-
   ewan, Saskatoon, 6 November 2006).

# Index

45, 63, 103, 127, 142; admission of, 22, 50, 55, 71, 78, 135; resources, 20
Newman, Warren, 126–7
New Zealand, 50
northern territories, 8, 63, 72, 147
Northwest Territories, 8, 110, 157; admission of, 22, 25
Nova Scotia: and Confederation, 133–4, 137; and the Constitution, 40, 47, 53–5; and equalization payments, 20, 23; and representation, 52, 78

O'Conner, W.F., 98–100
Official Language Act of Manitoba (1890), 57
Official Languages Act (1969), 21, 33; Commissioner of Official Languages, 81–2; impact of, 35–6, 58–9, 90, 150–1
Ontario, 86, 124; creation of, 22–3, 24, 54, 85, 88, 157; and House, 66; representation, 38, 52, 63, 147; and Senate, 47, 63, 78–80, 85
Onuf, Peter, 8, 157
opposition, the, 40, 57, 72, 76

Parliament: acts of, ix, 8, 20, 128, 131, 158–9; debates of, 7, 43–4, 66, 76, 107; as unique, 65–7
parliamentary: democracy, 9; government, 22, 43
parliamentary federalism, x, 6–7, 14, 40, 42, 62–8, 129, 137, 151–2, 160; and the Crown, 68–74; and the House, 84–91; and the Senate, 74–84
Parti Québécois, 10, 68, 75–6, 107, 152

partisanship, 90, 98, 106; and the House, 36, 53; impact on courts, 121; partisan neutrality, 95–6; and the Senate, 63, 91
party discipline, 6, 9, 87–8, 129, 158; discontent with, 89–90, 92; weakness of in American politics, 155
party system, 43, 82, 86–8, 90, 106, 108, 111, 149; party composition of the House, 53, 88–9, 107
patronage, 53, 63, 121
Pattullo, Duff, 27, 81, 118
Pearson, Lester, 105, 135, 151
Pepin-Robarts. *See* Task Force on Canadian Unity
Phillips, Susan, 147
popular: base of Commons, 64, 66; base of Senate, 75; constituent power, 44–5, 48, 50; opinion, 38, 46, 74; sovereignty, 48
Powell, Enoch, 74
power: in Constitution Act, 1867, xi, 6, 113; division of, xi, 4, 15, 30, 36, 41, 51, 62, 111, 120, 156, 159; executive, *which see*; geographical, 17, 19; legislative, *which see*; in U.S., 44–5
Prang, Margaret, 140–1
prerogative powers, 48–9, 67, 71, 84; compared to in monarchy, 68–9; dissolution of Parliament, 71–3, 77. *See also* prime minister
prime minister: prerogative powers of, 6, 9, 48–9, 51, 62–3, 72–3, 77, 84, 118, 156; and senators, 63, 77, 78, 81–2, 109
Prime Minister's Office (PMO), 38
Prince Edward Island, 19, 23, 38, 55–6, 78, 82
proportional representation (PR),